First World War
and Army of Occupation
War Diary
France, Belgium and Germany

GUARDS DIVISION
1 Guards Brigade
Headquarters
1 September 1916 - 30 September 1916

WO95/1213/1

The Naval & Military Press Ltd
www.nmarchive.com
Published in association with The National Archives

Published by

The Naval & Military Press Ltd

Unit 10 Ridgewood Industrial Park,

Uckfield, East Sussex,

TN22 5QE England

Tel: +44 (0) 1825 749494

www.naval-military-press.com

www.nmarchive.com

This diary has been reprinted in facsimile from the original. Any imperfections are inevitably reproduced and the quality may fall short of modern type and cartographic standards.

Contents

Document type	Place/Title	Date From	Date To
Heading	1916-1917 Guards Division 1st Guards Brigade. Bde Headquarters Sep. 1916-Jun. 1917.		
Heading	War Diary B.H.Q. 1st Guards Brigade September 1916-June 1917.		
Heading	War Diary		
War Diary	Meaulte	01/09/1916	09/09/1916
War Diary	Meaulte To Carnoy	10/09/1916	10/09/1916
War Diary	Carnoy	10/09/1916	12/09/1916
War Diary	Carnoy To S.23.c.7.6.	12/09/1916	12/09/1916
War Diary	400 Gds M.E. Of Bernafay Wood.	13/09/1916	14/09/1916
War Diary	S.23.b.7.6.	14/09/1916	15/09/1916
War Diary	Citadel F.21.d.	17/09/1916	19/09/1916
War Diary	T.19.a.0.1 1/2.	20/09/1916	25/09/1916
War Diary	J.19.a.0.1 1/2 To Carnoy	26/09/1916	27/09/1916
War Diary	Carnoy to F.13 Central.	28/09/1916	28/09/1916
War Diary	F.13 Central to E.18.d.	29/09/1916	29/09/1916
War Diary	Morlancourt	30/09/1916	30/09/1916
Heading	Divisional Operation Orders		
Heading	Operation Order File Oct 21st/15		
Operation(al) Order(s)	Guards Division Order No: 76.	12/09/1916	12/09/1916
Operation(al) Order(s)	Amendment To Guards Division Order No. 76.	13/09/1916	13/09/1916
Miscellaneous	G.D. No. 2240/G.	13/09/1916	13/09/1916
Operation(al) Order(s)	Instructions For Tanks, To Be Attached To Guards Division Order No. 76 Issued On 12th September 1916.	13/09/1916	13/09/1916
Miscellaneous	Instructions For Employment of Tanks.		
Miscellaneous	G.D. No. 2238/G.	12/09/1916	12/09/1916
Miscellaneous	G.D. No: 2246/G.	13/09/1916	13/09/1916
Miscellaneous	G.D.A.	12/09/1916	12/09/1916
Operation(al) Order(s)	Guards Division Order No. 77.	13/09/1916	13/09/1916
Miscellaneous	March Table. Issued With Guards Divn. Order No. 77.		
Operation(al) Order(s)	Guards Division Order No: 78.	15/09/1916	15/09/1916
Operation(al) Order(s)	Addition To Guards Division Order No. 78.	15/09/1916	15/09/1916
Operation(al) Order(s)	Guards Division Order No. 79.	16/09/1916	16/09/1916
Miscellaneous	G.D. No: 2288/G.	20/09/1916	20/09/1916
Miscellaneous	G.D. No. 2287/C.	20/09/1916	20/09/1916
Miscellaneous	Special Instructions For Action Of 2nd Guards Brigade.	23/09/1916	23/09/1916
Operation(al) Order(s)	Guards Division Order No: 82.	21/09/1916	21/09/1916
Operation(al) Order(s)	Amendment To Guards Division Order No. 82.	21/09/1916	21/09/1916
Operation(al) Order(s)	Instructions For Tanks, Issued With Guards Divisional Order No.82.	21/09/1916	21/09/1916
Operation(al) Order(s)	Amendment To Guards Division Order No. 82.	24/09/1916	24/09/1916
Operation(al) Order(s)	Guards Division Order No. 84.	24/09/1916	24/09/1916
Miscellaneous	G.D. No. 2307/C.	24/09/1916	24/09/1916
Operation(al) Order(s)	Guards Division Order No. 85.	26/09/1916	26/09/1916
Operation(al) Order(s)	Guards Division Order No: 86.	27/09/1916	27/09/1916
Map			
Map	Situation Map Scale-1:20,000.		
Heading	Orders From A & Q.		
Miscellaneous	Situation as Regards Ammunition and Supplies on Night of 14th/15th Sept. 1916.	14/09/1916	14/09/1916

Heading	Artillery Order & Instructions		
Heading	Operation Order File Oct. 20th/15		
Miscellaneous	Left Group G.D.A. Instructions No. 2.	14/09/1916	14/09/1916
Miscellaneous	A Form. Messages And Signals.		
Operation(al) Order(s)	Guards Divisional Artillery Order No: 49.	13/09/1916	13/09/1916
Miscellaneous	Table Of Tasks.		
Operation(al) Order(s)	Guards Divisional Artillery Order No: 52.	22/09/1916	22/09/1916
Miscellaneous	Table Of Tasks.		
Miscellaneous	G.D.A./814/56/A.	24/09/1916	24/09/1916
Heading	Medical Arrangements		
Heading	Operation Order File Oct 19th/15.		
Operation(al) Order(s)	Operation Order No. A21 By Lieut. Colonel J.G. Gill, R.A.M.C., A.D.M.S., Guards Division.	13/09/1916	13/09/1916
Miscellaneous	Medical Arrangements For Present Front.	11/09/1916	11/09/1916
Operation(al) Order(s)	Operation Order No. A 23 by Colonel S. Guise-Moores, C.B., A.M.S., A.D.M.S., Guards Division.	23/09/1916	23/09/1916
Miscellaneous	Field Ambulance Bearer Divisional Arrangements For Information Of Battalion Medical Officers.	14/09/1916	14/09/1916
Heading	1st Guards Brigade Operation Orders		
Operation(al) Order(s)	1st Guards Brigade Order No. 71.	09/09/1916	09/09/1916
Operation(al) Order(s)	1st Guards Brigade Order No. 72.	11/09/1916	11/09/1916
Operation(al) Order(s)	1st Guards Brigade Order No. 73.	13/09/1916	13/09/1916
Miscellaneous			
Operation(al) Order(s)	Amendment to 1st Guards Brigade Order No. 73.	13/09/1916	13/09/1916
Miscellaneous	Instructions For Employment Of Tanks.		
Operation(al) Order(s)	1st Guards Brigade Order No. 74.	13/09/1916	13/09/1916
Miscellaneous	Assembly March Table.		
Diagram etc	1st Guards Brigade Assembly Area.		
Miscellaneous	G.D. No. 2245/G.	13/09/1916	13/09/1916
Miscellaneous	1st Guards Brigade No. 237/4.	13/09/1916	13/09/1916
Operation(al) Order(s)	Amendment to 1st Guards Brigade Order No. 74.	20/09/1916	20/09/1916
Operation(al) Order(s)	1st Guards Brigade Order No. 74.	19/09/1916	19/09/1916
Miscellaneous			
Miscellaneous	March Table.		
Operation(al) Order(s)	1st Guards Brigade Operation Order No. 76.	16/09/1916	16/09/1916
Operation(al) Order(s)	1st Guards Brigade Order No. 76.	21/09/1916	21/09/1916
Operation(al) Order(s)	1st Guards Brigade Order No. 77.	21/09/1916	21/09/1916
Miscellaneous	1st Guards Brigade No. 262.	22/09/1916	22/09/1916
Operation(al) Order(s)	Supplement to 1st Guards Brigade Order No. 77.		
Operation(al) Order(s)	Amendments To 1st Guards Brigade Order No 77.	23/09/1916	23/09/1916
Operation(al) Order(s)	Supplement to 1st Guards Brigade Order No 77.	23/09/1916	23/09/1916
Operation(al) Order(s)	Amendment to 1st Guards Brigade Order No 77.		
Operation(al) Order(s)	Supplement to 1st Guards Brigade Order No 77.	23/09/1916	23/09/1916
Miscellaneous	2nd Bn Grenadier Guards.	23/09/1916	23/09/1916
Miscellaneous	A Form. Messages And Signals.		
Operation(al) Order(s)	Amendments To 1st Guards Brigade Order No 77.	23/09/1916	23/09/1916
Operation(al) Order(s)	1st Guards Brigade Order No 78.	24/09/1916	24/09/1916
Miscellaneous	March Table.		
Miscellaneous	Communications For Attack On Sept. 25th.	25/09/1916	25/09/1916
Miscellaneous	A Form. Messages And Signals.		
Operation(al) Order(s)	1st Guards Brigade Order No. 79.	26/09/1916	26/09/1916
Miscellaneous	A Form. Messages And Signals.		
Operation(al) Order(s)	1st Guards Brigade Order No. 80.	27/09/1916	27/09/1916
Operation(al) Order(s)	1st Guards Brigade Order No. 81.	28/09/1916	28/09/1916
Operation(al) Order(s)	1st Guards Brigade Order No. 82.	29/09/1916	29/09/1916
Operation(al) Order(s)	Amendment to 1st Guards Brigade Order No. 82.	29/09/1916	29/09/1916

Heading	Operation Order 2nd Guards Brigade		
Operation(al) Order(s)	Operation Order No. 63 By Lieutenant-Colonel B.N.S. Brooke, D.S.O. Commanding 2nd. Guards Brigade.	12/09/1916	12/09/1916
Operation(al) Order(s)	Operation Order No. 65 By Brigadier-General J. Ponson by, C.M.G., D.S.O. Commanding 2nd Guards Brigade.	22/09/1916	22/09/1916
Operation(al) Order(s)	Supplementary Orders To 2nd. Guards Brigade Order No. 65.	23/09/1916	23/09/1916
Operation(al) Order(s)	Supplementary Orders To 2nd. Guards Brigade Order No. 65.	24/09/1916	24/09/1916
Operation(al) Order(s)	Operation Order No. 68 By Brigadier-General J. Ponson by C.M.G. D.S.O. Commanding 2nd. Guards Brigade.	30/09/1916	30/09/1916
Operation(al) Order(s)	Supplementary Order To 2nd. Guards Brigade Order No. 68	30/09/1916	30/09/1916
Miscellaneous	2nd.G.B. No. 129/G.	13/09/1916	13/09/1916
Miscellaneous	2nd. Gds. Bde. No.129/G.	13/09/1916	13/09/1916
Miscellaneous	Copies To		
Heading	3rd Brigade Operation Orders		
Operation(al) Order(s)	3rd Guards Brigade. Operation Order No. 59.	14/09/1916	14/09/1916
Operation(al) Order(s)	3rd Guards Brigade. Operation Order No. 66.	22/09/1916	22/09/1916
Heading	Operation Orders From Other Brigades		
Operation(al) Order(s)	18th Infantry Brigade Operation Order No 87.	22/09/1916	22/09/1916
Operation(al) Order(s)	18th Infantry Brigade Operation Order No. 88.	23/09/1916	23/09/1916
Operation(al) Order(s)	41st Infantry Brigade Order No. 102.	13/09/1916	13/09/1916
Miscellaneous	Appendix "A" To Accompany 41st Inf. Bde. Order No. 102.		
Miscellaneous	Appendix "O" To 41st Inf. Bde. Order No. 102.		
Operation(al) Order(s)	After Order To:- 41st Infantry Brigade Order No. 102.	14/09/1916	14/09/1916
Operation(al) Order(s)	Appendix "B" To 41st Inf. Bde. Order No. 102.		
Miscellaneous	A Form. Messages And Signals.		
Operation(al) Order(s)	42nd Inf Bde Operation Order No. 76.	14/09/1916	14/09/1916
Miscellaneous	Appendix "A" To Accompany 42nd Inf Bde Operation Order No. 76.		
Miscellaneous	Order For Use Of "Tanks". Appendix B.		
Operation(al) Order(s)	Appendix "C" To 42nd Inf Bde Operation Order No. 76.		
Heading	Suggestions For The Attack		
Miscellaneous	H.Q. Gds: 1st Guards Brigade.	23/09/1916	23/09/1916
Miscellaneous	A Form. Messages And Signals.		
Miscellaneous	1st Guards Brigade.	24/09/1916	24/09/1916
Miscellaneous			
Miscellaneous		24/09/1916	24/09/1916
Heading	Narrative Of Operations X1st Guards Brigade During August & September 1916.		
Miscellaneous	Operations Carried Out By 1st Guards Brigade During August And September 1916.		
Miscellaneous	Appendix "A". September 15th.	15/09/1916	15/09/1916
Heading	Narratives Of Events 13th To 17th September 1916. 2nd Grenadier Gds. 2nd Coldstream Gds. 3rd Coldstream Gds. 1st Irish Gds. Congratulatory Messages.		
Miscellaneous	Narrative Of Events From Sept., 13th-17th, 1916.	13/09/1917	13/09/1917
Operation(al) Order(s)	1st Guards Brigade.	18/09/1917	18/09/1917
Miscellaneous	3rd Bn. Coldstream Guards. Operations From The 14th To 16th Sept., 1916.	14/09/1916	14/09/1916

Miscellaneous	The Brigade Major 1st Guards Brigade.	17/09/1916	17/09/1916
Miscellaneous	Attack Of The 1st Guards Brigade, September 15th & 16th. 1916.	15/09/1916	15/09/1916
Heading	Congratulatory Messages For Sept 15th.		
Miscellaneous	2nd Bn. Grenadier Guards.	16/09/1916	16/09/1916
Miscellaneous	2nd Bn. Coldstream Guards. 3rd Bn. Coldstream Guards.	18/09/1916	18/09/1916
Miscellaneous	1st Bn. Irish Guards.	18/09/1916	18/09/1916
Miscellaneous	Diary	12/09/1916	12/09/1916
Miscellaneous	1st Guards Brigade. Diary Of Operation 12th-17th September 1916.	12/09/1916	12/09/1916
Heading	Narratives Of Events 21st To 26th September 1916. Diary of Operations Brigade Headquarters 2nd Grenadier Guards 2nd Coldstream Guards 3rd Coldstream Guards 1st Irish Guards Congratulatory Messages.		
Miscellaneous	Diary Of Operations On September 25th 1916.	25/09/1916	25/09/1916
Miscellaneous	1st Guards Brigade-Narrative Of Operations 21st To 26th Sept. 1916.	21/09/1916	21/09/1916
Miscellaneous	Narrative Of Events From Sept. 24th-Sept. 26th 1916.	24/09/1916	24/09/1916
Miscellaneous	Report On Operations Carried Out By The 2nd Bn. Coldstream Guards From Sept., 21st-26th Inclusive.	21/09/1916	21/09/1916
Miscellaneous	Narrative Of Operations 20th-26th Sept., 1916.	20/09/1916	20/09/1916
Miscellaneous	1st Battalion Irish Guards. Narrative Of The Action 25th/26th September, 1916.	25/09/1916	25/09/1916
Heading	Congratulatory Messages For Operations On Sept. 25th 1916.		
Miscellaneous	C Form (Duplicate). Messages And Signals.		
Miscellaneous	A Form. Messages And Signals.		
Miscellaneous	All Units	28/09/1916	28/09/1916
Miscellaneous	General Sir H. Rawlinson, Commanding Fourth Army.	17/09/1916	17/09/1916
Heading	Lessons Learn From The Operations Of 15th & 25th September		
Miscellaneous	Lessons From The Recent Attack On Sept., 15th And Sept., 25th By 1st Guards Brigade.	15/09/1916	15/09/1916
Miscellaneous	2nd Bn. Grenadier Guards.	04/10/1916	04/10/1916
Miscellaneous	2nd Bn. Coldstream Guards.	04/10/1916	04/10/1916
Miscellaneous	3rd Bn. Coldstream Guards.	04/10/1916	04/10/1916
Miscellaneous	1st Bn. Irish Guards.	04/10/1916	04/10/1916
Miscellaneous	Report On The actions Of Sept., 15th And 25th, Regarding The Machine Guns Of The 1st Guards Brigade Machine Gun Company.	15/09/1916	15/09/1916
Miscellaneous	Report On The actions Of Sept., 25th And 26th, Of The 1st Guards Brigade Trench Mortar Battery.	25/09/1916	25/09/1916
Miscellaneous	1st Guards Bde., No. 329.	11/10/1916	11/10/1916
Miscellaneous	1st Guards Brigade. 2nd Guards Brigade. 3rd Guards Brigade.	08/10/1916	08/10/1916
Miscellaneous	XIV Corps "G".	05/10/1916	05/10/1916
Operation(al) Order(s)	Guards Division. Operations Of The 25th/26th September 1916.	25/09/1916	25/09/1916
Heading	Casualties		
Miscellaneous	Casualties-September 10th-17th, 1916.	10/09/1916	10/09/1916
Miscellaneous	Casualty Return.	23/09/1916	23/09/1916
Miscellaneous	Casualties September 10th-17th, 1916.	10/09/1916	10/09/1916
Miscellaneous	Summary		
Miscellaneous	Casualties. September 18th-30th, 1916.	18/09/1916	18/09/1916

Miscellaneous	Summary		
Miscellaneous	Casualties. September 15th/16th, 1916.	15/09/1916	15/09/1916
Miscellaneous	The Headquarters, 1st Guards Brigade.	24/09/1916	24/09/1916
Miscellaneous	2nd Battalion Grenadier Guards. Casualties For The Period 15th September.	15/09/1916	15/09/1916
Miscellaneous	2nd Battalion Coldstream Guards.	27/09/1916	27/09/1916
Miscellaneous	1st Guards Bde.	24/11/1916	24/11/1916
Miscellaneous	1st Guards Bde.	23/11/1916	23/11/1916
Miscellaneous	1st Guards Brigade	25/11/1916	25/11/1916
Miscellaneous	Trench Mortar Battery.	24/11/1916	24/11/1916
Miscellaneous	Headquarters, Guards Division.	27/09/1916	27/09/1916
Miscellaneous	Headquarters, Guards Division.	28/09/1916	28/09/1916
Miscellaneous	Conferences		
Heading	Previous to Attack Order for Sept 1916.		
Miscellaneous	Brigade Conference Held At Brigade Hd. Qrs., Meaulte, 27th Aug. 1916.	27/08/1916	27/08/1916
Miscellaneous	Conference Notes		
Miscellaneous	Communications During in Attack.	08/09/1916	08/09/1916
Miscellaneous	2nd Bn. Grenadier Guards.	07/09/1916	07/09/1916
Miscellaneous	Aeroplane Code.		
Miscellaneous	1st G.B. No. 237.	10/09/1916	10/09/1916
Miscellaneous	2nd Bn. Grenadier Guards. 2nd Bn. Coldstream Guards. 3rd Bn. Coldstream Guards. 1st Bn. Irish Guards.	12/09/1916	12/09/1916
Miscellaneous	Conference	11/09/1916	11/09/1916
Miscellaneous	German Troops.	11/09/1916	11/09/1916
Miscellaneous	C.R.E. Guards Div. No. 1027.	11/09/1916	11/09/1916
Miscellaneous	Conference held at Divisional Headquarters, August 28th.	28/08/1916	28/08/1916
Miscellaneous	Conference held at 2nd. Guards Brigade Hd. Qrs. 19th September 1916.	19/09/1916	19/09/1916
Heading	Intelligence Notes		
Miscellaneous	Our Line.		
Miscellaneous	System of Defence.		
Miscellaneous	German Lines.		
Miscellaneous	German Troops.		
Miscellaneous	Preliminary Report On Morval.		
Diagram etc	Morval		
Miscellaneous	Information About Les Boeufs From A Refugee.		
Diagram etc	Guards Dig. H.Q. 4th Sept 1916.		
Map			
Miscellaneous			
Map			
Miscellaneous	Situation at 15 pm.		
Map			

1916-1917
GUARDS DIVISION
1ST GUARDS BRIGADE

BDE HEADQUARTERS

SEP 1916-JUN 1917

Index.............................

SUBJECT.

No.	Contents.	Date.
	WAR DIARY B.H.Q. 1st GUARDS BRIGADE SEPTEMBER 1916 — June 1917	

(63,965). Wt.15,820—176. 2000. 9/21. Gp.164. A.&E.W.

W A R   D I A R Y

Army Form C. 2118.

WAR DIARY
or
INTELLIGENCE SUMMARY
(Erase heading not required.)

Instructions regarding War Diaries and Intelligence Summaries are contained in F. S. Regs., Part II. and the Staff Manual respectively. Title Pages will be prepared in manuscript.

Headquarters 1st Gds Bde

Vol 14

Place	Date	Hour	Summary of Events and Information	Remarks and references to Appendices
MEAULTE	Sept 1st	8.30am	Brigadier took commanding officers up to O.P. east of MARICOURT near SOMME to look at surrounding country.	
		12 noon	Casualties 2nd Gren Gds: O.R. wounded 1.	
"	Sept 2nd	9am	Brigadier went round billets of 1st Irish Gds.	
		12 noon	Casualties 2nd Gren Gds O.R. wounded 1. (gas)	
"	Sept 3rd	11am	Brigade church parade. The Chaplain General preached.	
		2pm	All units except 2nd Gren Gds paraded a detachment in fighting order.	
		5pm	2nd Gren Gds returned to billets in MEAULTE.	
	Sept 4th		Training interfered with by rain. Army Commander called at Bde H.Q.	
	Sept 5th		1st Irish Gds + 2nd Gren Gds carried out Bn training.	
		7pm	Message received saying that the Div was to be ready to move at short notice from 5am on Sept 6th owing to great French successes South of the SOMME. Verbal information from Div later explaining short notice to	

2449 Wt. W14957/M90 750,000 1/16 J.B.C. & A. Forms/C.2118/12.

Instructions regarding War Diaries and Intelligence Summaries are contained in F. S. Regs., Part II. and the Staff Manual respectively. Title Pages will be prepared in manuscript.

WAR DIARY
or
INTELLIGENCE SUMMARY
(Erase heading not required.)

Army Form C. 2118.

Place	Date	Hour	Summary of Events and Information	Remarks and references to Appendices
			mean two hours.	
MEAULTE	Sept 6th	1.am.	Previous orders to be ready to move cancelled. Div at 4 hours notice.	
		10.am.	4 hours notice removed – Training proceeded normally	
"	Sept 7th	2 pm.	Orders received for Bde to be ready to relieve 16th Div in GUILLEMONT sector + units warned accordingly.	APP 217
"	Sept 8th	5pm	1st Gds Bde Order No 70 issued.	APP. 218
	"	8.30am	Bde parade for Bde exercise in the attack in accordance with 1st Gds Bde Order No 70.	
"	"	11pm	Gds Div Order No 71 received	APP 219
"	Sept 9th	11am	Gds Div Order No 72 received.	APP 220
		4.15pm	1st Gds Bde Order No 71 issued.	APP 221.
MEAULTE to CARNOY	Sept 10th	10am	Bde moved to CARNOY in accordance with APP. 221. On arrival just W. of CARNOY it was found that 16th Div were not clear so Bde H.Q. 2nd Gds – 1st Irish Gds & M.G. Coy bivouaced on high ground W. of CARNOY until 2.30pm.	
		2pm.	Orders received to hold our Bn in readiness to move up in support of 3rd Gds Bde – 1st Irish Gds detailed for this purpose.	

Army Form C. 2118.

WAR DIARY
or
INTELLIGENCE SUMMARY
(Erase heading not required.)

Instructions regarding War Diaries and Intelligence Summaries are contained in F. S. Regs., Part II. and the Staff Manual respectively. Title Pages will be prepared in manuscript.

Place	Date	Hour	Summary of Events and Information	Remarks and references to Appendices
CARNOY	Sept 10th	8.10 pm	Orders received to send two coys to H.Q. 3rd Gds Bde at S.28 b.5.3.	
			Two coys 1st Irish Gds left.	
		9 pm		APP 222.
		12 mn	Gds Div Order No 73 received.	
"	Sept 11th	5.15 am	Orders received to send two more coys up to support 3rd Gds Bde by 9 am.	
		7.40 am	Two remaining coys ~~[illegible]~~ of 1st Irish Gds left to report at H.Q. 3rd Gds Bde.	
		12 noon	Casualties 2nd Gren Gds O.R. wounded 1.	
			3rd Cold Gds O.R. killed 1.	
			1st Irish Gds O.R. killed 3. wounded 10. accidentally wounded 6.	APP 223
		4 pm	Gds Div Order No 74 received	APP 224
		4 pm	Conference concerning future operations at Div H.Q.	" "
		6 pm	Conference at Bde H.Q. concerning future operations.	
		6 pm	Gds Div order No 75 received	APP 225.
		11.15 pm	1st Gds Bde Order No 72 issued.	APP 226.
"	Sept 12th	7 am	1st Irish Gds returned to bivouacs at CARNOY. ~~[illegible]~~ Two coys had been moved up to trenches east of GINCHY in support.	
		12 noon	Casualties 2nd Cold Gds O.R. wounded 5. (1 accidentally)	
			1 Irish Gds O.R. killed 3. wounded 9. (4 at duty)	

Instructions regarding War Diaries and Intelligence Summaries are contained in F. S. Regs., Part II. and the Staff Manual respectively. Title Pages will be prepared in manuscript.

WAR DIARY
or
INTELLIGENCE SUMMARY
(Erase heading not required.)

Army Form C. 2118.

Place	Date	Hour	Summary of Events and Information	Remarks and references to Appendices
CARNOY to S.23.c.7.6.	Sept 12th	8 pm	Gds Div Order No 73 received.	
		11 pm	Relief of 3rd Gds Bde carried out as per appendix 225. & reported complete.	
400 yds N.E of BERNAFAY wood.	Sept 13th		Enemy shelled neighbourhood of GINCHY intermittently throughout the day.	
		12 noon	Casualties 2nd Gren Gds Lt. Hon. M.B.H. TOWNELEY - BERTIE wounded	
			O.R. killed 3. wounded 6. (1 at duty)	
			2nd Cold Gds O.R. wounded 2. (1 at duty)	
			1st Irish Gds O.R. killed 3 wdd 4.	
		2 pm	Heavy guns shelled SUNKEN rd N of GINCHY	
		11.15 pm	1st Gds Bde Order No 73 issued.	
	Sept 14th	12.30 am	2nd Gren Gds attacked with one coy & 1 platoon Northwards down SUNKEN rd from GINCHY to FLERS. An advance of about 150 yds was made & the line of the orchard at N. end of Ginchy captured & consolidated. M.G. fire from N.W. stopped further advance.	

2449 Wt. W14957/M90 750,000 1/16 J.B.C. & A. Forms/C.2118/12.

Army Form C. 2118.

WAR DIARY
or
INTELLIGENCE SUMMARY
(Erase heading not required.)

Instructions regarding War Diaries and Intelligence Summaries are contained in F. S. Regs., Part II. and the Staff Manual respectively. Title Pages will be prepared in manuscript.

Place	Date	Hour	Summary of Events and Information	Remarks and references to Appendices
S.23.b.9.6.	Sept 14th		remainder of day fairly quiet	
		12.20	Casualties.	
		8pm	Assembly march carried out as per O.O. 74.	App. 22 B
		9pm	Bde H.Q. moved to battle H.Q. at S.24.c.6.1½	
	Sept 15th	1 am	Bde in position for assault	
			For details of Sept 15th & 16th see App	
CITADEL F.21.d	Sept 17th	7am	Relief by 62nd & 59th Bde complete	
	Sept 18th		Bde resting & reorganising. Drafts received.	
	Sept 19th		The Bde was to have relieved the 60th Inf Bde but owing to bad weather the relief was postponed.	
		2pm	Conference at 2nd Bde H.Q. outlining future operations.	
		7pm	Conference of C.O's at Bde H.Q.	

2449 Wt. W14957/M90 750,000 1/16 J.B.C. & A. Forms/C.2118/12.

Instructions regarding War Diaries and Intelligence Summaries are contained in F. S. Regs., Part II. and the Staff Manual respectively. Title Pages will be prepared in manuscript.

WAR DIARY
or
INTELLIGENCE SUMMARY
(Erase heading not required.)

Army Form C. 2118.

Place	Date	Hour	Summary of Events and Information	Remarks and references to Appendices
T. 19. a. 0.1½	~~Sept~~ Sept 20th	6 pm	Bde relieved 60th Inf Bde in accordance with Bde Order 74 & Gds Div Order No 80 owing to the appalling state of the ground the relief was not complete until 6.30 am. The condition of the tracks east of BERNAFAY wood ~~[illegible]~~ became a serious proposition at this time.	APP 230
	Sept 21st		On the whole a fairly quiet day. Desultory shelling all over our area.	
		12 noon	Casualties 2nd Gren Gds. O.R. wounded 1. 2nd Cold Gds O.R. killed 1. wounded 5.	
		8 pm	3rd Cold Gds & part of 2nd Cold Gds relieved by 6th Div as per Gds Div Orders 81 & 83 & 1st Gds Bde Order 76.	APP 231 232 233
		11.15 pm	1st Gds Bde Order No 77 issued.	
	Sept 22nd		The usual artillery activity - but very little damage done - weather fine & much aeroplane activity. Casualties. 3rd Cold Gds O.R. wounded 6.	

Instructions regarding War Diaries and Intelligence Summaries are contained in F. S. Regs., Part II. and the Staff Manual respectively. Title Pages will be prepared in manuscript.

WAR DIARY
or
INTELLIGENCE SUMMARY
(Erase heading not required.)

Army Form C. 2118.

Place	Date	Hour	Summary of Events and Information	Remarks and references to Appendices
T.19.a.0½	Sept 23rd		The usual artillery activity. The country had ~~that~~ dried up well & transport did not afford the same difficulties as two days before. During the previous two nights a support trench 150 yds in rear of our front line was dug & completed on night of Sept 23rd/24th. This trench built for assembly purposes.	
		12 noon	Casualties to 12 noon. 2nd Gren Gds O.R. killed 1 wded 2 2nd Cold Gds " 2 " 8 3rd Cold Gds 1 " 11 missing 1st Irish Gds 0 " 3 (one accidentally) No. 4 F. Coy 0 " 2 T.M. Bty 0 " 4 Capt The Rev. Father Browne wded.	
	Sept 24th		During the night 23/24th the new assembly support trench was completed. The other trench a communication trench in which it was hoped to assemble a Bn. for the assault was found to be beyond repair in the time so it was decided to dig another half finished one night through to the reserve line during	

Army Form C. 2118.

Instructions regarding War Diaries and Intelligence Summaries are contained in F. S. Regs., Part II. and the Staff Manual respectively. Title Pages will be prepared in manuscript.

WAR DIARY
or
INTELLIGENCE SUMMARY
(Erase heading not required.)

Place	Date	Hour	Summary of Events and Information	Remarks and references to Appendices
T 19. a. 0.1½	Sept 24th		the night of Sept 24/25. This was eventually done by dawn on 25th & the whole trench then ran from T 3. c. 2. 2 to T 8. b. 3. 0	
		6 am	Enemy opened heavy barrage on the right of our front & reserve lines. This was followed by a small attack on the 10th Inf Bde on our right. The enemy kept up quite a heavy barrage till 1 pm.	
		12 noon	Casualties	
		7 pm.	assembly march in accordance with ? Inf Bde Order No 78 carried out	
	Sept 25th	1.20 am	all units reported in their assembly positions.	
		12 noon.	all normal & enemy apparently suspecting no attack.	
			For orders & account of operations on Sept 25th & 26th see	

2449 Wt. W14957/M90 750,000 1/16 J.B.C. & A. Forms/C.2118/12.

Army Form C. 2118.

Instructions regarding War Diaries and Intelligence Summaries are contained in F. S. Regs., Part II. and the Staff Manual respectively. Title Pages will be prepared in manuscript.

WAR DIARY
or
INTELLIGENCE SUMMARY

(Erase heading not required.)

Place	Date	Hour	Summary of Events and Information	Remarks and references to Appendices
J. 19. a. 0. 1½ to CARNOY	Sept 26th	7pm.	About this hour 2nd Bn Irish Gds arrived at Bde H. Q to relieve the whole of the Bde. The relief was completed without difficulty by 11.30pm when the Bde was withdrawn into reserve as follows: 2nd & 3rd Bns Colds. Gds to CARNOY. 2nd Grend Gds & 1st Irish Gds to The CITADEL F.21.d. Bde M.G. Coy remained in the line. T.M. By to CARNOY.	
	Sept 27th	6.30pm	2nd & 3rd Bns Cold Gds moved to camps at F.13 central as per Order No 80 2nd Gren Gds - 1st Irish Gds moved to F.14.b. by verbal instructions a shower of rain at 6pm made the march across country a most difficult one.	APP. 235.
CARNOY to F.13 central.	Sept 28th	10-30am	Bde H.Q moved to F.13. central.	
		5pm.	M-G. Coy & T.M. By moved to F.14 b. Information received that the Div was going back into reserve near Amiens. See Gds Div warning order	APP 236.

2449 Wt. W14957/M90 750,000 1/16 J.B.C. & A. Forms/C.2118/12.

Army Form C. 2118.

Instructions regarding War Diaries and Intelligence Summaries are contained in F. S. Regs., Part II. and the Staff Manual respectively. Title Pages will be prepared in manuscript.

WAR DIARY
or
INTELLIGENCE SUMMARY
(Erase heading not required.)

Place	Date	Hour	Summary of Events and Information	Remarks and references to Appendices
F.13. central to E.18.d.	Sept 29th	4 pm.	2nd & 3rd Coldstream Gds & Bde H.Q. moved to SANDPIT camps E.18.d. see – weather wet & cross country tracks almost impassable for transport.	APP 237
MORLANCOURT	Sept 30th	2.30 pm.	Bde moved to billets at MORLANCOURT as per 1st Gds Bde Order No 82 & Gds Div Order No 87. The weather had become fine & the going across country was good –	APP 238
	Oct			

[signature]
Brig Gen
Comm'g 1st Gds Bde

2449 Wt. W14957/M90 750,000 1/16 J.B.C. & A. Forms/C.2118/12.

DIVISIONAL OPERATION ORDERS

Operation Orders
file
Oct 21st /15

SECRET

5

S E C R E T. Copy No......

=*=*=*=*=*=*=*=*=*=*=*=

Reference Map Sheet
57C S.W.

GUARDS DIVISION ORDER NO: 76.

=*=

1. The Fourth Army will attack the enemy's defences between COMBLES RAVINE and MARTINPUICH on Z day with the object of seizing MORVAL - LES BOEUFS - GUEUDECOURT and FLERS, and of breaking through the enemy's system of defence.

The French are undertaking an offensive simultaneously on the south and the Reserve Army on the north.

2. The attack will be pushed with the utmost vigour, all along the line, until the most distant objectives are reached.

The failure of a unit on a flank is not to prevent other units pushing on to their final objectives, as it is by such means that these units, which have failed, will be assisted to advance.

3. Preliminary Bombardment.

(a) Commencing on 12th September bombardment and wire cutting on hostile defensive system will take place from 6 a.m. to 6-30 p.m. daily.

(b) The preliminary bombardment on the day of the attack will be similar to that on previous days, there being no further increase of fire previous to ZERO.

(c) At 6-30 p.m. each evening, from 12th September inclusive, night firing will commence and continue till 6 a.m. Lethal shells will be used.

4 (a) The 6th Division is to attack on our right and the 14th Division on our left.

(b) The 2nd Guards Brigade will attack on the right of the Division - the 1st Guards Brigade on the left - the 3rd Guards Brigade will be in Divisional Reserve.

5. Forming up areas.

Forming up areas are shown on attached maps.

6. 1st and 2nd Guards Brigades will allot a forming up area for 75th and 76th Field Companies, R.E., respectively in their forming up areas.

Instructions as to movements of troops to their forming up areas will be issued separately.

7. Objectives allotted to Guards Brigades and neighbouring Divisions are shown on attached map.

First objective is marked			GREEN.
Second	-do-	-do-	BROWN.
Third	-do-	-do-	BLUE.
Fourth	-do-	-do-	RED.

8. The Infantry will advance to the attack of the GREEN Line at ZERO

to the attack of the BROWN Line at ZERO + 1 hour ~~45 minutes~~

to the attack of the BLUE Line at ZERO + ~~1~~ 2 hour ~~and 30 minutes~~.

to the attack of the RED Line at ZERO + 4 hours and 30 minutes.

9. **Artillery Barrages.** (a) 50% of Field Artillery covering the Division will be used for creeping barrage, and 50% for stationary barrage.

(b) Details of stationary barrages will be issued later. In all cases the stationary barrages will lift back, when the creeping barrage reaches it.

(c) At ZERO the creeping barrage will open 100 yards in front of our front trenches, and will advance at rate of 50 yards per minute until it is 200 yards beyond the first objective when it will become stationary.

At ZERO + ~~45~~ 1 hour the creeping barrage will become intense on a line 200 yards in front of first objective and will creep forward at rate of 50 yards per minute in front of that portion of the 1st Guards Brigade which is to advance to the second objective.

(d) At ZERO + 1 hours & 10 mins the creeping barrage will become intense on a line 200 yards in front of the first objective as far north as T.8.b.4.6., thence on a line 200 yards in front of 2nd objective and will advance at rate of 30 yards per minute until it has passed 200 yards beyond the third objective - when it will

will become stationary.

This barrage is to cover the advance of the tanks. There will be no creeping barrage in front of the infantry during their advance to third objective which commences at ZERO + ~~1 hr 30 minutes~~ 2 hours.

(e) At ZERO + 3 hours ~~45~~ 30 minutes the creeping barrage will become intense on a line 200 yards in front of the third objective - and will advance at rate of 30 yards per minute until it has passed 200 yards beyond fourth objective when it will become stationary. This barrage is to cover the advance of the tanks.

There will be no creeping barrage in front of the infantry during the advance ~~from the third~~ to the fourth objective which commences at ZERO + 4 hrs 30 minutes.

(f) In the attack on first and second objectives, gaps of 100 yards wide will be left in the creeping barrage for the routes of the tanks.

10. The flow of troops of 2nd Guards Brigade and 1st Guards Brigade must be maintained so as to ensure a strong attack being pressed against each successive objective.

Sufficient men will be left in each line captured to clear it of the enemy. No troops of 2nd and 1st Guards Brigades will be detailed to remain behind in objectives after they have been passed, for purposes of consolidation.

The task of the two leading Guards Brigades is to press the attack through to their ultimate objectives with every means at their disposal.

11. The 3rd Guards Brigade will advance at ZERO + 1 hour 30 minutes until its leading troops reach the south western outskirts of GINCHY when the Brigade will halt and await orders.

Special instructions as to action of Reserve Brigade will be issued.

12. Tanks will be employed to co-operate with the attack. Instructions as to their employment are attached.

Instructions will be issued as to movement of tanks to their departure positions, and as to time of their advance to the various objectives.

/13 R.E.

13. **R.E.** (a) 76th Field Company, R.E., will be at disposal of 2nd Guards Brigade and 75th Field Company, R.E., at disposal of 1st Guards Brigade for the attack.

55th Field Company, R.E., will be in Divisional Reserve.

(b) Pioneer Battalion will act under orders of C.R.E. and will be employed on improvements of communications forward as attack progresses.

14. **Royal Flying Corps.** (a) 9th Squadron, Royal Flying Corps will have ~~two~~ one Contact aeroplanes in the air from ZERO to dark on Z day and again from 6-30 a.m. to 9 a.m. on Z+ 1 day.

(b) Flares will be lit as follows:-

(i) On obtaining each objective.

(ii) At 12 noon and 5 p.m. on Z day.

(iii) At 6-30 a.m. on Z + 1 day.

Red Flares will be used by Infantry, Green Flares by Cavalry.

15. Watches will be synchronised at 12-30 p.m. and 6-30 p.m. on Y day by telephone from Divisional Head Quarters.

16. Special instructions will be issued on the following subjects:-

(a) Division of Artillery into Groups, and which fronts they support.

(b) Liaison between Artillery and Infantry also between neighbouring Infantry Brigades.

(c) Medical arrangements.

(d) Supply of - Rations.
Water.
S.A.A.
Light Trench Mortar Ammunition.
Hand Grenades.

17. All transport will be packed up, and ready to move forward at one hour's notice, after ZERO + 4 hours.

An Officer from each Brigade Transport will remain at Divisional Head Quarters, MINDEN POST - :

from ZERO + 2 hours onwards.

A channel of communication will thus be provided between Guards Brigades and their transport.

18. The Cavalry Corps is to be disposed in depth by 10 a.m. on Z day with its head at CARNOY ready to move at short notice.

As soon as the final objectives have been captured by the Infantry, the Cavalry will advance and seize the high ground ROCQUIGNY - VILLERS AU FLOS - RIENCOURT LES BAPAUME - BAPAUME.

The XIV Corps and also the XV Corps on our ~~right~~ LEFT will be prepared to support the Cavalry on the above line at the earliest possible moment.

19. <u>Prisoners</u>.

Prisoners will be sent to Divisional Collecting Station at CRATER POST, A.8.a.6.3. where they will be taken over and searched under A.P.M. arrangements.

Receipts will be given for prisoners and escorts will return to their units.

All captured documents should be sent with prisoners to Divisional Collecting Station, whence they will be forwarded under Divisional arrangements.

20. Advanced Brigade Head Quarters will be established as follows:-

2nd Guards Brigade	-	T.19.A.½.3½.
1st Guards Brigade	-	S.24.B.6.1½.
3rd Guards Brigade	-	DUMMY TRENCH S.23.B.5.2.

Advanced Divisional Headquarters will open at BERNAFAY WOOD (S.28.B.4.4) at 6 p.m. on Y day.

<u>A C K N O W L E D G E.</u>

C P Heywood

Lieut-Colonel,

12th September, 1916. General Staff, Guards Division.

Issued to Signals at 7-30 p.m.

Copy No. 1 General Staff.

2 "Q".

3 G.D.A.

4 C.R.E.

5 1st Guards Brigade.

6 2nd Guards Brigade.

7 3rd Guards Brigade.

8 Pioneer Battalion.

9 Divnl: Signals.

10 A.D.M.S.

11 A.P.M.

12 Divisional Train.

13 XIV Corps.

14 14th Division.

15 6th Division.

16 1st Cavalry Division.

17 War Diary.

****

SECRET

1st Gds Bde Order No 73

AMENDMENT TO GUARDS DIVISION ORDER NO. 76.

Cancel para. ~~8~~ 7 and substitute -

"The infantry will advance to the attack of the Green line at ZERO.

To the attack of the Brown Line at ZERO + 1 hour.

To the attack of the ~~BLUE~~ Blue Line at ZERO + 2 hours.

To the attack of the Red Line at ZERO + ~~2~~ 4 hours 30 minutes."

Para. ~~9~~ 8 (c), line 5.

For "at ZERO + 45 minutes", substitute "at ZERO + 1 hour".

Para. ~~9~~ 8 (d), line 1.

For "at ZERO + 1 hour" substitute "at ZERO + 1 hour 10 minutes".

Para. ~~9~~ 8. d last line, ~~on page 3, line 4~~.

For "at ZERO + 1 hour 30 minutes" substitute "at ZERO + 2 hours".

Para. ~~9~~ 8 (E) line 1.

For "at ZERO + 3 hours 45 minutes" substitute "at ZERO + 3 hours 30 minutes".

Para. 14 (a), line 1.

For "two contact aeroplanes" substitute "one contact aeroplane".

ACKNOWLEDGE.

C P Heywood.

Lieut.Colonel,
General Staff, Guards Division.

13th Sept.1916.

Copy to General Staff.
"Q".
G.D.A.
C.R.E.
1st Guards Brigade.
2nd Guards Brigade.
3rd Guards Brigade.
Pioneer Battn.
Divnl. Signals.
A.D.M.S.
A.P.M.
Divnl. Train.
XIV Corps.
14th Division.
6th Division.
1st Cavalry Division.
O.C., Tanks.
War Diary.

SECRET

G.D.No. 2240/G.

G.D.A.
C.R.E.
1st Guards Brigade.
2nd Guards Brigade.
3rd Guards Brigade.
A.D.M.S.
"Q".

Instructions as to action of Guards Brigade in Divisional Reserve.

Role of the Brigade in Divisional Reserve must largely depend on the success of the attack.

(a) If the attack is completely successful, the 1st and 2nd Guards Brigades should have sufficient weight to reach the fourth objective without the assistance of the Divisional Reserve.

The enemy's resistance would be temporarily broken and the Cavalry would be passed to the front.

The role of the 3rd Guards Brigade would then be to pass through the 1st and 2nd Guards Brigades and support the cavalry beyond the fourth objective.

(b) Should the attack be partially successful and the fourth objective reached in face of determined resistance on the part of the enemy, the 3rd Guards Brigade may be required to eventually relieve the 1st and 2nd Guards Brigades on the line of the fourth objective, or to move into a position of reserve in Squares T.8.c., and T.7.d.

(c) Should our advance be held up before reaching the fourth objective, it may be the role of the 3rd Guards Brigade to press home a fresh attack on the objective in which the enemy was holding out, passing through 1st and 2nd Guards Brigades.

This attack might be made either by day or night, but to be successful would require that adequate arrangements for artillery support were forthcoming.

(d) The situation may develop in such a manner as to demand the employment of the reserve brigade to a flank in order to safeguard

/the

Right or left flank of the Division should our attack be successful, while attacking troops of one or other flanks were held up. Such a role would probably demand an offensive movement in the first instance and the attack would have to be made with adequate artillery support.

(e) It is proposed as far as the situation allows to use the Reserve Brigade on a definite task, as a whole, and not to throw isolated battalions into the fight, thus losing the weight of an intact brigade.

(f) It should be noticed that favourable halting places for the reserve brigade are :-

(i) Southwest of GINCHY.

(ii) About squares T.8.c., T.7.d. The latter area should be defiladed from view as soon as the first objective about S.8.central is in our hands.

XIV Corps are being asked to keep us informed of the progress of the fight at S.8.central so that we may know when the area T.8.c., T.7.d. is defiladed from enemy observation.

(g) The necessity of keeping in close touch with the situation renders it advisable for Liaison Officers to be sent forward with the rear battalions of 1st and 2nd Guards Brigades.

G.O.C., 3rd Guards Brigade will arrange that this is done.

It is recommended that these officers return to 3rd Guards Brigade Headquarters as soon as the first objective is reached by troops of leading Brigades so that they may report the situation and give information as to heavily shelled areas to be avoided etc.,

ACKNOWLEDGE.

C P Heywood

13th Sept. 1916.

Lieut.Colonel,
General Staff, Guards Division.

Copy No............

SECRET.

G.D.No. 2241/G.

INSTRUCTIONS FOR TANKS,
to be attached to Guards Division Order No. 76
issued on 12th September 1916.

1. (a) Tanks will reach assembly position about S.29.b.4.4 on the evening of "X" day.

(b) Tanks will move from assembly position on Y/Z night in such time as to allow of their being in their forward positions at ZERO – 4 hours.

On arrival at these positions, tanks will be formed into three columns, numbered from right to left, each consisting of three tanks.

Tanks will be lettered -

A, B, C in No. 1 column.
D, E, F in No. 2 ,,
G, H, K in No. 3 ,,
and "L" Tank.

During operations, all references in messages to tanks and tank columns will be as above.

All arrangements will be made by Divisional Hd. Qrs. for (a) and (b).

2. Column No. 1 will advance to the attack of the Green Line at ZERO – 40.

Column No. 2 will advance to the attack of the Green Line at ZERO – 40.

Column No. 3 will advance to the attack of the Green Line at ZERO – 50.

Nos. 1, 2 & 3 columns will advance to the attack of the Blue Line (column No. 1 passing into the 6th Division area about T.9.central) at ZERO + 1 hour and 10 minutes.

Nos. 2 and 3 columns will advance to the attack of the Red Line at ZERO + 3 hours and 30 minutes.

3. A special task is allotted to "L" tank, viz. that of protecting the left flank of 1st Guards Brigade from hostile fire from direction of T.13.A.central. In this task, the

/two

two tanks of XV Corps on our left will assist.

~~"L" tank will at ZERO - 50 attack German trench from~~ T.13.B.2.5 to T.13.A.5.8, cruising in that neighbourhood and overcoming any opposition met with until the infantry of the 14th Division, who are advancing North-eastwards at ZERO from the line T.13.central - T.13.A.0.0, have cleared up the situation. "L" tank will as soon as, but not before, the enemy's resistance in T.13.A has been completely overcome withdraw to a position in reserve about S.24.central. On arrival at this point, O.C. "L" tank will report the position to 1st Guards Brigade Headquarters at S.24.B.6.1½ and there await fresh orders from Guards Division.

4. Orders as to withdrawal of tanks at the conclusion of operations or for the undertaking of fresh operations subsequent to the period dealt with in Guards Division Order No. 76 will be issued by XIV Corps and repeated through Guards Division to Guards Brigades concerned who will transmit these orders to the tanks - care being taken that those orders are delivered to each individual tank on their Brigade frontage.

As regards local co-operation between tanks and infantry in carrying out the tasks allotted in Guards Division Order No. 76, Company Commanders will notify Tanks their requirements, which requirements will be met by Tanks as long as it does not interfere with scheme of attack, and times and routes laid down in Guards Division Order No. 76.

5. Maps shewing routes of the Tanks and the special points in the enemy lines to be dealt with by them have been issued with Guards Division Order No. 76.

<u>ACKNOWLEDGE.</u>

Edward Seymour.

Captain,

13th September 1916. General Staff, Guards Division.

<u>Issued to Signals at 11-55 p.m.</u>

Copy No.

1 General Staff.	7 3rd Guards Bde.	13 XIV Corps.
2 "Q".	8 Pioneer Battn.	14 14th Division.
3 G.D.A.	9 Divnl. Signals.	15 6th Division.
4 C.R.E.	10 A.D.M.S.	16 1st Cavalry Division.
5 1st Guards Bde.	11 A.P.M.	17, 18 O.C. Tanks.
6 2nd Guards Bde.	12 Divnl. Train.	19 War Diary.

INSTRUCTIONS FOR EMPLOYMENT OF TANKS.

To accompany Guards Division Order No: 76.

Nine tanks will be allotted to Guards Division to work partly in Guards Division and partly in 6th Division area.

Departure positions and lines of advance of tanks are shewn on attached map.

Three tanks will be employed in each group and will normally advance in file.

ATTACK OF FIRST OBJECTIVE.

Tanks will start movement from their departure positions at a time so calculated that they reach their objective 5 minutes before the Infantry.

The Infantry will advance as usual behind a creeping barrage in which gaps, about 100 yards wide, will be left for the route of the tanks. The stationary barrage of both heavy and field artillery will be timed to be lifted off the objectives of the tanks some minutes before their arrival at these objectives.

After clearing up the first objective a proportion of tanks should be pushed forward a short way to prearranged positions as defensive strong points. If necessary a tank may be sent to assist the Infantry in clearing such points in the line as may be holding them up.

THE ATTACK OF THE 2ND OBJECTIVE.

Tanks and Infantry will advance together under the creeping barrage. Tanks will move as before in column and on well defined routes. The pace will be regulated to tank pace (30-50 yards per minute), but Infantry must not wait for any tanks that are delayed.

The action of the tanks will be as for the first objective.

THE ATTACK OF THE 3RD AND SUBSEQUENT OBJECTIVES.

The tanks will start sufficiently far in front of the Infantry to reach the third and fourth objectives some time before the Infantry being covered during their advance by a

creeping

creeping barrage.

The tanks will move as before in column.

Their action will be arranged so as to crush wire and keep down hostile rifle and machine gun fire.

The Infantry when they are advancing must not wait for any tanks that are delayed.

The following signals will be used:-

From Tanks to Infantry and Aircraft.

FLAG SIGNALS. -	RED Flag	-	Out of action.
	GREEN Flag	-	Am on objective.
	Other Flags	-	Are Inter-tank signals.
LAMP SIGNALS.	Series of T's	-	Out of action.
	Series of H's	-	Am on objective.

A proportion of the tanks will carry pigeons.

If tanks get behind time table or get out of action, infantry must on no account wait for them.

If the tanks succeed and the Infantry are checked the Tanks must endeavour to help them.

GENERAL NOTES.

Recent trials show that over heavily shelled ground a greater pace than 15 yards a minute cannot be depended on. This pace will be increased to 33 yards over good ground, and down hill on good ground it will reach 50 yards a minute.

=*=*=*=*=*=*=*=*=*=*=*=*=*=*=*=*=

SECRET

G.D. No.2238/G.

G.D.A.
C.R.E.
1st Guards Bde.
2nd Guards Bde.
3rd Guards Bde.
Pioneer Bn.
A.D.M.S.
Divnl. Train.

Reference Guards Division Order No. 76 para. 18 (d) the following are arrangements made for supply of articles mentioned.

1. Rations.

Dumps are situated as follows:-

(a) 12,000 preserved Rations at MINDEN POST. These will be issued on application to and by order of Guards Division A and Q office at MINDEN POST.

(b) 15,000 preserved rations near BERNAFAY WOOD at S.28.d.2.2.

The N.C.O. in charge will only issue on receipt of a written order signed by an officer.

Units may draw on this store in case of emergency and will notify Guards Division Q by wire the number of rations drawn.

(c) Rations will be issued at refilling points as follows for the next few days:-

13th inst. 1st and 2nd Guards Brigades.

Bread, preserved meat.
percentage of chewing gum.
4,000 Oxo cubes per Brigade.

3rd Guards Brigade.

Bread, fresh meat.
percentage of chewing gum.
4,000 Oxo cubes.

Note: Chewing gum and Oxo cubes to be consumed by order of Brigade Commanders.

<u>14th inst</u>. Preserved meat and biscuit for all Guards Brigades.

In addition sufficient bread and preserved meat for sandwiches.

Rum will be issued to the whole Division.

<u>15th inst</u>. Preserved meat and biscuit to all Guards Brigades.

2. <u>Water</u>.

The troughs on the W. side of BERNAFAY WOOD at S.28.d.3.5 are filled twice daily. Petrol tins will be filled from these troughs.

In case of emergency a store of full petrol tins will be kept at MINDEN POST ready to send out at once should the above supply fail.

It should, however, be noted that it takes a long time to send up these tins from MINDEN POST.

Samples of water from the wells in GINCHY have been sent for and will be submitted for analysis. If the analysis proves satisfactory it is hoped that a supply will be forthcoming from this village.

3. <u>Ammunition</u>.

A dump of S.A.A., grenades, and Stokes Mortar ammunition has been established on the W. edge of BERNAFAY WOOD. Units will draw on this dump.

4. Brigades will be responsible for the transport of Stores and Ammunition from the dump at BERNAFAY WOOD. The Division will maintain these dumps.

5. A store of charcoal and coke in limited quantites will be formed at S.28.d.2.2.

C. Darell

Lieut-Colonel,

12th September 1916. A.A. & Q.M.G. Guards Divn.

SECRET

G.D.No: 2246/G.
****

G.D.A.
C.R.E.
1st Guards Brigade.
2nd Guards Brigade.
3rd Guards Brigade.
=*=*=*=*=*=*=*=*=*=*=

With reference to Guards Division Order No: 76, the 20th Division will be in XIV Corps Reserve.

H. L. Aubrey-Fletcher Capt

~~Lieut-Colonel,~~

13th September, 1916.

General Staff, Guards Division.

SECRET

HEADQUARTERS,
GUARDS' DIVISION.
No. 2229/G
Date 12/9/16

G.D.A.
C.R.E.
1st Guards Brigade.
2nd Guards Brigade.
3rd Guards Brigade.
Pioneer Battn.
Divnl. Signals.
A.D.M.S.
A.P.M.
Divnl. Train.
XIV Corps.
14th Division.
6th Division.
1st Cavalry Division.
"Q".

---

1. Reference Guards Division Operation Order No. 76.

2. The day of attack (Z day) will be the 15th September.

3. Zero hour will be in the early morning, probably between 6 and 6.30 a.m. The exact time will be notified later.

4. ACKNOWLEDGE.

C P Heywood

Lieut. Colonel,

12th September 1916. General Staff, Guards Division.

SECRET

Copy No. 5

GUARDS DIVISION ORDER NO. 77.

The following instructions are issued in connection with Guards Division Order No. 76.

1. ~~Special instructions for Tanks are attached.~~

2. Movement on Y/Z night to forming up areas, as allotted in map attached to Guards Division Order No. 76, will be carried out in accordance with attached March Table.

3. R.E.Dumps.

(a) Advanced R.E. dumps have been established at S.24.B.9.8 and T.19.C.2.4.

These dumps will not be drawn on except subsequent to the commencement of operations, or to provide stores to be carried forward in the attack.

(b) A main R.E. dump has been established on the West side of BERNAFAY WOOD. This dump may be drawn on at any time.

Dumps (a) and (b) contain Sandbags - French wire - Pickets - and Barbed wire.

(c) A mobile reserve of R.E. stores will be kept parked near MINDEN POST.

4. Traffic.

Traffic moving westward from GUILLEMONT STATION (S.24.c) will not use the road through TRONES WOOD - such traffic will be diverted southwards from S.24.c.4.2 on to the main GUILLEMONT - MONTAUBAN ROAD.

1st Guards Brigade will maintain a post till further orders at S.24.c.4.2 to control traffic.

5. Details of standing barrages and artillery distribution, also details of Medical arrangements will be issued separately.

ACKNOWLEDGE.

C P Heywood

Lieut.Colonel,
General Staff, Guards Division.

13th Sept. 1916.

<u>Issued to Signals at 6.30 p.m.</u>

Copy No. 1 General Staff.
2 "Q".
3 C.D.A.
4 C.R.E.
5 1st Guards Brigade.
6 2nd Guards Brigade.
7 3rd Guards Brigade.
8 Pioneer Battn.
9 Divnl. Signals.
10 A.D.M.S.
11 A.P.M.
12 Divnl. Train.
13 XIV Corps.
14 14th Division.
15 6th Division.
16 1st Cavalry Division.
17 C.C., Tanks.
18 War Diary.

M A R C H   T A B L E.

Issued with Guards Divn. Order No. 77.

Unit.	Present Position.	Destination.	Starting point.	Time.	Route.	Notes.
2 battalions) 1st Gds. Bde.)	CARNOY area.	Forming up area.	Road junction A.8.c.	8 p.m.	MONTAUBAN	Units East of CARNOY must move to starting point by Cross Roads A.14.A.5.2 or road junction A.13.b.5.3.
75th Field Coy R.E.	CARNOY area.	"	"	8.40 pm.	"	
2 battalions) 2nd Gds. Bde.)	CARNOY area.	"	"	9 p.m.	"	
76th Field Coy R.E.	CARNOY area.	"	"	9.40 p.m.	"	
3rd Guards Bde.	L.3.B.	"	"	10 p.m.	CARNOY MONTAUBAN.	3rd Guards Brigade will be clear of L.3.B. HAPPY VALLEY by 8 p.m. and will move by Cross country tracks to an assembly area F.17.d. Detailed area will be pointed out by "Q".
55th Field Coy. R.E.	CARNOY area.	"	"	11.20 p.m.	MONTAUBAN.	
Pioneer Battn. (4th Coldstreams)	MINDEN POST AREA.	"	"	11.30 pm.	CARNOY MONTAUBAN.	

S E C R E T.

Copy No.......

GUARDS DIVISION ORDER NO: 78.

Reference Map Sheet 57C S.W.

1. The attack of the XIV and XV Corps will be continued tomorrow morning.

2. The objectives of the Guards Division will be as follows:-
1st Objective.
BLUE Line between T.9.d.8.7 and N.33.c.2.0.
2nd Objective.
LES BOEUFS from T.10.a.8.4 - SUNKEN ROAD T.10.a.3.10 - thence to SUNKEN ROAD T.4.d.7.0 to T.4.b.5.3 - thence SUNKEN ROAD to Cross Roads at T.34.a.2.9.

3. The attack will be carried out by the 61st Infantry Brigade on the Right, and the 3rd Guards Brigade on the Left.
Dividing Line between Brigades will be :-
Line T.8.b.5.0 - T.3.d.2.7 - N.34.a.8.2.
Dividing Line between 3rd Guards Brigade and XV Corps :-
Line from T.8.a.2.6 to N.33.B.2.0. - N.34.a.2.9. There will be no troops attacking on Right of 61st Infantry Brigade.

4.(a) Infantry will advance to the attack of the 1st Objective at such time as to be within 100 yards of the creeping barrage (which will commence 250 yards in front of BLUE Line) at ZERO 10 minutes. Creeping barrage will creep on at ZERO + 10 at rate of 50 yards a minute to 200 yards beyond BLUE Line.
(b) Infantry will advance to the attack of the 2nd Objective at ZERO + 35 minutes at which hour creeping barrage will become intense 200 yards beyond BLUE Line, and will advance at pace of 50 yards per minute until it has passed 200 yards beyond 2nd Objective.
(c) Standing Barrages on 1st and 2nd Objectives will lift back as creeping barrages reach them.

5. Troops of 1st and 2nd Guards Brigades in GREEN Line will be in Divisional Reserve and will not move forward with the attack. They will not be withdrawn tonight.

6. 61st Infantry Brigade will move up to its front of attack (now held by 2nd Guards Brigade) tonight, leaving TRONES WOOD at 12 midnight, or as soon after that hour as possible. Details as to guides and routes to be arranged between 61st Infantry Brigade and 2nd Guards Brigade.

7. 60th Infantry Brigade will be in Divisional Reserve at WATERLOT FARM at 7 a.m. tomorrow.

8. ZERO hour will be 9-25 a.m.

9. Watches will be synchronised by telephone, from Divisional Head Quarters.

A C K N O W L E D G E.

C P Heywood
Lieut-Colonel.
General Staff, Guards Division.

15th September, 1916.
Issued to Divnl: Signals at 9-45 p.m.

Copy No. 1 General Staff.
2 "Q"
3 G.D.A.
4 C.R.E.
5 1st Guards Bde.
No. 6 2nd Guards Bde.
7 3rd Guards Bde.
8 Pioneer Bn.
9 6th Division.
10 61st Infy. Bde.
No. 11 60th Inf. Bde.
12 14th Division
13 XIV Corps.
14 20th Division
15 War Diary.

ADDITION TO GUARDS DIVISION ORDER NO. 78.

1. With reference to Guards Division Order No. 78, the following changes in Headquarters will take place at 8 a.m. tomorrow, the 16th instant:-

2. 3rd Guards Bde. H.Q.	to S.24.b.7.3 (now occupied by 1st Guards Bde.
1st Guards Bde.	to DUMMY TRENCH (now occupied by 3rd Guards Bde.
61st Infantry Brigade	to T.19.a.1.4 (now occupied by 2nd Guards Bde.)
2nd Guards Brigade	to S.23.d.5.5.

A C K N O W L E D G E.

E Seymour

Captain for
Lieut-Colonel,

15th September 1916. General Staff. Guards Divn.

Issued to General Staff.
"Q".
G.D.A.
C.R.E.
1st Guards Bde.
2nd Guards Bde.
3rd Guards Bde.
Pioneer Bn.
6th Division.
61st Inf. Bde.
60th Inf. Bde.
14th Division.
XIV Corps
20th Division.
War Diary.

S E C R E T .

Copy No 5

GUARDS DIVISION ORDER NO. 7[illegible]

1. Guards Division (less Artillery) will be relieved tonight by 20th Division on the front between T.14.B.9.8 and the boundary between XV Corps and Guards Division (a line between T.7.B.7.0 - T.3.A.3.10).

Relief to be completed by 5.30 a.m. tomorrow.

(a) The Right sector.

(Now held by 61st Inf. Bde. and 2nd Guards Brigade) will be relieved by 60th Infantry Brigade.

The Left Sector.

(Now held by 3rd Guards Brigade and 1st Guards Brigade) will be relieved by 59th Infantry Brigade.

Details of relief to be arranged between Brigades concerned.

(b) 61st Inf. Bde. Headquarters and 2nd Guards Brigade Headquarters are at T.19.A.4.6.

3rd Guards Brigade Headquarters are at S.24.B.5.3.

1st uards Brigade Headquarters are at S.23.D.10.5.

2. Field Coys. R.E. and Pioneer Battalion will complete tasks allotted for tonight before withdrawing.

3. (a) On completion of relief the Division will be disposed as under -

3rd Guards Brigade	CARNOY.
2nd Guards Brigade	CITADEL (F.21.b.3.2).
1st Guards Brigade	CITADEL.

(b) Field Coys. R.E. and Pioneer Battalion return to their former billets.

(c) 1st Line transport to former billets.

4.) On completion of relief 20th Division will be disposed

61st Infantry Brigade	TRONES WOOD	- Hd.Qrs. N. end of TRONES WOOD.
60th Infantry Brigade	RIGHT SECTOR	- Hd.Qrs. T.19.A. 4.6.
15th Infantry Brigade	WATERLOT FARM Area	Hd. Qrs. WATERLOT FARM.
59th Infantry Brigade	LEFT SECTOR	Hd.Qrs. S.24.D.5.3.

(d) Travelling kitchens will meet troops near cross roads just S.W. of BERNAFAY WOOD to provide thom with a hot meal.

5. G.O.C. Guards Divisien will hand over command of the line to G.O.C. 20th Division at 8 a.m. on September 17th, at which hour Divisional Headquarters will close at BERNAFAY WOOD and open at FORKED TREE (L.2.B.)

A C K N O W L E D G E.

C P Heywood

Lieut-Colonel,

16th September 1916. General Staff. Guards Divn.

Issued to Si nals at 7.30 p.m.

Copy No. 1	General Staff.	10	A.D.M.S.
2	"Q".	11	A.P.M.
3.	G.D.A.	12	Divnl. Train.
4	C.R.E.	13	61st Inf. Bde.
5	1st Guards Bri ade.	14	60th Inf. Bde.
6	2nd Guards Bri ade.	15	20th Division.
7	3rd Guards Bri ade.	16	14th Division.
8	Pioneor Bn.	17	6th Division.
9	Divnl. Signals.	[illegible]	XIV Corns.
		19	1st Cavalry Division.
		20	War Diary.

SECRET.

Q.D.No: 2288/G

1st Guards Brigade.
2nd Guards Brigade.
3rd Guards Brigade.
C.R.E.

(1). The Major General wishes to point out the necessity of pushing on with the construction of assembly trenches for the attack.

These trenches are of special importance owing to the probability that the attack will take place in the afternoon.

(2). In considering the number of troops to be employed by 1st and 3rd Guards Brigades in the forthcoming attack, consideration must be given to the following factors -

A. The distance to the final objective is at least 1,500 yards.

B. The possibility of having to form defensive flanks if the attack to North or South of us were held up.

C. The probability of a counter-attack.

The Germans have recently brought up reinforcements.

D. The necessity of having a strong reserve in the BROWN Line in case of our men being driven back by counter-attack from LES BOEUFS.

It is the Major General's opinion that for the attack all four battalions of 1st and 3rd Guards Brigades should be assembled well forward -

To attempt to bring up troops, after the attack has started, from such areas as T.7.D or GINCHY is not advisable - They may suffer heavy casualties on the way, and must be out of touch with operations at commencement of the attack.

ACKNOWLEDGE.

C P Heywood

Lieut-Colonel,

20th September, 1916.

General Staff, Guards Division.

SECRET

G.D. No. 2287/G.

C.D.A.
C.R.E.
1st Guards Bde.
2nd Guards Bde.
3rd Guards Bde.
A.D.M.S.
"Q".

---

1. The attack proposed for the 22nd will now be postponed to 23rd.

Certain alterations in the place of attack will be made which will involve our handing over 600 yards on the right of our attacking front to 6th Division who will now be attacking on our right.

2. This re-adjustment will be carried out tomorrow night under orders which will be issued later.

It will involve 1st Guards Brigade being relieved on 600 yards of frontage South of SUNKEN ROAD, T.3.D.4.0, by 6th Division, and also the relief of 3rd Guards Brigade on 300 yards of frontage by 1st Guards Brigade.

This will put the Division, on completion of relief tomorrow night, on a frontage of approximately 1,000 yards of which the Southern 500 yards will be held by 1st Guards Brigade and the Northern half by 3rd Guards Brigade.

3. No alteration will be made in arrangements for tonight's relief.

4. In the new plan of attack 2nd Guards Brigade will be kept complete in Divisional Reserve.

A C K N O W L E D G E .

C P Heywood

Lieut-Colonel,

20th September 1916. General Staff. Guards Divn.

SECRET

G.D. No. 2301/G.

1st Guards Bde.
~~2nd Guards~~ Bde.
~~3rd Guards~~ Bde.

Special Instructions for action of 2nd Guards Brigade.

(Brigade in Divnl. Reserve).

1. The distribution of the 2nd Guards Brigade is given in Guards Division Order No. 82.

2. It is not the intention of the Major-General to use the 2nd Guards Brigade on September 25th until the situation after the attack has cleared.

At the same time the situation may demand the sending forward of one or even two Battalions to reinforce 1st or 3rd Guards Brigades early in the action - in certain eventualities. If required, these Battalions would be ordered to move in the first instance to area T.7.D. or the reserve line T.8.A and B.

3. The most probable tasks of the Reserve Brigade are

(A) to carry out a new attack on 26th against any portion of our objectives which are still held by the enemy. Forming up and preparations for such an attack would be made on night of 25th/26th.

or

(B) to relieve the 1st and 3rd Guards Brigades on the line gained.
This relief would be most likely to take place on night 26th/27th.

4. Reconnaissance necessary to ensure that Battalions can move by the most covered route to reserve line in T.8.A and B should be carried out.

A C K N O W L E D G E.

C.P. Heywood

Lieut-Colonel,
General Staff. Guards Divn.

23rd September 1916.

S E C R E T.
****

Copy No.....5.....

GUARDS DIVISION ORDER NO: 82.

Reference Map 57.C.,S.W.
1/20,000 - (attached)

(1). (a) The Fourth Army will renew the attack on "Z" day in combination with attacks by the French to the South and the Reserve Army to the North.

(b) The objectives of the XIV Corps include MORVAL and LES BOEUFS, and those of the XV Corps, GUEUDECOURT.

(c) The attack of the XIV Corps will be carried out by the 5th Division on the Right, the 6th Division in the Centre and the Guards Division on the Left; the 56th Division will form a defensive flank to the South of the 5th Division.

The 21st Division will be attacking on our Left.

(2). The 1st Guards Brigade will attack on the Right; and the 3rd Guards Brigade on the Left.

2nd Guards Brigade(less 1 Battalion) will be in Divisional Reserve.

1 Battalion, 2nd Guards Brigade will be in Corps Reserve. 2nd Guards Brigade will notify Divisional Head Quarters the name of the Battalion detailed.

PRELIMINARY BOMBARDMENT.

(3). A steady bombardment of hostile positions will be commenced at 7 a.m. on "Y" day and will be continued to 6-30 p.m. It will re-commence at 6-30 a.m. on "Z" day.

The ground in front and rear of the German trenches which are being bombarded will be searched occasionally with 18 Pdr: shrapnel and H.E.Shell.

There will be no intensive fire previous to the hour of ZERO. Night firing will be carried out nightly between the hours of 6-30 p.m. and 6-30 a.m.

4.

(4). FORMING UP AREAS.

Forming up areas are shewn on attached map.

1st and 3rd Guards Brigades will allot forming up areas to 75th and 55th Field Companies, R.E., respectively within their areas.

Instructions for movements to forming up areas will be issued separately.

(5). Objectives allotted to Guards Brigades and neighbouring Divisions, also dividing lines, are shewn on attached map.

First Objective is marked......GREEN.

2nd Objective is marked........BROWN.

3rd Objective is marked........BLUE.

(6). The Infantry will advance to the attack of the GREEN Line at ZERO

to the attack of the BROWN Line at ZERO + one hour

to the attack of the BLUE Line at ZERO + two hours.

(7). BARRAGES.

(a) 50% of Field Artillery covering the Division will be used for creeping barrage and 50% for stationary barrage.

(b) In all cases the stationary barrage will lift back when the creeping barrage meets it.

(8). (A) At ZERO the creeping barrage will commence 100 yards in front of our front trenches.

It will advance at rate of 50 yards per minute until it is 200 yards beyond the GREEN Line when it will become stationary.

(B) At ZERO + one hour

the creeping barrage will commence 200 yards in front of the GREEN Line and will advance at the rate of 50 yards per minute until it has passed 200 yards beyond the BROWN Line when it will become stationary.

(C) At ZERO + two hours

the creeping barrage will commence 200 yards in front of the BROWN Line, and will advance at rate of 50 yards per minute, until it has passed 200 yards beyond the BLUE Line, when it will

will become stationary.

(9) Details of stationary barrages will be notified later.

(10). (a) The task of the two leading Guards Brigades is to press the attack through to the BLUE Line.

A sufficient flow of troops must be maintained by 1st and 3rd Guards Brigades, from ZERO onwards, to ensure that the attack made from the BROWN Line is strong and well supported.

(b) Special arrangements must be made to deal with resistance in LES BOEUFS and thus prevent the possibility of the enemy cutting off our troops which have gained the BLUE Line.

(c) 1st and 3rd Guards Brigades will garrison and consolidate the BROWN Line with a portion of their Reserves, when the attack pushes forward to the BLUE Line.

(d) On gaining the BLUE Line patrols will be sent forward, and any ground from which good observation can be gained will be occupied.

Such points will be consolidated and eventually joined up with our line.

(11) 75th Field Company, R.E. and 55th Field Company, R.E., will be
R.E. at disposal of 1st and 3rd Guards Brigades respectively for the attack.

76th Field Company, R.E., and Pioneer Battalion (4th Bn: Coldstream Guards) will be in Divisional Reserve.

(12) One Contact Patrol will be in the air from ZERO till 6-30 p.m.

(13) Flares will be lit by leading Infantry lines on obtaining each objective, and also at 6 p.m. on "Z" day.

(14) Watches will be synchronised at 6 p.m. on "Y" day and at 8 a.m. on "Z" day by telephone from Divisional Head Quarters.

(15) Separate instructions will be issued on the following points:-

(A) Division of Artillery into groups and the fronts they support.

(B) Medical arrangements.

(C) Supply of Rations.
Water.
S.A.A.
Light Trench Mortar Ammunition.
Hand Grenades.

16.

(16) Ammunition portions of 1st Line Transport will be collected on the South West side of BERNAFAY WOOD - to the South of the GUILLEMONT - MONTAUBAN road, and remainder of 1st Line Transport in the neighbourhood of MINDEN POST by 12 noon on "Z" day. An Orderly from each Brigade Transport will be in waiting at Advanced Divisional Head Quarters, BERNAFAY WOOD, and an Officer from each Brigade Transport at Divisional Head Quarters MINDEN POST from 12 noon on "Z" day to receive instructions.

(17) PRISONERS.

Prisoners will be dealt with as per paragraph 19, G.D.O. No: 76.

(18) For the attack, Advanced Head Quarters will be as follows:-

Divisional Head Quarters........BERNAFAY WOOD.(S.28.B.4.4.)

1st Guards Brigade ....T.19.A.½.3½.

3rd Guards Brigade..............S.24.B.6.1½.

2nd Guards Brigade..............DUMMY TRENCH.
(S.23.B.5.2.)

(19) "Z" day will be September 23rd.

Hour of ZERO will be notified later - it will probably be in the afternoon.

C.P. Heywood

ACKNOWLEDGE.

Lieut-Colonel,
General Staff, Guards Division.

21st September,1916.

Issued to Divnl:Signals at 12 noon.

Copy No: 1 General Staff.
2 "Q".
3 G.D.A.
4 C.R.E.
5 1st Guards Brigade.
6 2nd Guards Brigade.
7 3rd Guards Brigade.
8 Pioneer Battalion.
9 Divnl. Signals.
10 A.D.M.S.
11 A.D.V.S.
12 A.P.M.
13 Divnl.Train.
14 O.C.Supply Column.
15 Senior Supply Officer.
16 Camp Commandant.
17 Sanitary Section.
18 S.A.A.Sections,Guards D.A.C.
19 D.A.D.O.S.
20 XIV Corps.
21 5th Division.
22 6th Division.
23 20th Division.
24 21st Division.
25 War Diary.

****

S E C R E T .

Copy No ....5...

AMENDMENT TO GUARDS DIVISION ORDER NO. 82.

Para. 8.C.

line 2 - for "100 yards"

substitute "200 yards"

A C K N O W L E D G E .

C P Heywood

Lieut-Colonel,

21st September 1916.

General Staff. Guards Divn.

Copy No. 1	General Staff.	14	O.C. Supply Column.
2	"Q".	15	Senior Supply Officer.
3	C.D.A.	16	Camp Commandant.
4	C.R.E.	17	Sanitary Section.
5	1st Guards Brigade.	18	S.A.A. Sections, Guards D.A.C.
6	2nd Guards Brigade.	19	D.A.D.O.S.
7	3rd Guards Brigade.	20	XIV Corps.
8	Pioneer Battalion.	21	5th Division.
9	Divnl. Signals.	22	6th Division.
10	A.D.M.S.	23	20th Division.
11	A.D.V.S.	24	21st Division.
12	A.P.M.	25	War Diary.
13	Divnl. Train.		

S E C R E T.
****

Copy No 5

AMENDMENT TO GUARDS DIVISION ORDER NO. 82.
****

Para. 19.

"Z" day will be September 25th.

A C K N O W L E D G E.
****

E Seymour. Captain
for Lieut-Colonel,

21st September 1916. General Staff. Guards Divn.

Copy No. 1 General Staff.
2 "Q".
3 C.D.A.
4 C.R.E.
5 1st Guards Brigade.
6 2nd Guards Brigade.
7 3rd Guards Brigade.
8 Pioneer Battalion.
9 Divnl. Signals.
10 A.D.M.S.
11 A.D.V.S.
12 A.P.M.
13 Divnl. Train.
14 O.C. Supply Column.
15 Senior Supply Offr.
16 Camp Commandant.
17 Sanitary Section.
18 S.A.A. Sections.
19 D.A.D.O.S.
20 War Diary.

****

SECRET

Copy No....5.....

INSTRUCTIONS FOR TANKS,
Issued with Guards Divisional Order No. 82.
****

1. Three Tanks under Captain Hiscocks are allotted to the Quards Division for the operations on "Z" day. They will be kept in Divisional Reserve.

2. These Tanks will be in their assembly position at the South-west corner of TRONES WOOD by 5 p.m. on "Y" day, at which hour an orderly will be sent by Captain Hiscocks to Quards Divisional Headquarters.

3. At ZERO hour, the three Tanks will proceed from their assembly position to a point about T.13.central, avoiding the roads in getting to this point.

.. On arrival, Captain Hiscocks and two orderlies will report at 1st Quards Brigade Headquarters at T.19.A.½.8½. and will there await orders from Divisional Headquarters.

4. An advanced dump of petrol, 120 gallons, will be maintained at T.13.central.

5. From 5 p.m. on "Y" day, all orders ^from Divnl.Hd.Qrs. affecting Tanks will be sent direct to Captain Hiscocks.

ACKNOWLEDGE.

E Seymour.
Captain,
General Staff, Quards Division.

21st Sept. 1916.

Issued to Signals at 2-30 pm.

Copy No.1 General Staff.
2 "Q"
3 C.D.A.
4 C.R.E.
5 1st Quards Bde.
6 2nd Quards Bde.
7 3rd Quards Bde.
8 Pioneer Battn.
9 Divnl. Signals.
10. A.D.M.S.
11 A.D.V.S.
12 A.P.M.
13 Divnl. Train.
14 O.C.Supply Column.
15 Senior Supply Officer.
16 Camp Commandant.
17 Sanitary Section.
18 S.A.A.Sections, Gds. D.A.C.
19 D.A.D.O.S.
20 XIV Corps.
21 5th Division.
22 6th Division.
23 20th Division.
24 21st Division.
25 O.C.Heavy Machine Gun Section.
26 O.C.Heavy Machine Gun Sub-Section, allotted to Quards Division.
27. War Diary.

S E C R E T.
****

AMENDMENT TO GUARDS DIVISION ORDER NO. 82.
****

Para. 8 (a) line 1,

For "100 yards" -

Substitute "200 yards".

A C K N O W L E D G E.
****

E Seymour Capt
for Lieut-Colonel,

24th September 1916. General Staff. Guards Divn.

Issued to C.D.A.
C.R.E.
1st Guards Brigade.
2nd Guards Brigade.
3rd Guards Brigade.
Pioneer Bn.
Divnl. Signals.
XIV Corps.
6th Division.
21st Division.

****

S E C R E T. Copy No...5.......

QUARDS DIVISION ORDER NO. 84.
****

(1) Movement to forming up areas will be carried out as under :-

A. 1st and 3rd Quards Brigades and attached Field Companies R.E. will be assembled in their forming up areas by dawn on September 25th.

B. 2nd Quards Brigade (less 2 battalions) and 76th Field Coy. R.E. will be assembled in TRONES WOOD and the vicinity by 11 a.m. 25th September, moving from CARNOY by Companies at 5 minutes interval.

Cross country tracks will be used.

C. The battalion of 2nd Quards Brigade in Corps Reserve (3rd Bn.Grenadier Quards) will be in position at "THE CRATERS" A.8.A. by ZERO.

C.O., battalion will report his arrival at the rendezvous to 6th Division Advanced Headquarters (A.3.C.1.6). Any orders for movement of this battalion will be sent by XIV Corps through 6th Division Advanced Hd.Qrs., where an officer of 3rd Bn.Grenadier Quards will remain in waiting.

D. One battalion 2nd Quards Brigade will remain at CARNOY.

(2) Divisional Headquarters will close at MINDEN POST and open at BERNAFAY WOOD (S.28.B.4.4) at 10.30 a.m. on September 25th.

ACKNOWLEDGE.

C P Heywood
Lieut.Colonel,
General Staff, Quards Division.

24th September 1916.

Issued to Signals at 11 a.m.

Copy No.1 General Staff.	7 3rd Quards Bde.	13 Camp Commandant.
2 "Q"	8 Pioneer Battn.	14 XIV Corps.
3 Q.D.A.	9 Divnl. Signals.	15 6th Division.
4 C.R.E.	10 A.D.M.S.	16 20th Division.
5 1st Quards Bde.	11 A.P.M.	17 21st Division.
6 2nd Quards Bde.	12 Divnl. Train.	18 War Diary.

****

S E C R E T.   G.D.No. 2307/G.

~~"Q".~~
G.D.A.
~~C.R.E.~~
1st Guards Brigade.
~~2nd Guards Brigade.~~
3rd Guards Brigade.
Pioneer Battn.
Divnl. Signals.
A.D.M.S.
A.P.M.

~~O.C., Heavy M.G.Sub-Section,~~
~~Attchd Guards Division.~~

---

1. With reference to Guards Division Order No. 82, dated 21st September 1916.

2. ZERO hour will be 12.35 p.m. on September 25th.

The French are attacking at the same hour.

This hour is only to be communicated to those whom it immediately concerns, and in no case should it be communicated by telephone.

3. Acknowledge by wire.

C P Heywood

24th September 1916.

Lieut.Colonel,
General Staff, Guards Division.

S E C R E T.

Copy No.....5.......

GUARDS DIVISION ORDER NO. 85.

1. (a) 2nd Guards Brigade will relieve 1st and 3rd Guards Brigades in the line to-night. Details of relief to be arranged between Brigades concerned.

(b) Divisional boundaries remain as for the attack, i.e.,

Southern boundary.

T.8.d.4.5 - just south of SUNKEN ROAD to T.4.c.4.7 - LES BOEUFS CHURCH - T.4.b.3.4.

Northern boundary.

T.7.b.9.6 - T.2.a.8.6 - N.32.d.8.4 - N.33.central - N.34.a.3.2.

2. Machine Gun Companies of 1st and 3rd Guards Brigades will remain in the line to-night and will be relieved by 2nd Guards Brigade Machine Gun Company on night of 27th/28th September.

3. On completion of relief Brigades will be disposed as follows :-

2nd Guards Brigade.

Brigade Headquarters	-	T.19.a.½.3½
4 battalions.	- -	Forward Area.

3rd Guards Brigade.

Brigade Headquarters	-	S.24.b.6.1½
2 battalions	- -	CARNOY.
2 battalions	- -	TRONES WOOD Area.

1st Guards Brigade. - - CARNOY.

4. 55th and 75th Field Coys. R.E. will continue to work to-night on sectors of the line to which they are at present attached.

ACKNOWLEDGE.

C.P. Heywood.

Lieut.Colonel,
General Staff, Guards Division.

26th Septr. 1916.

Issued at 11 am.

Copy No.1 General Staff.	6 2nd Guards Bde.	11 XIV Corps.
2 "Q"	7 3rd Guards Bde.	12 6th Division.
3 C.D.A.	8 Pioneer Battn.	13 21st Division.
4 C.R.E.	9 Divnl Signals.	14 A.P.M.
5 1st Guards Bde.	10 A.D.M.S.	15 War Diary.

5

Copy No......

SECRET.

GUARDS DIVISION ORDER NO: 86.

1. (A). XV Corps are attacking certain trenches North and North West of GUEUDECOURT today at 2-15 p.m.

(B) To deceive the enemy as to exact point of attack XIV Corps will demonstrate with Artillery [illegible] fire.

2. The Heavy Artillery are bombarding LE TRANSLOY and the trenches between N.29.B.2.8 and N.36.A.5.8 from 7 a.m. to ZERO plus 10 minutes.

3. At ZERO, Field Artillery of Guards and 6th Divisions are to place a stationary barrage on trenches between N.29.B.2.8 and N.36.A.5.8., and will open a creeping barrage 200 yards in front of front trenches held by our Infantry - this barrage will advance until LE TRANSLOY line is reached; when the bombardment will cease.

4. ZERO will be 2-15 p.m. today.

A C K N O W L E D G E.

C P Heywood

Lieut-Colonel,

27th September,1916.

General Staff, Guards Division.

Issued to Signals at 8-45 a.m.

Copy No. 1 General Staff.
2 "Q".
3 G.D.A.
4 C.R.E.
5 1st Guards Brigade.
6 2nd Guards Brigade.
7 3rd Guards Brigade.
8 Pioneer Battalion.
9 A.D.M.S.
10 Divnl: Signals.
11 21st Division.
12 6th Division.
13 XIV Corps.
14 War Diary.

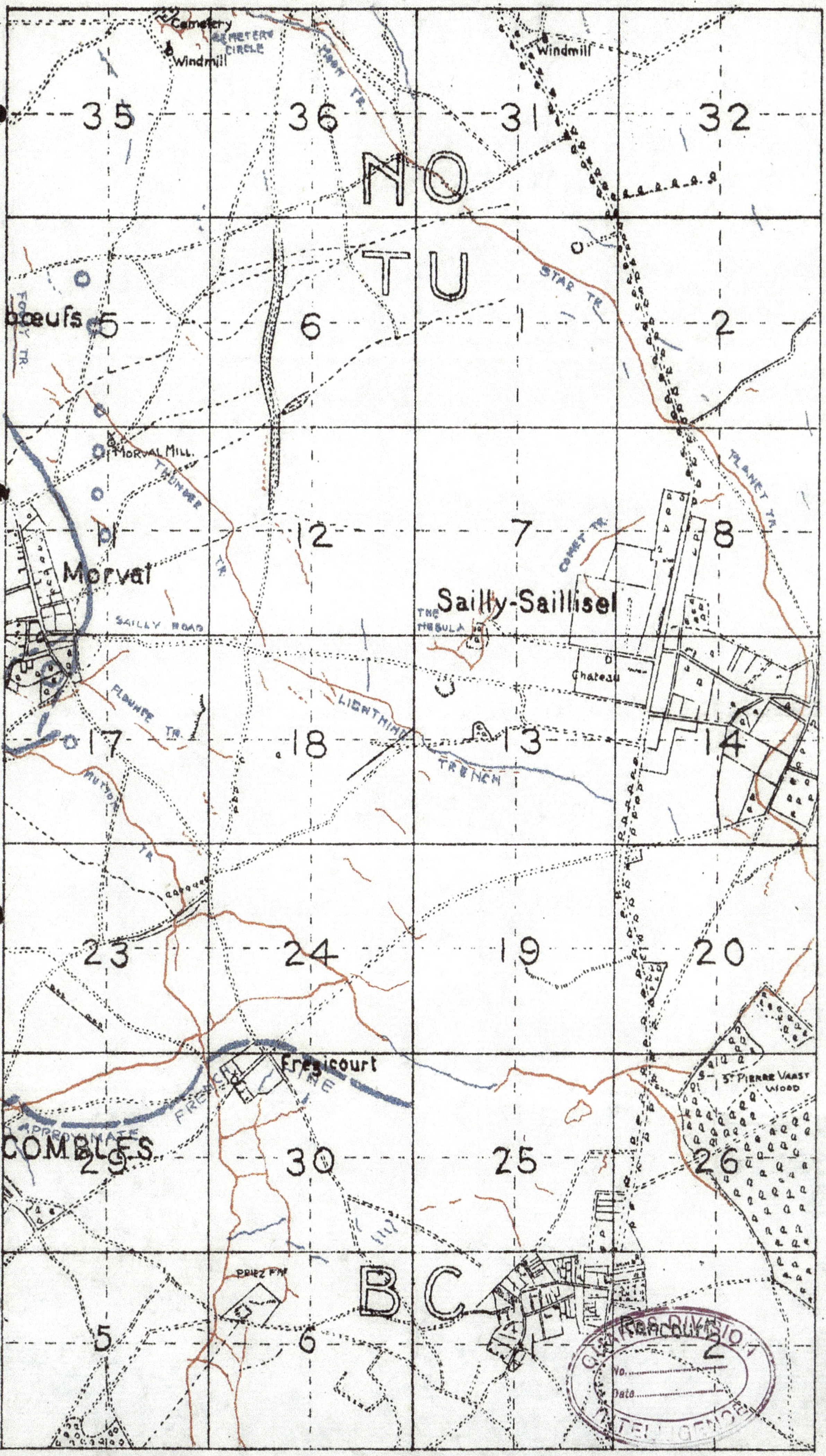
Cemetery
CEMETERY CIRCLE
Windmill
Windmill
35
36
31
32
NO
TU
boeufs
5
6
1
2
STAR TR.
MORVAL MILL
THUNDER TR.
11
12
7
8
Morval
Sailly-Saillisel
COMET TR.
PLANET TR.
SAILLY ROAD
THE NEBULA
Chateau
FLOUNCE TR.
LIGHTNING TRENCH
17
18
13
14
MUTTON TR.
23
24
19
20
Fregicourt
St PIERRE VAAST WOOD
APPROXIMATE FRENCH LINE
COMBLES
29
30
25
26
PRIEZ FM
BC
5
6
2
Rancourt
GUARDS DIVISION
No.
Date.
INTELLIGENCE

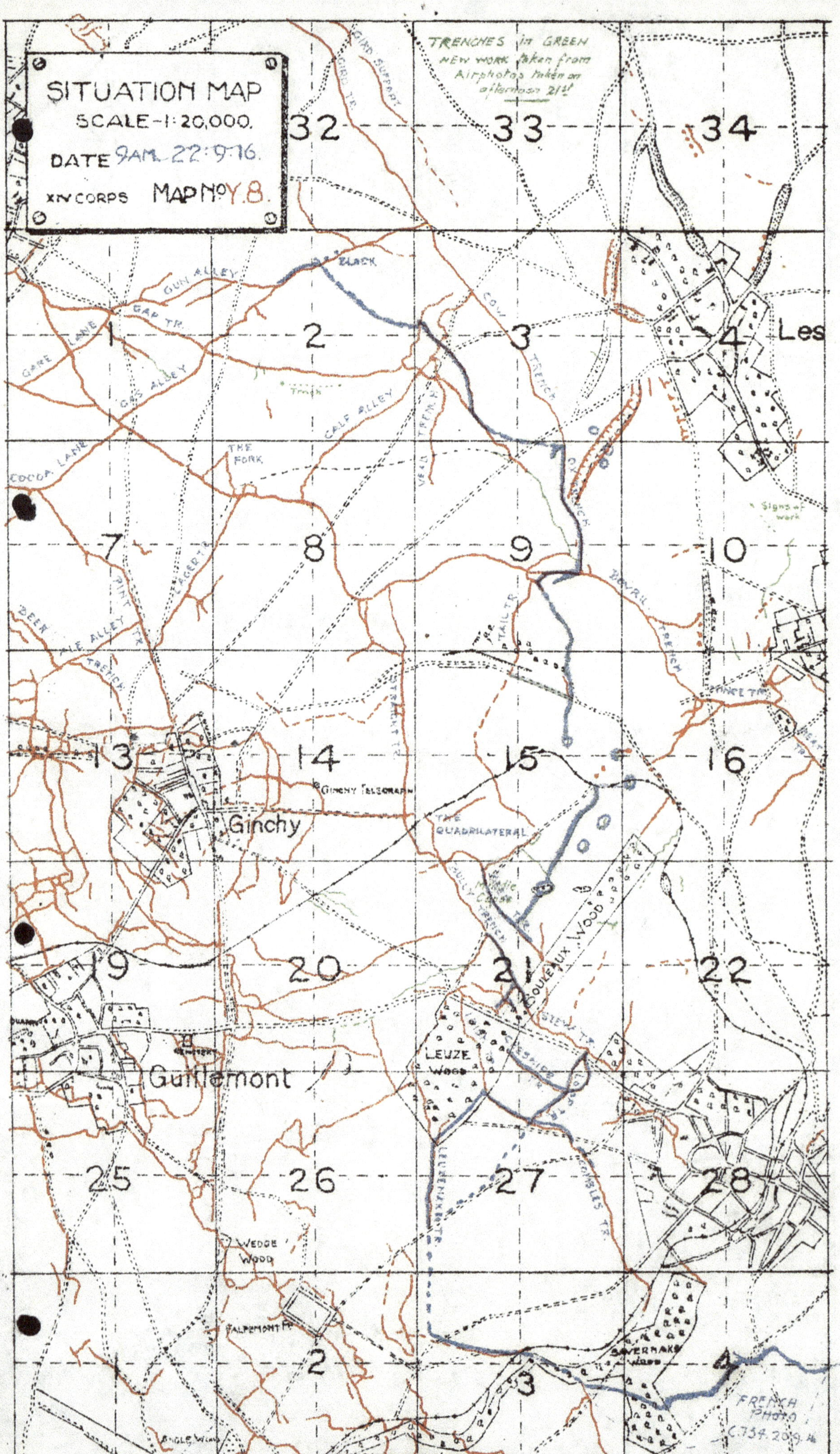

SITUATION MAP
SCALE - 1:20,000.
DATE 9AM. 22.9.16.
XIV CORPS
MAP No Y.8.
TRENCHES in GREEN
NEW WORK taken from Airphotos taken on afternoon 21st
32
33
34
1
2
3
4
Les
7
8
9
10
13
14
15
16
19
20
21
22
25
26
27
28
1
2
3
4
GUN ALLEY
GAP TR.
GAS ALLEY
CALF ALLEY
COCOA LANE
THE FORK
BLACK
Signs of work
Ginchy
GINCHY TELEGRAPH
THE QUADRILATERAL
BOULEAUX WOOD
Guillemont
LEUZE WOOD
WEDGE WOOD
FALFEMONT FM
SAVERNAKE WOOD
ANGLE WOOD
OAKHANGER WOOD
FRENCH PHOTO C.734 20.9.16

ORDERS FROM A & Q.

S E C R E T.

G.D.No. 2255/G.

1st Guards Brigade.
2nd Guards Brigade.
3rd Guards Brigade.
Pioneer Battalion.
Transport Officer, 1st Gds.Bde.
Transport Officer, 2nd Gds.Bde.
Transport Officer, 3rd Gds.Bde.
S.A.A. Section, D.A.C.
C.R.A.

SITUATION AS REGARDS AMMUNITION AND SUPPLIES ON NIGHT OF 14th/15th SEPT. 1916.

1. AMMUNITION.

(a) S.A.A.

144,000 rounds are being dumped to-night at the Headquarters of the 1st Guards Brigade and a similar number at Headquarters of the 2nd Guards Brigade.

Brigades have also brought up a supply from the BERNAFAY WOOD dump.

A dump of over one million rounds is on edge of BERNAFAY WOOD.

The S.A.A. carts of the 1st and 2nd Guards Brigade will proceed to-night to the west edge of TRONES WOOD to form a mobile reserve under the hands of Brigade Commanders.

S.A.A. carts will be left under a guard, the animals returning to CARNOY.

When the animals are required, Brigades will warn "Q" office at MINDEN POST.

Failing receipt of any instructions, animals will be sent up as soon as the 2nd objective is attained.

The transport of the 3rd Guards Brigade remains under the orders of the Brigade Commander, who has made his own arrangements.

(b) Grenades and Trench Mortar Ammunition.

Dump at BERNAFAY WOOD.

(c) S.A.A. Section remains at present under the instructions of Divisional Headquarters.

/2. Water

2. WATER.

A pipe line is laid from MONTAUBAN to tanks near Divisional Headquarters in BERNAFAY WOOD. It is anticipated that this supply will be working to-night. This pipe line will be carried on East as soon as possible.

An 8" pipe line has been laid from CARNOY to MONTAUBAN. The Corps anticipate that this supply will be in working order to-night.

Petrol tins full of water will be sent from MINDEN POST to the supply dump at BERNAFAY WOOD.

All empty tins that units cannot fill will be returned to this supply dump; if they cannot be filled from the supplies at BERNAFAY trough they will be filled under Divisional arrangement at MINDEN POST.

3. Supply Dumps as already notified.

4. The first line transport of the 1st and 2nd Guards Brigades move to-morrow to MINDEN POST.

The first line transport of the 3rd Guards Brigade remai at the CITADEL.

Communication will be maintained through "Q" office, MINDEN POST.

5. In the event of the A. echelon of the D.A.C. being ordered forward, the S.A.A. Section will come under the command of the O.C., D.A.C.

The position of the A. echelon D.A.C. will be notified t Brigades and Brigade Transport Officers.

Ammunition can then be drawn from either dumps or from the A. echelon D.A.C. which now takes the place of the old Brigade Ammunition Columns.

Orderlies will be sent to the Headquarters of Infantry Brigades by the O.C., D.A.C. when this change takes place.

/6. New

6. New dumps as formed will be notified by wire to all concerned.

C.M. Hayward Lt.Col.

Lieut.Colonel,
A.A. & Q.M.G., Guards Division.

14th September 1916.

ARTILLERY ORDERS & INSTRUCTIONS

Operation Order
File
Oct 20th/15

Ref. G.D.A. Order No. 99
of 13.9/16.
+ maps issued to Brigades.
Ref. French Maps.

Secret

LEFT GROUP G.D.A. INSTRUCTIONS No. 2.

Sept 14th. 1916.

(In continuation of message L.G. 97, issued this morning)

1/ Left Group under the command of Lt. Col. F. A. Buzzard R.F.A. comprises:–

24th Bde. R.F.A. (3. 6 gun 18 pdr. Btys.)
(1. 4 gun How. Bty.)
61st. Bde. R.F.A. 3. 4 gun 18 pdr Btys
76th Bde. R.F.A. {3. 4 gun 18 pdr Btys.}
{1. 4 gun. How. Bty.}

2/ Left Group will, in tomorrow's attack, support 1st. Guards Brigade, Headquarters of which will be at S.24.b. 6.1½. from 4 a.m. tomorrow.

3/ The O.C. 24th Bde. R.F.A. will be responsible for the maintenance of the Creeping Barrage.

4/ 61st Bde (Right) and 76th Bde (Left) will form standing barrages as follows. Dividing line T.8.b.3.4 – T.3.a.5.2½. – N.34.a.5.2. zero to +12' along trench T.8.d.3.7. – a.1.5 (Green line)
+12' to +1 hr. 50' along trench T.3.d.1.7. – a.1½.9½ (Blue line)
+1 hr. 50' to +4 hrs 20' along line T.34.c.5.2. – a.½.9. (Red line.)
+ 4 hrs 20' onwards – 200 yds beyond Red line.

5./ D/76 (How.) Bty. (Left) and 43rd (How) Bty (Right) will fire as laid down in G.D.A. Orders. Dividing line as in para. 4 above.

Continued.

Liason. 6/ (a) Lt. Colonel Bryant, will act as Liason officer with 1st. Guards Brigade from 4·30 A.M. on Sept 15th.

(b) O.C. 24th. Bde R.F.A. will have an officer, not below the rank of captain, ready to relieve Lt. Col. Bryant at any time after 8 A.M. on the 15th. on receipt of orders from Left Group.

(c) Liason officers (Subalterns) with Battn. Hdqrs will be provided as follows:—

With 2nd. Bn. Coldstream Gds from 61st. Bde. R.F.A.
" 3rd. " " " from 61st. Bde. R.F.A.
" 1st. " Irish Gds from 76th. Bde R.F.A.
" 2nd. " Grenadier Gds from 24th. Bde. R.F.A.

These officers, whose names will be reported to this office, will be at 1st. Gds. Bgde. Hdqrs., S 24·b·6·1½ by 4·30 A.M. tomorrow and will be guided thence to Battn. Hdqrs.

They will have with them visual apparatus, signallers, and at least 1½ miles of light wire.

The 1st. Gds. Bde. will be establishing visual stations, and these stations will be warned to look out for F.O.O's messages and to transmit them. Artillery brigades will also establish visual stations to keep touch with F.O.O's.

The call TP should be sent to call the attention of these stations and messages addressed "Artillery GAIN" should reach the liason officer at 1st. Gds. Bde Hdqrs. with little delay.

7/ Every endeavour must be made to acquire and transmit information, not only regarding our own troops, but regarding progress on their flanks.

8/ A brigade, when it advances from its present position will come under the orders of G.D. Artillery direct unless it is otherwise informed.

9/ Headquarters Left Group will open at West side of TRONES WOOD near North end. S23.b.7½.3½. at 6 P.M. this evening.

10. The 1st Gds. Bde. will advance tomorrow from the line T.14.a.1.1. – T13 b 9.5 – 7.3. – T13 b 0.1

11/ Zero hour will be 6.20 a.m. tomorrow.

12/ Acknowledge by wire.

H Vaughan
Lt. R.F.A.
Adj. Left Group. G.D.A.

Copies to.

24th. Bde. R.F.A.
61st. " "
76th. " "
Right Group
1st. Guards Brigade.
G.D.A. (For transmission to Group on Left).

"A" Form.

MESSAGES AND SIGNALS.

Army Form C. 2121.

No. of Message............

Prefix.......... Code............m.

Office of Origin and Service Instructions.

Words | Charge

Sent

At..........m.

To..........

By..........

This message is on a/c of:

..........Service.

SECRET

(Signature of "Franking Officer.")

Recd. at..........m.

Date..........

From..........

By..........

TO 1st Gds Bde
~~2nd Gds Bde~~
~~3 Gds Bde~~

* Sender's Number	Day of Month	In reply to Number	AAA
G 442	13		

Herewith copy of Gds Div Artillery orders AAA the essential points (which have not ~~yet~~ been dealt with in G. Div Operation order No 76) are marked by Blue Chalk. AAA acknowledge.

From Guards Div

Place

Time 8 pm

The above may be forwarded as now corrected.

(Z)

C Heywood Lt Col

..........*Censor.*

Signature of Addressor or person authorised to telegraph in his name.

* This line should be erased if not required.

(A1) O. Ltd., London— W.14042/M.44. 150,000 Pads. 12/15. Form C.2121.

S E C R E T.

Copy No: 1.....

GUARDS DIVISIONAL ARTILLERY ORDER NO: 49.

1. The Fourth Army will attack the enemy's defences between COMBLES RAVINE and MARTINPUICH on Z day with the object of seizing MORVAL - LES BOEUFS - GUEUDECOURT and FLERS, and of breaking through the enemy's system of defence.

The French are undertaking an offensive simultaneously on the south and the Reserve Army on the north.

2. The attack will be pushed with the utmost vigour, all along the line, until the most distant objectives are reached.

The failure of a unit on a flank is not to prevent other units pushing on to their final objectives, as it is by such means that these units, which have failed, will be assisted to advance.

3. Preliminary Bombardment.

(a) Commencing on 12th September bombardment and wire cutting on hostile defensive system will take place from 6 a.m. to 6.30 p.m. daily.

(b) The preliminary bombardment on the day of the attack will be similar to that on previous days, there being no further increase of fire previous to ZERO.

(c) From 6.30 p.m. - 6 a.m. each evening from 12th Sept: inclusive night firing will be carried out by Groups in accordance with instructions already issued.

4. (a) The 6th Division is to attack on our right and the 14th Division on our left.

(b) The 2nd Guards Brigade will attack on the right of the Division - the 1st Guards Brigade on the left - the 3rd Guards Brigade will be in Divisional Reserve.

5. Objectives allotted to Guards Brigades and neighbouring Divisions are shown on attached Map.

First Objective is marked GREEN.
Second " " " BROWN.
Third " " " BLUE.
FOURTH " " " RED.

6. The Infantry will advance to the attack of the GREEN Line at ZERO.

to the attack of the BROWN Line at ZERO plus 1 hour
" " " " " BLUE Line at ZERO plus 2 hours
" " " " " RED Line at ZERO plus 4 hours 30 mins.

7. The task of the two leading Guards Brigades is to press the attack through to their ultimate objectives with every means at their disposal.

The 3rd Guards Brigade will advance at ZERO + 1 hour 30 mins: until its leading troops reach the South Western outskirts of GINCHY where the Brigade will halt and await orders.

8. Tanks will be employed to co-operate with the attack, instructions as to their employment are attached.

9. Right and Left Groups will cover the front of the Right and Left Guards Brigades respectively, and will be responsible for the barrages on the front of their Brigades.

Tasks are shown in attached sheet.

10. (a) 74th & 76th Brigades (less Howitzer Batteries) will be detailed to move forward on receipt of orders from this Head Quarters, to positions about T.7.d., T.8.c. (74th Bde: on the right) to the close support of the Infantry - This order will be given when Guards Division has captured the BLUE Line, unless our troops on the flanks are held up and make advance impossible.

When they advance they will continue to cover the advance of their respective Guards Brigades, and will come under the orders of the G.O.C., Guards Brigade concerned - to whom communication will be established.

Failing other orders to the contrary or opportunity for individual action they will continue to thicken the Standing Barrage in front of their Guards Brigade front.

(b) D.A.C. will detail a portion of a section of the D.A.C. to be prepared to advance to supply ammunition to these Brigades at Zero hour.

Orderlies will be supplied by these detachments D.A.C., to 74th & 76th Brigades respectively.

11. <u>Liaison</u>. Each Group will send a senior Officer and party to Guards Brigade Head Quarters as Liaison Officer.

A Liaison Officer will also be attached to and accompany each Battalion Head Quarters of the 1st and 2nd Guards Brigades.

12. All transport will be pulled up and ready to move forward at one hours notice after ZERO plus 4 hours.

13. (a) 9th Squadron, Royal Flying Corps will have two contact aeroplanes in the air from ZERO to dark on Z day and again from 6.30 a.m. to 9 a.m. on Z plus 1 day.

(b) Flares will be lit as follows :-

(i) On obtaining each objective.
(ii) At 12 noon and 5 p.m. on Z day.
(iii) At 6.30 a.m. on Z plus 1 day.

Red flares will be used by Infantry, Green flares by Cavalry.

14. The Cavalry Corps is to be disposed in depth by 10 a.m. on Z day with its head at CARNOY ready to move at short notice.

As soon as the final objectives have been captured by the Infantry, the Cavalry will advance and seize the high ground ROCQUIGNY - VILLERS AU FLOS - RIENCOURT LES BAPAUME - BAPAUME.

The XIVth Corps and also the XVth Corps on our left will be prepared to support the Cavalry on the above line at the earliest possible momement.

Gaps through which the Cavalry can move forward, which must be kept free from shell fire will be notified later.

The Cavalry will not enter villages, so fire can be maintained on the latter continously.

15. Day of attack(Z day) will be 15th Sept:

Zero hour will be in the early morning probably between 6. and 6.30 a.m.

Exact time will be notified later.

16. Head Quarters Guards Divisional Artillery will open at BERNAFAY WOOD(S.28.b.4.4.) at 6 p.m. on Y day.

~~ACKNOWLEDGE.~~ ack'd RSG

Issued at :-..5 p.m......

13th September 1916.

Major R.A.

Brigade Major, Guards Divnl: Arty.

Copies to:-

1-4.	Guards Division.
5.	R.A. XIVth Corps.
6.	6th Div: Arty:(Centre Div: Artilleries)
7.	7th Div: Arty.
8.	Right Group.
9.	Left Group.
10-13.	61st Bde: R.F.A.
14-18.	74th Bde: R.F.A.
19-23.	75th Bde: R.F.A.
24-28.	76th Bde: R.F.A.
29-33.	24th Bde: R.F.A.
34-37.	38th Bde: R.F.A.
38.	D.A.C.
39.	XIVth Corps Heavy Arty.
40-41.	Office.
42.	War Diary.

TABLE OF TASKS.

Reference :- 57C S.W. 1/20,000 & 57C S.W.3. 1/10,000.

Right Group will find Barrages on Right Guards Brigade front, and Left Group on Left Guards Brigade front.

50 % of 18-Pdrs: will be employed on Standing, and 50 % on Creeping Barrages.

All fire will be kept within Guards Division area.

2. (a) STANDING BARRAGES.

(i) GREEN Line along Trench T.14.b.8½.7. - T.8.d.4.5. - T.8.a.1.5.

(ii) BLUE Line. along Trench T.9.b.6.2½. - N.33.c.1½.0.

(iii) RED Line. Along RED Line T.4.b.6.2. - N.28.c.0.0.

(b) TIMES.

Standing Barrage commences on GREEN Line at ZERO.
Lifts from GREEN Line to BLUE Line at ZERO + 12 mins.
Remains on BLUE Line from ZERO + 12 mins to ZERO + 1 hour 50 mins.
Lifts from BLUE Line to RED Line at ZERO + 1 hour 50 mins.
Remains on RED Line from ZERO + 1 hour 50 mins: to ZERO + 4 hours 20 mins.
Lifts from RED Line to 200 yards beyond RED Line at ZERO + 4 hours 20 mins.

(c) Gaps will be left in the Stationary Barrage on the GREEN Line at least 50 yards on either side of the spots where the tanks arrive.

3. CREEPING BARRAGES.

(a) At ZERO. Creeping Barrage will start 100 yards in front of the Infantry and will creep forward at the rate of 50 yards a minute to 200 yards beyond the GREEN Line, when it will become stationary.
During this period gaps 100 yards wide will be left along the route of Tanks.

(b) At ZERO + 1 hour. The Creeping Barrage in front of that portion of the first Guards Brigade which is to advance to the BROWN Line (i.e. position N. of T.8.b.3½.4.), will creep forward at the rate of 50 yards a minute to 200 yards beyond the BROWN Line, when it will become stationary.
During this period gaps 100 yards wide will be left along the route of Tanks.

During (a) and (b) the Creeping Barrage immediately covers the advance of the Infantry.

(c) At ZERO + 1 hour 10 mins: Creeping Barrage will advance at the rate of 30 yards a minute and join the stationary barrage on BLUE Line.
During (c) Creeping barrage covers the advance of the Tanks.

(d) At ZERO + 1 hour 50 mins: Creeping barrage will lift and form a stationary barrage 200 yards beyond the BLUE Line.
This is to allow the Tanks to move up and down the objectives and destroy more obstacles covering them.

(e) At ZERO + 3 hours 30 mins: Creeping barrage will creep forward at the rate of 30 yards per minute and join the Stationary barrage on the RED Line. This is to cover the advance of the Tanks.

(f) At ZERO + 4 hours 20 mins: Creeping barrage will lift to 200 yards beyond RED Line to enable the Tanks to move up and down the objectives and destroy more obstacles covering them.

4. 4.5" Howitzers.

(a) ZERO to Zero + 12 mins: Communication Trenches between GREEN and BLUE Lines.

(b) ZERO + 12 mins: to ZERO + 1 hour 40 mins: Communication Trenches between BROWN-GREEN Line and BLUE Line. Fire to be kept 200 yards beyond the Creeping barrage.

(c) ZERO + 1 hour 45 mins: to ZERO + 2 hours 15 mins: All 4.5" Hows: will fire P.S. Shell at LES BOEUFS Village. Rapid rate of fire.

From ZERO + 2 hours 15 mins: to ZERO + 4 hours 20 mins: Howitzers will be prepared to put up barrage on RED Line

After ZERO + 4 hours 20 mins: Howitzers will be prepared to barrage 200 yards beyond RED Line.

5. Rate of Fire.

(a) Intense Fire will be for 18-Pdrs: 4 rounds per gun a minute.
for 4.5" Hows: 2 rounds per gun a minute.

At normal times rate of fire will be 18-Pdrs: 1 round per gun a minute.
and for 4.5" Hows: 20 rounds per gun per hour.

(b) Fire will be intense at ZERO.
ZERO + 1 hour.
ZERO + 2 hours.
ZERO + 4 hours 30 mins.

to cover the advance of the Infantry. In each case this fire will remain intense for such time as the situation demands.

6. The First Objective differs slightly from the GREEN Stationary Barrage Line, as the former does not follow the Trench all the way but runs from T.15.a.1.9. - T.8.d.7.6. - T.8.b.3½.4. and along Trench to T.8.a.5.1.
Other objectives coincide with Coloured Stationary Barrage Lines.

SECRET.

Copy No: 39

GUARDS DIVISIONAL ARTILLERY ORDER NO: 52.

24
22nd September 1916.

1. (a) Fourth Army will renew the attack on "Z" day in combination with attacks by the French to the South and the Reserve Army to the North.

(b) The objectives of the XIVth Corps include MORVAL and LES BOEUFS, and those of the XVth Corps, GUEUDECOURT.

(c) The attack of the XIVth Corps will be carried out by the 5th Division on the Right, the 6th Division in the Centre and the Guards Division on the Left; the 56th Division will form a defensive flank to the South of the 5th Division.

The 21st Division will be attacking on our Left.

2. 1st Guards Brigade will attack on the Right and 3rd Guards Brigade on the Left.

Boundary between Brigades,
T.3.c.2½.8. - T.3.a.8.1½. - N.33.d.9½.0. - N.34.c.4½.4.

2nd Guards Brigade will be in Reserve.

3. OBJECTIVES.

(a) 1st Objective - GREEN LINE.
T.3.d.4.0. - T.3.a.5.5. - N.33.c.4.2. - N.33.c.1½.5.

(b) 2nd Objective - BROWN LINE.
T.4.c.4.6½. - T.4.a.2½.1. - T.3.b.9.3. - T.4.a.0.9½. - N.33.d.7.4. - N.33.central. N33c7.8

(c) 3rd Objective - BLUE LINE.
T.4.b.5.4. - N.34.c.7.0. along SUNKEN Road to N.34.a.2.3.

4. PRELIMINARY BOMBARDMENT.

A steady bombardment of hostile positions will be commenced at 7 a.m. on "Y" day and will be continued to 6.30 pm. It will recommence at 6.30 am on "Z" day.

Group Commanders will arrange to search/ occasionally with 18-Pdrs:, the ground in front and rear of the German trenches which are being bombarded by Heavy Artillery.

There will be no intensive fire previous to the hour of ZERO. Night firing will be carried out nightly between the hours of 6.30 pm and 6.30 am.

5. The Infantry will advance,
to the attack of the GREEN Line at ZERO.
to the attack of the BROWN Line at ZERO plus 1 hour.
to the attack of the BLUE Line at ZERO plus 2 hours.

6. (a) The task of the two leading Guards Brigades is to push the attack through to the BLUE Line.

(b) 1st and 3rd Guards Brigades will garrison and consolidate the BROWN Line with a portion of their reserves when the attack pushes forward to the BLUE Line.

(c) On gaining the BLUE Line patrols will be sent forward, and any ground from which good observation can be gained will be occupied.

Such points will be consolidated and eventually joined up with our line.

7. <u>ORGANIZATION OF DIVISIONAL ARTILLERY.</u>

<u>Right Group.</u>

Comdr: Lieut: Col: A.B. Bethell, D.S.O. H.Q., S.29.a.6.3.
24th Brigade R.F.A.
74th Brigade R.F.A.
75th Brigade R.F.A.

<u>Left Group.</u>

Comdr: Lieut: Col: F.A. Buzzard, H.Q., S.23.b.9.5.
61st Brigade R.F.A.
76th Brigade R.F.A.
93rd Brigade R.F.A.

In addition 14th Horse Arty Bde will support Guards Division up to Zero + 1 hr 10 mins

8. Right Group will support, supply Liaison Officer to, and form barrages on the front of 1st Guards Brigade, and Left Group on front of 3rd Guards Brigade.

9. 50% of the ~~18 Pdrs. of~~ Divisional Artillery will be used for Creeping Barrage and 50% for Standing Barrage.

Details of Barrages and Tasks are given in attached Sheet.

10. <u>TANKS.</u>

Three Tanks have been allotted to the Division. They will be kept in Divisional Reserve.

At ZERO hour they will proceed from their assembly position at S.W. corner of TRONES WOOD to a point about T.13.central, avoiding the roads in getting to this point.

They will there await orders from Divisional H.Q.

11. One contact patrol will be in the air from ZERO till 6.30 pm.

12. Flares will be lit by leading Infantry lines on obtaining each objective, and also at 8 p.m. on "Z" day.

13. Watches will be synchronized to Groups at 6.15 pm on "Y" day, and 8.15 am on "Z" day.

14. For the attack, Advanced Headquarters will be as follows :-

Divisional Headquarters Divisional Arty: H.Q.,	BERNAFAY WOOD.(S.28.b.4.4.)
1st Guards Brigade,	T.19.a.½.3½.
3rd Guards Brigade,	S.24.b.6.1½.
2nd Guards Brigade,	DUMMY TRENCH(S.23.b.5.2.).

15. "ZERO" hour will be notified later - it will probably be in the afternoon. of 25th Sept.

ACKNOWLEDGE.

[signature]
Major R.A.

Issued at:- 11.30 am.

Brigade Major, Guards Divnl: Arty.

Copy No:	No: 1	R.A. XIVth Corps.
	2	Guards Division.
	3	Left Centre Artillery.
	4	7th Div: Arty.
	5-8	61st Brigade R.F.A.
	9-13	74th Brigade R.F.A.
	14-18	75th Brigade R.F.A.
	19-23	76th Brigade R.F.A.
	24-28	24th Brigade R.F.A.
	29-33	93rd Brigade R.F.A.
	34	D.A.C.
	35	XIVth Corps Heavy Artillery.
	36-37	Office.
	38	War Diary.
	39	1st Guards Brigade.
	40	2nd Guards Brigade.
	41	3rd Guards Brigade.
	42-44	14th Brigade RHA

TABLE OF TASKS.

1. STANDING BARRAGES.

(a) 1st Standing Barrage Line - Along trench T.3.d.4.0. - T.3.a.5.5. - N.32.d.7½.4.

2nd Standing Barrage Line.- Along SUNKEN ROADS T.4.c.4.6½. - T.4.a.2½.1. - T.3.b.9.3. - T.4.a.0.9½. - N.33.d.7.5.- N.33.b.8.2.

3rd Standing Barrage Line - Road T.4.b.½.2. - N.34.a.2.3.

(b) (i) Standing Barrage will open on 1st Standing Barrage Line at ZERO.

14th Horse Artillery Brigade will form Standing Barrage on portion of 1st Standing Barrage Line extending from the extreme left to 250 yards to the South.

(ii) At ZERO plus 3 mins: Standing Barrage(except 14th Horse Arty: Bde:) will lift to 2nd Standing Barrage Line, the Left Group opening out to cover whole of Left Group area on that line.

Right Group will not fire within 50 yards of the left of 6th Division.

14th Horse Arty: Bde: will lift at ZERO plus 7 mins: on to trench N.33.c.4.1½. - 1½.5½. and remain there until ZERO plus 11 mins:, when it will lift and search valley in N.33.b until ZERO plus 1 hour 10 mins:, at which time it returns to its own Division.

(iii) At ZERO plus 1 hour 8 mins: Right Group Standing Barrage will lift on to Road T.4.a.8½.0. - T.4.a.2.8. and fire H.E. It will remain Stationary on this line until ZERO plus 2 hours when it will lift on to 3rd Standing Barrage Line and return to Shrapnel.

At ZERO plus 1 hour 10 mins: Left Group Standing Barrage will lift on to 3rd Standing Barrage Line.

(iv) At ZERO plus 2 hours 4 mins: Whole Standing Barrage will lift on to Line of new works East of BLUE Line.

2. CREEPING BARRAGE.

(a) Creeping Barrage will open at ZERO 200 yards in front of the Infantry, and will creep forward at the rate of 50 yards per minute, to a line 200 yards East of First Objective (GREEN Line) where it will become Stationary.

(b) At Zero plus 1 hour it will creep forward, at the same pace, to a line 200 yards East of Second Objective(BROWN LINE) where it will become Stationary.

(c) At ZERO plus 2 hours it will creep forward, at the same pace, to a line 200 yards East of 3rd Objective(BLUE Line) where it will become Stationary.

3. RATES OF FIRE FOR STANDING AND CREEPING BARRAGES.

(a) Intense fire (4 rounds per gun a minute).

From ZERO to ZERO plus 3 mins:
" ZERO plus 6 mins: to ZERO plus 11 mins.
" ZERO plus 1 hour to ZERO plus 1 hour 3 mins:
" ZERO plus 1 hour 6 mins: to ZERO plus 1 hour 10 mins:
" ZERO plus 2 hours to ZERO plus 2 hours 15 mins:

(b) Slow Fire. (1 round per battery a minute).

From ZERO plus 11 mins: to ZERO plus 1 hour.

(c) At other times up to 2 hours 15 mins: Normal rate of Fire(one round per gun per minute).

(d) After 2 hours 15 mins: fire will be slow, and slacken off according to situation. - If situation unknown fire will periodically go to Normal rate.

The above rates will be altered according to the situation, and if the state of the guns requires.

4. HOWITZERS.

(a) Right Group.

(i) At ZERO - 3 hours. The three Howitzer Batteries of Right Group will fire a total of 700 rounds of Poison Shell at the quickest rate practicable into LES BOEUFS into an area of 100 yards square round HOUSE 9.(T.4.a.7.6. (see enlarged map of LES BOEUFS recently circulated).

(ii) From ZERO to ZERO plus 1 hour.

One Battery SUNKEN ROAD T.3.d.7.3½. - T.4.c.4.8.
One " SUNKEN ROAD T.3.d.6.5. - T.3.b.9.3.
One " Road T.3.b.3.1½. - T.3.b.9.3.

(iii) From ZERO plus 1 hour to ZERO plus 1 hour 6 mins.

Three Batteries - Main Street from CHURCH - Cross Roads T.4.a.0.9½.

(iv) From ZERO plus 1 hour 6 mins: to ZERO plus 2 hours.

2 Batteries - 3rd Standing Barrage Line.
One Battery - SUNKEN ROAD T.4.b.2.4. - N.34.a.5.4.

(v) From ZERO plus 2 hours - onwards.

2 Batteries - New Work East of 3rd Objective.
1 Battery - Remains on SUNKEN ROAD T.4.b.2.4. - N.34.a.5.4. keeping clear of Infantry in 3rd Objective.

(b) Left Group.

(i) "A" Battery.

ZERO to ZERO plus 3 mins:	Road T.3.a.5½.4. - Cross Roads T.3.a.8½.8. and Trench T.3.a.6½.6. - 5.7.
ZERO plus 3 mins: to ZERO plus 1 hour 9 mins.	SUNKEN ROAD T.4.a.0.9½. - N.33.d.7.5.
ZERO plue 1 hour 9 mins: to ZERO plus 2 hours.	3rd Standing Barrage Line.
ZERO plus 2 hours - onwards.	Road N.34.d.8.7½. - N.35.a.2.1½.

(ii) "B" Battery.

ZERO to ZERO plus 8 mins.	Trench N.33.c.4.2. - 1½.5½.
ZERO plus 8 mins: to ZERO plus 2 hours.	Road N.33.d.7.5. - N.33.b.8.2. lifting to Northern portion of the Road, when Infantry approach BROWN LINE.
ZERO plus 2 hours - onwards.	SUNKEN Road N.34.b.5.8½. - N.35.a.0.9.

(iii) Rates of Fire.

(a) Intense (2 rounds per gun a minute).

From ZERO to ZERO plus 5 mins.
.. ZERO plus 1 hour to ZERO plus 1 hour 8 mins.
.. ZERO plus 2 hours to ZERO plus 2 hours 5 mins.

(b) At other times up to ZERO plus 2 hours 15 mins: Medium rate of fire(40 rounds per gun per hour).

(c) After ZERO plus 2 hours 15 mins: Slow rate of fire, and slacken off according to the Situation.

The above rates will be altered according to the Situation and if the state of the guns requires.

\-

S E C R E T.   G.D.A./814/56/A.

H.Q. No. 1st Guards Bde.

Head Quarters Guards Divisional Artillery (Left Artillery) will close at MINDEN POST and open at BERNAFAY WOOD(S.28.b.4.4.) at 10.30 a.m. on Sept: 25th.

Staff Captain & D.T.M.O. will remain at MINDEN POST.

[signature]

Major R.A.

24th September 1916.   Brigade-Major, Guards Divnl: Arty.

MEDICAL ARRANGEMENTS

Operation Order
file
Oct 19/15

SECRET. OPERATION ORDER Nº A21 Copy Nº 6....

by

Lieut.Colonel J.G.GILL, R.A.M.C.,

A.D.M.S.,GUARDS DIVISION.

(Reference Guards Division Order Nº 76)

(Reference Sheet 57 c. S.W.)

1. The Guards Division will attack on Z day.

2. The following Medical Arrangements will be made.

(A) PRIOR TO ATTACK REACHING 3rd OBJECTIVE.

The pre-existing Medical Arrangements (see No. 429/3 attached) for clearing the line hold good.

In addition,

(I) A Bearer Division will be held in reserve behind each attacking Brigade in Dugouts at S.23.d.5.2. and old German trench at S.30.a.5.3.

(II) A DIVISIONAL BEARER RESERVE consisting of one Bearer Division will be held in readiness to support at BRIQUETERIE.

(III) A Tent subdivision will establish an A.D.S. at S.30.b.5.6.

(IV) One Tent subdivision complete will move on the evening previous to Z day to BRIQUETERIE and park there until further orders are issued.

(V) A Tent subdivision will remain in Reserve at CARNOY.

(VI) As the attack progresses Bearer Divisions will push forward stretcher squads and maintain touch with battalion Medical Officers.

(B) ON ATTACK REACHING 3rd OBJECTIVE.

(I) Divisional Reserve Bearer Division will move up to neighbourhood of GUILLEMONT.

(II) Casualties will be conveyed to A.D.S. at S.30.b.5.6.

(C) ON ATTACK REACHING FOURTH OBJECTIVE.

(I) A Divisional Collecting Station will be established as soon as possible by a Tent subdivision at GINCHY where casualties will be collected and treated pending clearance.

3. All A.D.Ss. and Ambulance Posts will be indicated by flags and directing posts.

4. Walking wounded will be directed to CORPS WALKING ~~WOUNDE~~ WOUNDED COLLECTING POST at A.14.c.6.1., near CARNOY.

5. In the event of a Divisional Collecting Station being formed the number of cases remaining requiring clearance will be notified from time to time to A.D.M.S.

6. All transport will be packed up and ready to move forward at one hour's notice after ZERO plus 4 hours.

7. All reports to be sent to A.D.M.S. at Advanced Divisional Headquarters (S.28.b.4.4.), via A.D.S. at S.30.b.5.6., from ZERO.

8. ZERO will be communicated later.

J. G. Colt
Lieut. Colonel,
A.D.M.S., Guards Division.

13th Sept. 1916.

Copies to:-

Nº 1 ; Nº 3 F.A.
" 2 ; Nº 4 F.A.
" 3 ; Nº 9 F.A.
" 4 ; 'G' Guards Division.
" 5 ; Adv.'Q' Guards Division.
" 6 ; 1st Guards Bde.
" 7 ; 2nd " "
" 8 ; 3rd " "
" 9 ; D.D.M.S.,XIV Corps.
" 10 ; A.D.M.S.,14th Division.
" 11 ; A.D.M.S., 6th Division.
" 12 ; Office.
" 13 ; Diary.
" 14 ;

A.D.M.S., Nº 429/3

MEDICAL ARRANGEMENTS FOR PRESENT FRONT.

(1) POSITIONS OF MEDICAL UNITS.

Battalion Aid Posts in Dugouts at T.14.c.4.9.; combined Aid Posts for 2 battalions.
Right Battalion Aid Post.at T.25.b.1.3.
Advanced Bearer Post.(3 squads) in dugouts at S.24.d.9.5.
Ambulance Posts.BERNAFAY WOOD (S.22.d.9.1.)
BRIQUETERIE (A.4.b.4.5.)
Adv.Ambulance post at S.30.a.8.4.

Advanced Dressing Station. CARNOY.

Bearer Reserve Posts.in dugouts in TRONES WOOD (S.29.b.5.5.) and at BRIQUETERIE.

(2) CLEARANCE OF FRONT LINE.

By Battalion Stretcher Bearers to Aid Posts. From Right Battalion Aid Post to advanced ambulance post by ambulance bearers. From combined aid post at T.14.c.4.9. to Ambulance Post at BERNAFAY WOOD by ambulance bearers, - using relays of bearers at TRONES WOOD. Advanced ambulance post is cleared by Ford Cars to Cross roads at S.W. corner of BERNAFAY WOOD, where cases are transferred to large ambulance cars.
BERNAFAY WOOD Ambulance Post is cleared by Horsed Ambulance Wagons to S.W. corner of WOOD where cases are transferred to large ambulance cars.

(3) All cases requiring re-drsssing are dressed at Ambulance Post at BRIQUETERIE and at A.D.S., CARNOY, prior to removal to Corps M.D.S. at BRONFAY FARM (F.29.b.)

(4) Walking wounded are directed to Corps W.W.C.P. at A.14.c.6.1.

11th Sept.1916.

(sd) F.D.G.Howell, Captain, R.A.M.C.,
for A.D.M.S., Guards Division.

SECRET. OPERATION ORDER Nº A 23 CopyNº......

by

COLONEL S. GUISE-MOORES, C.B., A.M.S.,
A.D.M.S., GUARDS DIVISION.

(Reference Guards Division Order Nº 82, as amended)
(Reference Sheet, 57 c, S.W.)

1. The 1st & 3rd Guards Bdes. will attack at ZERO hour on Z day, in conjunction with 6th Division (on the right) and 21st Division (on the left).

The 2nd Guards Bde. (less 1 battalion) will be held in Divisional Reserve.

2. Disposition of Medical Units prior to attack

(a) A Tent subdivision will form an A.D.S. at S.30.b.5.6.

(b) A Tent subdivision will form an A.D.S. and Wagon post at T.13.c.8.8.

(c) A Tent subdivision (less personnel at ambulance post BERNAFAY WOOD) will be held in reserve at CARNOY.

(d) TheBearer Divisions of Nos. 3 & 4 F.As. will be held in readiness in trenches, in near vicinity of S.30.b.5.6. and T.13.c.8.8., to commence clearance of the front area.

(e) The Bearer Division of Nº 9 F.A. will be held in reserve at S.30.a.4.2.

(f) Ambulance wagons will be held in readiness at S.30.a.2.1.

3. The Bearer Divisions will be placed under the command of Major A.D.FRASER, who will be responsible for clearance of the front area.

4. The O.C., Divisional Bearers will maintain touch with Battalion Medical Officers by means of liaison Officers and men specially detailed for the purpose.

5. If conditions allow, the O.C., Divisional Bearers will establish an Ambulance and Wagon Post in neighbourhood of T.7.d.central, when the attacking troops have reached their ultimate objective. The position of this post will be communicated to Battalion Medical Officers as soon as possible.

6. The O.C., Divisional Bearers will instruct Battalion Medical Officers to report their positions to him, giving map references, by means of walking wounded.

7. The O.C., Divisional Bearers will place himself in communication with Brigade Headquarters concerned, in order that information regarding progress of attack may be obtained.

8. General plan of method of clearance of casualties.

(a) Battalion stretcher bearers will convey cases in ~~direc~~ direction of T.13.c.8.8. until touch is obtained with ambulance bearer squads. These squads will be pushed forward as far as possible in order to reduce the 'carry' of battalion stretcher bearers. Ambulance Bearer squads will be under the command of Bearer Officers.

8.cont.

(b) On stretcher cases reaching ambulance post at T.13.c.8.8., they will be dressed and conveyed by Horsed Ambulance Wagons to A.D.S.at S.30.b.5.6. Cases requiring redressing will receive attention prior to transference to Motor Ambulance Cars plying from this position to Corps. M.D.S. at BRONFAY FARM (F.29.b.)

9. Walking wounded, after receiving attention, will be directed to Corps W.W.C.P. at A.14.c.6.1. (near CARNOY).

10. O.C., Divisional Bearers will arrange to have G.S. wagons (horsed) available to supplement ambulance wagons if required.

11. All reports will be sent to A.D.M.S. at Advanced Divisional Headquarters (S.28.b.4.4.) via A.D.S. at S.30.b.5.6.

12. Z day will be Sept. 25th. ZERO hour will be communicated later.

23rd Sept.1916.

J Gun Mooney[?]
COLONEL,
A.D.M.S., Guards Division.

Copies to:-

№ 1 :	№ 3 F.A.
" 2 :	№ 4 F.A.
" 3 :	№ 9 F.A.
" 4 :	'G' Guards Division.
" 5 :	'Q' Guards Division.
" 6 :	1st Guards Bde.
" 7 :	2nd Guards Bde.
" 8 :	3rd Guards Bde.
" 9 :	D.D.M.S., XIVth Corps.
" 10 :	A.D.M.S., 5th Division.
" 11.:	A.D.M.S., 6th Division.
" 12 :	A.D.M.S., 21st Division.
" 13 "	A.D.M.S., 56th Division.
" 14 :	Office.
" 15 :	Diary.

Field Ambulance Bearer Divisional Arrangements for information of Battalion Medical Officers.

Advanced Dressing Station.	All cases occurring in front of, and in the vicinity of GUILLEMONT will be dealt with at the Advanced Dressing Station (S.30 b 5.6) on MONTAUBAN – GUILLEMONT Road.
Collection of Wounded.	The majority of bearers will be posted here before the attack. They will push forward and get in touch with Medical Officers of Battalions as soon as possible after the attack on the 3rd Objective, No 4, Field Ambulance following the 1st Brigade and No 9, Field Ambulance the 2nd Bde. If possible they will clear the cases from the front area, first. No 3, Field Ambulance bearers will work from behind, forwards
Information from Battalion Medical Officers.	It would facilitate the work of Field Ambulance bearers, if the position of cases unable to walk was indicated, by posting a rifle in the ground, butt upwards, and if Battalion Medical Officers sent back by walking wounded or other available means, messages as to the position and numbers of Casualties etc., addressed:– "Advanced Dressing Station, Guards Division"

Copies to H.Q. 1st Gds Bde
2nd
3rd
All Batt. M.O.s Gds Divn

[signature] Fraser.
Major, R.A.M.C.
O.C. Gds Divnl Bearers

14.9.16.

1st Guards Brigade Operation Orders

SECRET.   Copy No. 13.

221

1st Guards Brigade Order No.71.

Reference Map - ALBERT
Combined Sheet. 1/40,000.   9th September 1916.

1. The Brigade will move to bivouacs about CARNOY tomorrow September 10th in accordance with attached March Table.

2. First Line Transport will be Brigaded and march in rear of 75th Field Coy., R.E. under the Orders of Bde., Transport Officer. There will be an interval of 50 yards between the Transport of each Unit.

3. Advanced parties from all Units will report to the Staff Captain at 8-30 A.M. tomorrow at Cross-roads F.18.c.

4. The party attached to 183 Tunnelling Coy., will rejoin their Units at CARNOY tomorrow.

5. Completion of movements and position of Unit H.Q., will be reported to this Office.

6. Position of Brigade H.Q., in CARNOY Area will be notified later.

Acknowledge.

W B Smith
Captain,
Brigade Major, 1st Guards Brigade.

Issued to Signals at :- 4.15 pm

Copy No. 1 2nd Bn. Grenadier Guards.
2 2nd Bn. Coldstream Guards.
3 3rd Bn. Coldstream Guards.
4 1st Bn. Irish Guards.
5 Bde., Machine Gun Company.
6 1st Guards T.M.Battery.
7 75th Field Coy., R.E.
8 NO. 3 Coy., Train.
No. 9 Bde.,Transport Officer.
10 Guards Division.
11 O.C., Signals.
12 Staff Captain.
13, 14, 15 & 16 Retained.

S E C R E T.   Copy No. 16.

226

1st Guards Brigade Order No. 72.

11th Sept., 1916.

Reference Map -
57 C. S.W. 1/20,000.

1. The 1st Guards Brigade will relieve the left section now held by 3rd Guards Brigade from T.14.a.2.3. to T.13 central. to-morrow night September 12th/13th.

2. The Boundaries of the Brigade will be :-

(a) On the right T.14.a.2.3. - GINCHY CHURCH - T.13.d.3.3. - HIGH HOLBORN at S.24.b.7.4. junction of CORNISH ALLEY and KNOX Trench S.24.d.2.8. - thence Railway to S.29.b.5.9. - S.29.a.6.3. - thence track Westwards through BERNAFAY WOOD.

(b) On the Left T.13. central - S.E. corner of DELVILLE WOOD. S.18.d.6.10. (PILSEN ALLEY inclusive to 41st Division) NORTHERN corner of TRONES WOOD - S.28. central. - MONTAUBAN CARNOY Road (inclusive to this Division and Division on left) S.28.c.6.6. - S.27.c.7.4.

3. (a) The 2nd Bn. Grenadier Guards will relieve all Infantry in the Area mentioned in para. 2. East of the DELVILLE WOOD HUILLEMONT Road. Battn., H.Q., will be at T.19.a.5.0.

(b) The 1st Bn. Irish Guards will be in Brigade Support in BERNAFAY WOOD and the trenches between TRONES WOOD and the DELVILLE GUILLEMONT Road.
Battn., H.Q., will be in BERNAFAY WOOD.

(c) The 2nd and 3rd Battn's. Coldstream Guards will remain in their present bivouacs.

4. (a) Arrangements for relief of Bde.,M.G.Company will be made direct between O.C's. concerned. On completion of relief O.C., 1st Gds.Bde. M.G.Company will arrange to have one section in the line under the Orders of O.C., 2nd Bn. Grenadier Guards.

(b) Another section will be held in Reserve in the Area between BERNAFAY WOOD and the GINCHY DELVILLE WOOD Road.

(c) H.Q., will also be established in the Area mentioned in b above.

(d) Remainder of Machine Gun Company will remain in their present bivouacs.

5. (a) 1st Guards T.M.Battery will arrange relief direct with 3rd Guards T.M.Battery and on completion of relief will arrange to have two guns in the line under orders of O.C., 2nd Bn. Grenadier Guards.

(b) Two other guns will be held in Reserve in the Area between BERNAFAY WOOD - ~~GUINCHY~~ GUILLEMONT DELVILLE WOOD Road.

(c) Remainder of 1st Guards T.M.Battery will remain in present bivouacs.

6. Completion of relief will be reported by 14th Corps Code 'A'.

7. Details as to relief by 2nd Bn. Grenadier Guards and 1st Bn. Irish Guards will be issued to-morrow to Units concerned.

8. Brigade H.Q. will close at CARNOY and open at S.23.d.2.3. (DUMMY TRENCH) at 9 P.M. to-morrow 12th inst..

Acknowledge.

J.M. Gibbs

for Captain,
Brigade Major, 1st Guards Brigade

Issued to Signals at :- 11.15 pm

Copy No.1 2nd Bn. Grenadier Gds.,
3 2nd Bn. Coldstream Gds.,
3 3rd Bn. Coldstream Gds.,
4 1st Bn. Irish Gds.,
5 Bde., M.G. Company.
6 1st Guards T.M.Battery.
7 75th Field Coy., R.E.
8 No. 4 Field Ambulance.
9 No. 3 Coy., Train.
10 Guards Division.
11 3rd Guards Brigade.
12 2nd Guards Brigade.
13 Bde., Transport Officer.
14 Staff Captain.
15 Signal Officer.
16) Retained.
17)

SECRET. Copy No. 12

1st Guards Brigade Order No 75.

Reference Map Sheet. 13th September 1916.
57 c S.W.

1. The fourth Army will attack the enemy's defences between COMBLES RAVINE and MARTINPUICH on Z day with the object of seizing MORVAL - LES BOEUFS - GUEUDECOURT and FLERS, breaking through the enemy's system of defence.
The French are undertaking an offensive simultaneously on the South of the Reserve Army on the North.

2. The attack will be pushed with the utmost vigour, all along the line, until the most distant objectives are reached.
The failure of a unit on a flank is not to prevent other units pushing on to their final objectives, as it is by such means that these Units, which have failed, will be assisted to advance.

3. Preliminary bombardment.
(a) Commencing on 12the September bombardment and wire cutting on hostile defensive system will take place from 6 a.m. to 6.30 p.m. daily.
(b) The preliminary bombardment on the day of the attack will be similar to that on previous days, there being no increase of fire previous to ZERO.
(c) At 6.30 p.m. each evening from 12th September inclusive, night firing will commence and continue until 6 a.m. Lethal shells will be used.

4. (a) The 2nd Guards Brigade will attack on the right of the Division the 1st Guards Brigade the left and the 3rd Guards Brigade will be in Divisional Reserve.
(b) The 41st Brigade of the 14th Division will attack on the left of the 1st Guards Brigade.
(c) Boundaries are shewn on attached map.

5. Forming up areas.
Forming up areas are shown on attached maps.
Instructions as to movement of troops to their forming up areas will be issued separately.

6. Objectives allotted to Guards Brigades and neighbouring Division are shewn on attached map.

First objective	is	marked		Green.
Second	"	"	"	Brown.
Third	"	"	"	Blue.
Fourth	"	"	"	Red.

7. The Infanty will advance to the attack of the GREEN line at ZERO.
To the attack of the brown line at ZERO + ~~[illegible] minutes~~. 1 hour
To the attack of the blue line at ZERO + 2 hours ~~and 30 minutes~~.
To the attack of the Red Line at ZERO + 4 hours and 30 minutes.

8. Artillery Barrages.
(a) 50% of Field Artillery covering the Division will be used for creeping barrage, and 50% for stationary barrage.
(b) Details of stationary barrages will be issued later. In all cases the stationary barrages will lift back when the creeping barrage reached it.
(c) At ZERO the creeping barrage will open 100 yards in front of our trenches and will advance at rate of 50 yards per minute until it is 50 yards beyond the first objective when it will become stationary.

The task of the Brigade is to press the attack through to their ultimate objectives with every means at our disposal.

12. Tanks will be employed to co-operate with the attack.
Instructions as to their employment are attached.
Instructions will be issued as to movement of tanks to their departure positions and as to time of their advance of their various objectives.

13. <u>Royal Flying Corps</u>
(a) 9th Squadron, Royal Flying Corps will have one Contact Aeroplanes in the air from ZERO to dark on Z day and again from 6.30 a.m. to 9 a.m. on Z + 1 day.
(b) Flares will be lit as follows:-
(1) On obtaining each objective.
(2) At 12 noon and 5 p.m. on Z day by leading troops.
(3) At 6.30 a.m. on Z + 1 day by leading troops.
Red flares will used by Infantry, Green flares by Cavalry.

14. An orderly with a watch will visit all Battalion H.Q. about 1 p.m. and 7 p.m. on Y day so that time may be checked.

15. Special instructions will be issued on the following subjects,
(a) Medical arrangements.
(b) supply of rations, water, S.A.A. Light T.M.Amn. and hand grenades.
(c) Communications.

16. All Transport will be packed up and ready to move forward at 1 hours notice after ZERO + 4 hours.
The Brigade Transport Officer will remain at Divisional H.Q. MINDEN POST from ZERO + 2 hours onwards.
On Y day after 7.30 p.m. the road running North from Cross roads S 23 d 4.2 will be clear of all wheeled traffic.

17. As soon as the final objectives have been captured by the Infantry the Cavalry will advance and seize the High ground ROCQUIGNY - VILLERS - AU FLOS - RIENCOURT - LES - BAPAUME - BAPAUME.
The XIVth Corps will be prepared to support the Cavalry on the above line at the earliest possible moment.

18. <u>Prisoners.</u> will be sent via Brigade Headquarters to Divl. collecting station at CRATER POST A 8 a 6.3 where they will be taken over and searched under A.P.M. arrangements.
Receipts will be given for prisoners and escort will return to their units.
All captured documents should be sent with prisoners to Divl. collecting station whence they will be forwarded under Divisional arrangements.

19. <u>Dumps.</u>
R.E. Dumps of sandbags and wire have been established along the GUILLEMONT - WATERLOT FARM road in the Brigade area.
A water dump is being established at advanced Brigade Headquarters at S 24 b 6.1½.
Dumps of Bombs and S.A.A. are also being established along the GUILLEMONT - WATERLOT FARM ROAD in the Brigade area.

20. Brigade Headquarters will be established at S 24 b 6.1½ from 4 a.m. onwards on Z day.
Acknowledge.

Captain.
<u>Brigade Major, 1st Guards Brigade.</u>

Issued through Signals at:-

Copy No 1. 2/Gren. Gds.
2. 2/Cold.Gds.
3. 3/Cold.Gds.
4. 1/Irish Gds.
5. Bde.M.Gun Coy.
6. 1st Gds.T.M.Bty.
7. 76th Field Coy. R.E.
8. No 3 Coy. Gds.Divl. Train.
9. Guards Division.
10. 2nd Guards Bde.
11. 3rd Guards Bde.
12. 61st Inf. Bde.
13. Left Group G.D.A.
14. Field Ambulance.
15. Bde. Transport Officer.
16. Staff Captain.
17.
18. } Retained.

Amendment to 1st Guards Brigade Order No 73.

Cancel para 7 and substitute -

"The Infantry will advance to the attack of the Green Line at ZERO".

To the attack of the Brown line at ZERO + 1 hour.

To the attack of the blue line at ZERO + 2 hours.

To the attack of the red line at ZERO + 4 hours 30 minutes.

Para 8 ([illegible]) line 5.

For "at ZERO + 45 minutes" substitute
"at ZERO + 1 hour."

Para 8 (d) line 1.

For "at ZERO + 1 hour" substitute
"at ZERO + 1 hour 10 minutes.

Para 8 (d) last line on page 3.

For "at ZERO + 1 hour 30 minutes" substitute
"at ZERO + 2 hours."

Para 8. (E) line 1.

For "at ZERO + 3 hours 45 minutes" substitute
"at ZERO + 3 hours 30 minutes."

Para 14 (a) line 1.

For "two contact aeroplanes" substitute
"one contact aeroplane."

Captain.

13th Sept. 1916. Brigade Major, 1st Guards Brigade.

2nd Bn Grenadier Guards.
2nd Bn Coldstream Guards.
3rd Bn Coldstream Guards.
1st Bn Irish Guards.
Bde. Machine Gun Coy.
1st Guards T.M.Battery.
75th Field Coy.
Guards Division.
2nd Guards Brigade.
3rd Guards Brigade.
41st Infantry Brigade.
Brigade Transport Officer.
Staff Captain.
No 3 Coy. Guards Divl. Train.
Left Group., Guards Divl. Artillery.

INSTRUCTIONS FOR EMPLOYMENT OF TANKS.

To accompany 1st Guards Brigade Orders No 73.

Nine tanks will be allotted to Guards Division to work partly in Guards Division and partly in 6th Division area.

Departure positions and lines of advance of tanks are shewn on attached map.

Three tanks will be employed in each group and will normally advance in file.

ATTACK OF FIRST OBJECTIVE.

Tanks will start movement from their departure positions at a time so calculated that they reach their objective five minutes before the Infantry.

The Infantry will advance as usual behind a creeping barrage in which gaps about 100 yards wide will be left for the route of the tanks. The stationary barrage of both heavy and field artillery will be timed to be lifted off the objectives of the tanks some minutes before their arrival of these objectives.

After clearing up the first objective a proportion of the tanks should be pushed forward a short way to pre-arrange positions as defensive strong points. If necessary a tank may be sent to assist the Infantry in clearing such points in the line as may be holding them up.

THE ATTACK OF THE SECOND OBJECTIVE.

Tanks and Infantry will advance together under the creeping barrage. Tanks will move as before in column and on well defined routes. The pace will be regulated to tank pace (20 to 30 yards per minute) but Infantry must not wait for any tanks that are delayed.

The action of the tanks will be as for the first objective.

THE ATTACK OF THE THIRD AND SUBSEQUENT OBJECTIVES.

The tanks will start sufficiently far in front of the Infantry to reach the third and fourth objectives sometime before the Infantry being covered during their advance by a creeping barrage.

The tanks will move as before in column.

Their action will be arranged so as crush wire and keep done hostile rifle and machine gun fire.

The Infantry when they are advancing must not wait for any tanks that are delayed.

The following signals will be used.

From tanks to Infantry and Aircraft.

FLAG SIGNALS. - Red flag - Out of action.
Green flag - Am on objective.
Other flags - Are inter-tank signals.

LAMP SIGNALS. Series of T's - Out of action.
" " E's - Am on objective.

A proportion of the tanks will carry pigeons.

If tanks get behind time table or get out of action Infantry must on noaccount wait for them.

If the tanks succeed and the Infantry are checked, the tanks must endeavour to help them.

GENERAL NOTES.

Recent trials show that over heavily shelled ground a greater pace than 15 yardsa minute cannot be depended on. This pace will be increased to 25 yards over good ground, and down hill on good ground it will reach 30 yards a minute.

SECRET. Copy No. 9

1st Guards Brigade Order No 74.

Orders for assembly for the assault.

Ref. Map. ALBERT Combined Sheet 1/40,000 — 13th Sept. 1916.

---

1. (a) On the night Sept. 14/15th 2nd Bn Coldstream Guards and 3rd Bn Coldstream Guards will relieve troops of 2nd Bn Grenadier Guards in their forming up areas as shewn in map issued with 1st Guards Brigade Orders No 73.
   (b) Arrangements are being made for 41st Brigade to take over the ground in their area at present held by 2nd Bn Grenadier Guards.

2. March Table for Units moving to their assembly areas is attached.

3. The assembly march must be carried out in absolute silence and there must be no smoking.
   Between dawn and ZERO there will be no movement.

4. Precautions will be taken to ensure that a larger number of fires than usual are not lighted.

5. Between dawn and ZERO there will be no movement in assembly positions of troops.

6. Arrival in assembly positionswill be reported at once to advanced Brigade Headquarters.

Captain.

ACKNOWLEDGE. Brigade Major, 1st Guards Brigade.

Issued through signal at :-

Copy No 1. 2nd Bn Grenadier Guards.
2. 2nd Bn Coldstream Guards.
3. 3rd Bn Coldstream Guards.
4. 1st Bn Irish Guards.
5. Bde. Machine Gun Coy.
6. 1st Guards Brigade T.M.Battery.
7. 75th Coy. R.E.
8. Guards Division.
9. Retained.

ASSEMBLY MARCH TABLE.

UNIT.	Starting point.	Time.	Route.	Remarks.
2/Gren.Gds.	-	On relief.	Shortest route.	(a) Support Coy. will not await relief but will wait until 2nd and 3rd Cold.Gds. have passed East of the WATERLOT - GUILLEMONT Road. (b) Guides should reconnoitre routes to Battn. assembly lines. (c) M.G.Coy. and T.M.Detachment will report in assembly line. (d) Guides for Coys. taking over front line will be provided at West end of track through TRONES WOOD at S 23.d.5.0
2/Cold.Gds.	A.8.c	8 p.m.	Cross rds. A 14 a 5.2 MONTAUBAN. N. end of BERNAFAY WOOD	(a) To move by Coys. at 100 yards interval. (b) Guides for front line will meet Battns. at Western end of the track through TRONES WOOD S 23 d 5.0. (c) M.G.Sections join Battns. before moving off from billets.
3/Cold.Gds.	A.8.c	8.15 p.m.	track through centre of TRONES WOOD.	
1/Irish Gds.	S 30 a 2.8	8.15 p.m.	most direct tracks.	(a) M.G.Section to report before Battn. marches off from BERNAFAY WOOD.
Bde.M.G.Coy.	A 8 c	8.30 p.m.	as for 2nd C.G.	(a) Sections to be attached to 2nd and 3rd C.G. to join these Bns. before they march off from bivouacs.
T.M.Battery.	A 8 c	8.35 p.m.	- do -	Detachment to be attached to 2nd Bn Grenadier Gds. to report to O.C. 2/Gren.Gds. at the assembly line of that Battn.
75th Field Coy.	A 8 c	8.40 p.m.	- do -	To pick up work platoons at N.end of BERNAFAY WOOD.

1st Guards Brigade

Assembly Area

(Less 2nd - 3rd Bns Coldstream Gds)

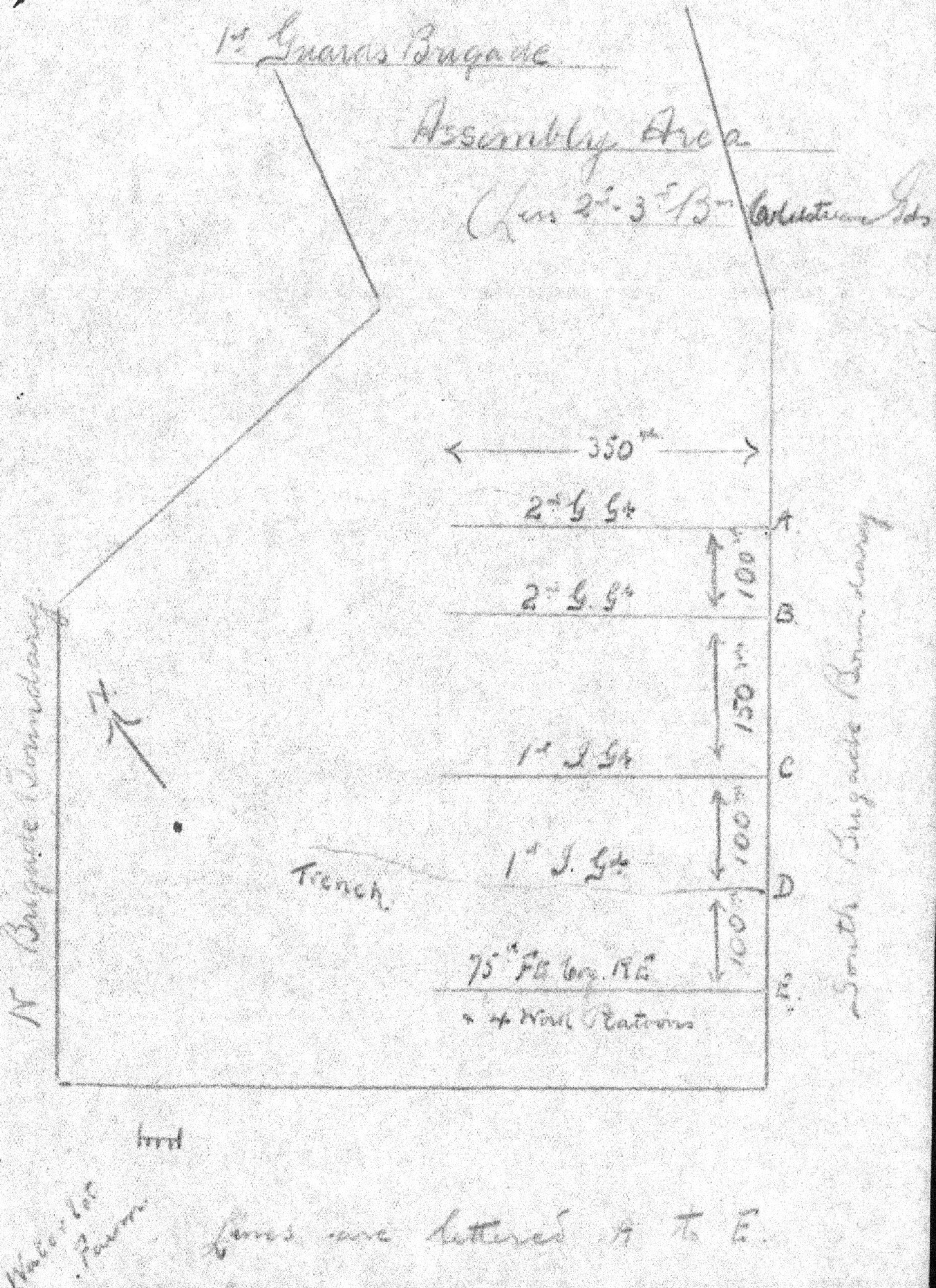

Lines are lettered A to E.

Lateral pegs on 2 Coy frontage are 10 yds apart.

Forward Direction line boards are 25 yds apart one central line – two on flanks.

1st Guards Brigade.
2nd Guards Brigade.
3rd Guards Brigade.
G.D.A.
C.R.E.
Pioneer Battalion.
"Q".

Div Signals

G.D.No. 2245/G.

HEADQUARTERS
No. 237/4
Date 13/9/16
FIRST GUARDS BRIGADE

The S.O.S. Signal for XIV Corps, from 6 p.m. to-morrow September 14th, will be 3 blue rockets fired in rapid succession.

This message will be repeated until acted upon by the artillery.

The Bde Bombing Officer is arranging for the exchange of

All red rockets in possession of units ~~will be~~ & the issue of blue ones in their place

withdrawn and returned to the Division as soon as blue rockets have been issued.

<u>ACKNOWLEDGE.</u>

[signature]

Captain,

13th Sept. 1916. General Staff, Guards Division.

1st Guards Brigade No 837/4.

2nd Bn Grenadier Guards.
2nd Bn Coldstream Guards.
3rd Bn Coldstream Guards.
1st Bn Irish Guards.
Bde. Machine Gun Coy.
1st Guards T.M.Battery.

The S. O. S. Signal for XIVth Corps, from 6 p.m. tomorrow Sept. 14th. will be 3 blue rockets fired in rapid succession.

This message will be repeated until acted upon by the Artillery.

The Brigade Bombing Officer is arranging for the exchange of all red rockets in possession of Units and the issue of blue ones in their place.

Captain.

13th Sept. 1916.

Brigade Major, 1st Guards Brigade.

SECRET.   Copy No. 16

Amendment to 1st Guards Brigade Order No.74.

20th Sept., 1916.

Cancel the para. 2 and column 4 of March Table and substitute.

On completion of relief Battalions will be disposed as follows:-

(a) 3rd Bn. Coldstream Gds., will relieve 12th Rifle Brigade and 12th K.R.R. in Right Sub-sector of Brigade front.

(b) 2nd Bn. Coldstream Gds., will relieve 6th Oxford & Bucks and 6th K.S.L.I. in Left Sub-sector of Brigade front.

(c) 1st Bn. Irish Gds., will be in Brigade Support about GUILLEMONT Station.

(d) 2nd Bn. Grenadier Gds., will be in Brigade Reserve in TRONES WOOD.

Advanced parties from 2nd Bn. Grenadier Guards and 1st Bn. Irish Guards should be sent as soon as possible to look for accommodation in their allotted areas and should report progress to the Staff Captain at West end of track through centre of TRONES WOOD at 6-30 P.M.

M B Smith
Captain,
Brigade Major, 1st Guards Brigade.

Issued through Signals at 4-15 P.M.

Copy No. 1 2nd Bn. Gren.Gds.,
2 2nd Bn. Cold.Gds.,
3 3rd Bn. Cold.Gds.,
4 1st Bn. Irish Gds.,
5 Bde., M.G.Company.
6 1st Guards T.M.Btty.,
7 75th Field Coy., R.E.
8 4th Field Ambulance.

Copy No. 9 Bde., Transport Officer.
10 Bde., Supply Officer.
11 Guards Division.
12 60th Infantry Bde.,
13 Staff Captain.
14 O.C., Signals.
15)
16) Retained.

SECRET.   Copy No. 5

(230)

1st Guards Brigade Order No. 74

Ref. Maps - ALBERT 1/40,000.   September 19th, 1916.
57C S.W. 1/20,000.

1. On night of 20th/21st Sept., 1st Guards Brigade will relieve 60th Infantry Brigade in the trenches from T 9 d 6.8 to T 3 c 6.1.

2. On completion of relief battalions will be disposed as follows :-

(a) 2nd Gren.Gds., 2 coys. in front line from T 9 d 6.8 to T 9 b 4.6.
1 company in Support from T 9 d 6.8 to T 9 d 2.8.
1 company in Reserve.

(b) 1st Irish Gds., 1 company in front line from T 9 b 4.6 to SUNKEN ROAD T 9 a 8.8.
2 coys. in Support from T 9 d 2.8 to T 8 d 8.6.
1 company in Reserve.

(c) 2nd Cold.Gds., 3 platoons in front line from SUNKEN ROAD T 9 a 8.8 to T 3 c 6.1.
9 platoons in Support ~~from SUNKEN ROAD T 8 d 2.5 to T 8 a [illegible]~~.
1 company in Reserve.

This should read "in triangle from T 8 d 5.5 Eastwards to T 8 d 8.6 Southwards to T 8 d 8.0. Northwards to T 8 d 5.5 and also trench running thence NW for 100 x."

(d) 3rd Cold.Gds., will be in Reserve in TRONES WOOD.

3. Relief of M.G.Company and T.M.Battery will be arranged direct between O.C's concerned.
O.C., 1st Guards T.M.Battery will arrange to take over the 2 guns of 60th T.M.Battery in position about T 9 b 4.9.
O.C., 1st Guards T.M.Battery will arrange for his battery to carry up as much ammunition as possible for these guns on night of relief and subsequent nights.

4. 1st Line Transport will remain in its present position. Arrangements will be made by the Bde., Transport Officer direct with Units to have any Transport such as Cookers bivouaced on the W. side of TRONES WOOD.

5. There is a Bde., Bomb Store at T 13 c 5.5 near the point at which the ambulances stop.

6. Brigade H.Q., will close at the CITADEL and open at T 19 a 1.2 at 9 P.M.

ACKNOWLEDGE.

W. B. Smith
Captain,
Brigade Major, 1st Guards Brigade.

Issued to Signals at :- 7.45pm

Copy No.1	2nd Bn. Grenadier Gds.,	Copy No.9	Bde., Transport Officer.
2	2nd Bn. Coldstream Gds.,	10	Bde., Supply Officer.
3	3rd Bn. Coldstream Gds.,	11	Guards Division.
4	1st Bn. Irish Gds.,	12	60th Infantry Bde.,
5	Bde. M.G. Company.	13	Staff Captain.
6	1st Guards T.M. Battery.	14	O.C., Signals.
7	75th Field Coy., R.E.	15)	
8	4th Field Ambulance.	16)	Retained.

MARCH TABLE.

UNIT.	Starting point.	Time.	Taking over from.	Remarks.
2/Gren.Gds.	Camp.	6.45 p.m.	3 front line 12th K.R.R. 12/R.B.	(a) Battns will move by Coys. at 100 yds interval. (b) Owing to state of roads Lewis Guns will be taken up as far as possible on limbers.
2/Cold.Gds.	"	7.5 p.m.	3 front line plats from 6/Ox & Bucks 7th Ox. & Bucks. 1 support plat. from 6/Ox & Bucks 2 support coys. from 6/K.S.L.I.	(c) Route for all Units - CARNOY - MONTAUBAN - N.W. end of BERNAFAY WOOD.
3/Cold.Gds.	"	7.15 p.m.	-	(d) Guides will meet Battns. at W. ~~edge~~ end of track through centre of TRONES WOOD.
1/Irish Gds.	"	6.55 p.m.	6th Ox. & Bucks. 12th ~~Rifle Bde.~~ KRR ✻	(e) The Coys. and Battan. in reserve will send advanced parties to meet the Brigade Major, at W. end of track through TRONES WOOD at 6.30 p.m.
Bde.M.G.Coy.	"	7.25 p.m.		
T.M.Battery.	"	7.30 p.m.		

✻ 1 coy ~~[illegible]~~ 1/I G in front line take over from 6/Ox & Bucks
2 coys 1/I G. in support from 12/K.R.R.

SECRET. **Copy No. 14**

1st Guards Brigade Operation Order No 76.

16th September 1916.

1. The Guards Division will be relieved tonight 16/17th Sept. by the 59th Brigade in the GREEN LINE and by the 14th Division in the BROWN LINE, and the extension towards LES BOEUFS.

2. (a) O.C. 2nd Bn Grenadier Guards will issue orders for the relief of all Units of the 1st Guards Brigade in the GREEN LINE.
(b) They will be relieved by 10th K.R.R. who are 230 strong.
(c) Eight Guides will be at Western edge of TRONES WOOD on the track at 10.15 p.m. to lead the K.R.R. by half Companies and distribute them along the GREEN LINE in Guards Divl. area.
(d) Company Commanders and Machine Gun Officer of a K.R.R. Battalion will be sent to Headquarters, 2nd Bn Grenadier Guards. to go over the line. They will report about 6 p.m.

3. Officer Commanding, 3rd Bn Coldstream Guards will arrange the relief of all the troops of the 1st Guards Brigade in the BROWN LINE and its continuation in the direction LES BOEUFS CHURCH.
8 guides will report at 1st Guards Brigade Headquarters between TRONES WOOD and BERNAFAY WOOD as early as they can be sent down.

4. The Brigade will bivouac at the CITADEL F 21 b 3.2 Route CARNOT the CITADEL.

5. Battalions will collect South of the MARICOURT - FRICOURT Road.

6. Battalion Quartermasters will be ordered to take over Camps.

7. The Brigade Transport Officer will arrange about all 1st Line Transport which will be in its former billets.

8. 75th Field Coy. R.E. will return to their former billets.

9. Battalion cookers with a hot meal will be at the BRIQUETERIE A 4 b 5.7. This meal will be served as detachments pass.

10. An Officer of each Unit of those left behind with the 1st Line Transport has been detailed to meet detachments of Units at the South West corner of BERNAFAY WOOD.

A C K N O W L E D G E.

W B Smith
Captain.
Brigade Major, 1st Guards Brigade.

Issued through signals at :-

Copy No 1. 2nd Bn Grenadier Guards.
2. 2nd Bn Coldstream Guards.
3. 3rd Bn Coldstream Guards.
4. 1st Bn Irish Guards.
5. Bde. Machine Gun Coy.
6. 1st Guards T.M.Battery.
7. Brigade Transport Officer.
8. 75th Field Coy. R.E.
9. Guards Division.
10. 2nd Guards Brigade.
11. 3rd Guards Brigade.
12. Staff Captain.
13.)
14.)
15.) Retained.
16.)

233

SECRET. **Copy No.** 15.

1st Guards Brigade Order No 76.

21st September 1916.

Reference Map 57.c. 1/20,000.

1. Troops of the 2nd and 3rd Bn Coldstream Guards holding trenches S. of the GINCHY - LES BOEUFS Road will be relieved by the 16th and 18th Infantry Brigades.

2. (a) The Right front Coy. and Right support Coy. of 3/Cold.Gds. will be relieved by 2 Coys. of the 1st Buffs, 16th Inf. Bde. The leading Company will be at Brigade Headquarters at 7 p.m. and guides to H.Q. 3rd Bn Coldstream Guards will be provided by Brigade Headquarters.

(b) The remaining 2 Coys of the 3rd Bn Coldstream Guards will be relieved by 2nd D.L.I. 18th Inf. Bde. Guides will be provided from Brigade H.Q. to Bn. H.Q. This Battalion will arrive at Brigade H.Q. at 7.15 p.m.

(c) Coys. of 2nd Bn Coldstream Guards South of the GINCHY - LES - BOEUFS Road will be relieved by 11th Essex, 18th Inf. Bde. Guides to Battalion H.Q. will be provided by Brigade H.Q. These Coys. will arrive at Brigade H.Q. at 7.45 p.m.

3. (a) On completion of relief 3rd Bn Coldstream Guards will relieve 1st Bn. Grenadier Guards of 3rd Guards Brigade in the line N. of 3rd Bn Coldstream Guards as far as communication trench T.3.c.4.8. Dividing line between 1st and 3rd Guards Bde. is communication trench from T 3 c 4.8 to T 8 a 4.8. Details of this relief will be arranged direct between O.C. 3rd Bn Coldstream Guards and O.C. 1st Bn Grenadier Guards.

(b) Troops of 2nd Bn Coldstream Guards relieved by 6th Divn. S. of SUNKEN ROAD will on completion of relief be bivouaced between TRONES and BERNAFAY WOOD.

O.C's M.G.Coy. and T.M.Battery will arrange direct with O.C.'s M.G.Coy.'s and T.M.Btys. concerned for relief of necessary guns.

There are two M.G's in the area to be taken over from 1st Bn Grenadier Guards - Guides for two relieving guns of 1st Guards Machine Gun Coy. will be at trench junction T 8 b 0.4 at 8.30 p.m. tonight.

4. Completion of reliefs will be reported to this Office by XIVth Corps Code.

ACKNOWLEDGE.

W B Smith

Captain.
Brigade Major, 1st Guards Brigade.

Issued through signals at :- 3.30pm

Copy No. 1	2nd Bn Grenadier Guards.	11. 16th Inf. Bde.
2	2nd Bn Coldstream Guards.	12. 18th Inf. Bde.
3	3rd Bn Coldstream Guards.	13.)
4.	1st Bn Irish Guards.	14.)
5	Bde. Machine Gun Coy.	15.) Retained.
6	1st Guards Bde. T.M.Battery.	16.)
7	75th Field Coy. R.E.	
8	Guards Division.	
9	2nd Guards Brigade.	
10	3rd Guards Brigade.	

SECRET. Copy No. 16

1st Guards Brigade Order No 77.

21st September 1916.

Ref. Map.
57.c.1/20,000.

1. The 4th Army will renew the attack on Z day in combination with the attacks by the French to the South and Reserve Army to the North.

2. (a) The Guards Division will form part of the attack of the XIVth Corps.

(b) 1st Guards Brigade will attack on the right and 3rd Guards Brigade on left of Guards Division.

(c) 18th Infantry Brigade of 6th Division will be attacking on the right of 1st Guards Brigade.

ATTACKING TROOPS.

3. The attack of 1st Guards Brigade will be carried out by 2nd Bn Grenadier Guards on the right and 1st Bn. Irish Guards on the left.

The 2nd Bn Coldstream Guards will be in support on the right and 3rd Bn Coldstream Guards in support on the left.

PRELIMINARY BOMBARDMENT.

4. A steady bombardment of hostile positions will begin at 7 a.m. on Y day and will be continued to 6.30 p.m. It will begin again at 6.30 a.m. on Z day.

Night firing will be carried out nightly from 6.30 p.m. to 6.30 a.m.

There will be no intensive fire previous to ZERO.hour.

FORMING UP AREAS.

5. Forming up areas, boundaries and objectives are shown on the attached map -

The first objective is Marked GREEN.
The second objective is marked BROWN.
The third objective is marked BLUE.

FORMATION FOR ATTACK.

6. The 2nd Bn Grenadier Guards and 1st Bn Irish Guards will form up in two lines - one in the firing line and one in the support line.

The 2nd Bn Coldstream Guards will form up in the communication trench from T 8 a 9.4 to T.3.c.3.8.

The 3rd Bn Coldstream Guards will form up in the trench from T 8 a 9.4 to T 8 d 5.5.

The 1st Guards Brigade Machine Gun Coy. will assemble with one section at the head of 2nd Bn Coldstream Guards - one section in rear of 2nd Bn Coldstream Guards and one section on right of 3rd Bn Coldstream Guards.

The 1st Guards Brigade Trench Mortar Battery will form up with two guns on right of front line and two guns on right of support line.

The 75th Field Coy. R.E. and work platoons will form up in trenches T 8 d.

7. The Infantry will advance to the attack of the GREEN Line at ZERO - to the attack of the BROWN Line at ZERO + 1 hr. To the attack of the BLUE Line at ZERO + 2 hours.

BARRAGES.

8.(a) 50% of Field Artillery barrage will be used for creeping barrage and 50% for stationary barrage.

(b) In all cases the stationary barrage will lift back when the creeping barrage meets it.

9.(a) At ZERO the creeping barrage will start 100 yards in front of our front line trenches. It will advance at the rate of 50 yards a minute until it is 200 yards beyond the GREEN Line when it will become stationary.

(b) At ZERO + 1 hour the creeping barrage will start 200 yards in front of the GREEN Line and will advance at the rate of 50 yards a minute until it has passed 200 yards beyond the BROWN Line when it will become stationary.

(c) At ZERO + 2 hours the creeping barrage will start 100 yards in front of the BROWN Line and will advance at the rate of 50 yards a minute until it has passed 100 yards beyond the BLUE Line when it will become stationary.

(d) Other permanent barrages are being arranged along certain Sunken roads.

TASKS.

10.(a) The task of the Division is to press the attack through to the BLUE Line. a sufficient flow of troops will be maintained from ZERO onwards to ensure that the BROWN Line is strong and well supported.

(b) The attack on all objectives will be carried out by 2nd. Bn Grenadier Guards on the right and 1st Bn Irish Guards on the left.

The 2nd and 3rd Bns. Coldstream Guards will be in support under Command of Lt.Col.J.V.CAMPBELL. D.S.O.,

METHOD OF ASSAULT.

11. The assault will be carried out by leading Battalions in two waves at 75 yards distance.

ACTION OF SUPPORT BATTNS.

12. As soon as the front and support lines are vacated by 2nd Bn Grenadier Guards and 1st Bn Irish Guards the 2nd Bn Coldstream Guards and 3rd Bn Coldstream Guards will occupy them.

All movement to these lines by supporting Units should be by the Communication trench from T 8 a 9.4 to T 8 c 3.8.

Similarly 2nd and 3rd Bns. Coldstream Guards will occupy the GREEN and BROWN Lines as soon as they are vacated by 2nd Bn Grenadier Guards and 1st Bn Irish Guards.

As soon as the 2nd Bn Grenadier Guards and 1st Bn Irish Gds. have gained the BROWN Line 2nd and 3rd Bns. Coldstream Guards will each send a Company as clearing up parties in LES BOEUFS. These two Companies must shelter in shell holes behind the BROWN Line during the pause at that line. They must on no account become mixed up with 2nd Bn Grenadier Guards and 1st Bn Irish Guards. They will carry a special supply of P. bombs and Mills Grenades for dealing with cellars.

b The 2nd and 3rd Bns. Coldstream Guards are responsible for making good each objective as captured and for guarding either flank if threatened, paying special attention to the right flank.

Lt.Col.J.V.CAMPBELL. D.S.O., Commanding supporting Battns. will be prepared to give such additional support as may be required to carry out the attack on the final objective - bearing in mind the necessity for holding positions already captured.

MACHINE GUNS.

13. (a) At the first favourable opportunity after the GREEN Line has been captured, O.C. Machine Gun Coy. will send I section forward to it. In this line and in his subsequent move to the BROWN line two guns will always be on the right flank ready to assist in the formation of a defensive flank.

(b) Similarly when the BROWN and BLUE Lines have been captured one section will be sent forward to help in the consolidation of each of these lines.

Thus when the final objective has been captured there should be 4 guns in the BLUE Line and 8 in reserve in the BROWN Line.

STOKES T.M..

14. (a) Previous to the assault two guns will be established in the right of the Brigade area. These two guns will move forward at the first favourable opportunity and establish themselves on the right of the GREEN Line.

(b) Two other guns will be in reserve in the front line and will only move forward to the GREEN Line if order to do so by Lt. Col.J.V.CAMPBELL. D.S.O., or by the Brigadier.

R.E. and WORK PLATOONS.

15. 75th Field Coy. R.E. and work platoons will move forward from their assembly area to the trench about T 8 b 3.0 as soon as this trench is clear of 3rd Bn Coldstream Guards. They will be ready to move forward on receipt of orders from Brigade H.Q. and consolidate ground gained. O.C. 75th Coy. R.E. will detail one Officer and three orderlies in liaison with O.C. supporting Battns.

PATROLS.

16. When the BLUE line has been captured patrols will be sent forward and any ground from which good observation can be gained will be occupied.

Such points will be consolidated and eventually joined up with our line.

CONTACT PATROL & FLARES.

17. One contact aeroplane will be in the air from ZERO till 6.30 p.m. on Z day. Flares will be lit by leading Infantry lines on obtaining each objective and also at 6 p.m. on Z day.

18. Watches will be synchronised at 7 p.m. on Y day and at 9 a.m. on Z day.

1st LINE TRANSPORT.

19. Ammunition portions of 1st Line Transport will be collected on the South side of BERNAFAY WOOD to the South of the GUILLEMONT MONTAUBAN Road and remainder of 1st Line Transport in the neighbourhood of MINDEN POST by 12 noon on Z day.

Brigade Transport Officer will detail an orderly to be in waiting at Advanced Divisional Headquarters, Bernafay Wood ~~to the~~ and will himself be at MINDEN POST from 12 noon on Z day.to receive instructions.

PRISONERS.

20. Prisoners will be sent back to the Corps Cage at the CRATERS A 8 a under escort. In future correspondence will not be taken off prisoners except off Officers. Officers documents will be removed as soon as they are captured and sent to the Corps Cage with their escort.

DUMPS.

21. An advanced Brigade Dump of Bombs - S.A.A. - Stokes Mortar ammunition - R.E. material and rations has been established about T 8 c Central.

EQUIPMENT.

22. The equipment to be carried by the assaulting troops will be the same as that laid down for the attack on Sept. 15th.

23. Arrangements have been made for the Brigade on our Right to open enfilade machine and trench mortar fire on the GREEN LINE from about T 9 d 3.9 at ZERO. This fire will be continued until the creeping barrage passes beyond the GREEN Line.

MEDICAL arrangements.

24. Medical arrangements will be notified later.

Brigade Headquarters.

25. Brigade Headquarters will be at T 19 a ½.3½. An Advanced Brigade Report Centre will be established in the communication trench T 8 b - T 3 c on Sept. 22nd.

Pigeons will be supplied to the Battalions on Z day as follows:-

3 to 2nd Bn Grenadier Guards.

3 to 1st Bn Irish Guards.

6 to 3rd Bn Coldstream Guards.

As soon as all pigeons have been released pigeon men must return at once to Brigade Headquarters.

26. Z day will be Sept. 25th ZERO hour will be notified later - it will probably be in the afternoon.

ACKNOWLEDGE.

[signature]

Captain.

Brigade Major, 1st Guards Brigade.

Issued through signals at :- 11.15 p.m.

Copy No 1. 2nd Bn Grenadier Guards.
2. 2nd Bn Coldstream Guards.
3. 3rd Bn Coldstream Guards.
4. 1st Bn Irish Guards.
5. Bde. Machine Gun Coy.
6. 1st Guards Bde. T.M.Bty.
7. 75th Field Coy. R.E.
8. Right Group G.D.A.
9. Guards Division.
10. 2nd Guards Brigade.
11. 3rd Guards Brigade.
12. 18th Inf. Bde.
13. B.T.O.
14. Sigs.
15. Staff Captain.
16. Retained.

1st Guards Brigade No. 262.

2nd Bn Grenadier Guards.
2nd Bn Coldstream Guards.
3rd Bn Coldstream Guards.
1st Bn Irish Guards.

The forthcoming attack differs from the last in that the whole scheme is not such an ambitious one. The distance to the first objective is about 300 yards - to the second objective 800 yards and to the last objective about 1,300 yds. In each case the objective is a clearly defined one and not merely a line drawn across the map.

Between our present front line and the 1st objective there is only "No Man's Land". - During the next two nights this should be actively patrolled to ensure that our attack is not taken by surprise by some unknown trench and in order that Officers and N.C.O's may have a knowledge of the ground.

It would also be of great assistance to the Artillery if reports as to the actual distance to the GREEN LINE were sent in.

The ground slopes down to LES BOEUFS beyond which there is a distinct hollow with a plateau the same level as LES BOEUFS beyond. On reaching the final objective Officers and N.C.O's should understand the necessity for pushing patrols out to command this hollow and give warning or prevent counter-attacks forming up here.

Large scale maps of LES BOEUFS have been sent to all Battalions. These should be carefully studied by all Officers and N.C.O's and especially by those of the Coys. detailed for the cleaning up of LES BOEUFS.

All runners and signallers should know the position of the advanced Brigade Report Centre and that the best means of approach to it will probably be down the communication trench T 3 c and T 8 b.

Finally it cannot be too much impressed on assaulting troops the necessity for clinging to our own barrage. It will be an attack in which this should be comparatively easy and on which the success of the whole operation may depend.

W B Smith

Captain.

22nd Sept. 1916. Brigade Major, 1st Guards Brigade.

S E C R E T.

Supplement to 1st Guards Brigade Order No 77.

The following extracts for medical arrangements on Z day are forwarded for your information and necessary action.

1. Disposition of Medical Units prior to attack.

(a) A Tent sub-division will form an A.D.S. at S 30 b 5.6
(b) A tent sub-division will form an A.D.S. and Wagon Post at T 13 c 8.8.
(c) A tent sub-division (less personnel at Ambulance Post BERNAFAY WOOD) will be held in reserve at CARNOY.
(d) The Bearer Divisions of Nos. 3 and 4 F.A.'s will be held in reserve at S 30 a 4.2.
(e) The Bearer Division of No 9 F.A. will be held in reserve at S 30 a 4.2.
(f) Ambulance Wagons will be held in readiness at S 30 a 2.1.

2. The Bearer Divisions will be placed under the Command of Major A.D.FRASER. who will be responsible for clearance of the front area.

3. The O.C.Divisional bearers will maintain touch with Battalion Medical Officers by means of liaison Officers and men specially detailed for the purpose.

4. If conditions allow, the O.C. Divisional Bearers will establish an ambulance and Wagon Post in neighbourhood of T 7 d central, when the attacked troops have reached their ultimate objective. The position of this post will be communicated to Battalion Medical Officers as soon as possible.

5. The O.C., Divisional Bearers will instruct Battalion Medical Officers.to report their positions to him, giving map references, by means of walking wounded.

6. The O.C. Divisional Bearers will place himself in communication with Brigade Headquarters concerned, in order that information regarding progress of attack may be obtained.

7. General Plan of method of clearance of casualties.

(a) Battalion stretcher bearers will convey cases in direction of T 13 c 8.8 until touch is obtained with ambulance bearer squads. These squads will be pushed forward as soon as possible in order to reduce the 'carry' of Battalion stretcher bearers. Ambulance Bearer Squads will be under the Command of Bearer Officers.
(b) On stretcher cases reaching ambulance post at T 13 a 8.8 they will be dressed and conveyed by horsed ambulance wagons to A.D.S. at S 30 b 5.6. Cases requiring redressing will receive attention prior to transference to Motor Amb. cars plying from this position to Corps M.D.S. at BRONFAY FARM. (F 29 b).

8. Walking wounded, after receiving attention, will be directed to Corps W.W.C.P. at A 14 c 6.1 (near CARNOY).

9. O.C. Divisional Bearers will arrange to have G.S.wagons (horsed) available to supplement ambulance wagons if required.

10. All reports will be sent to A.D.M.S. atxAdvanced Divl. Headquarters (S 28.b.4.4) via A.D.S. at S 30.b.5.6.)

Captain.
Brigade Major, 1st Guards Brigade.

Issued through signals at :-
Copy No 1. 2nd Bn Grenadier Guards.
2. 2nd Bn Coldstream Guards.
3. 3rd Bn Coldstream Guards.
4. 1st Bn Irish Guards.
5. Bde. Machine Gun Coy.
6. 1st Guards T.M.Battery.
7. 75th Field Coy. R.E.
8. Guards Division.
9. 2nd Guards Brigade.
10. 3rd Guards Brigade.
11. 18th Infantry Brigade.
12. Brigade Transport Officer.
13. Staff Captain.
14. Signals.
15.)
16.) Retained.

SECRET.

Ammendments to 1st Guards Brogade Order No 77.

Para 11. insert.

Waves for assaulting Battalions.
To prevent overcrowding two waves will attack the 1st onjective, subsequent waves being sent forward to thicken up the line as required.
Battalion Headquarters will therefore not leave the assaulting ~~line~~ trench with the leading waves but will control the progress of the attack by sending up such support as is required and will follow on when they consider the time is suitable to do so.

Para 25 add.

PIGEONS.
It is not necessary to send more than one pigeon at a time with messages.

Captain.
Brigade Major, 1st Guards Brigade.

23/9/1916.

SECRET.

Supplement to 1st Guards Brigade Order No 77.

All Units are responsible for reconnoitring and knowing the routes to their assembly positions for the attack on Z day.

W B Smith

Captain.

23/9/1916. Brigade Major, 1st Guards Brigade.

S E C R E T.

Amendment to 1st Guards Brigade Order No 77.

Para 9. (a) Amend to read.

At ZERO the creeping barrage will start 200 yards in front of our front line trenches etc.

Captain.
Brigade Major, 1st Guards Brigade.

Issued to all recipients of
1st Guards Bde. O. No 77.

<u>S E C R E T.</u>

Supplement to 1st Guards Brigade Order No 77.

Units attacking on flanks of the Brigade.

1. The 11th Essex of 18th Infantry Brigade will be attacking on Z day on the right of 2nd Bn Grenadier Guards.
They will attack the 2nd objective.
The 1st West Yorks of the same Brigade will go through the 11th Essex and attack the 3rd objective.
This Brigade will stand fast during our attack on the first objective but will assist our attack with Machine Gun and Stokes Mortar fire.

2. The 2nd Scots Guards of the 3rd Guards Brigade will attack on the left of the 1st Bn Irish Guards. They will attack the first and second objectives.
The 1st Bn Grenadier Guards will go through them and attack the 3rd objective.

W B Smith
Captain.
Brigade Major, 1st Guards Brigade.

23/9/1916.

2nd Bn Grenadier Guards.
2nd Bn Coldstream Guards.
3rd Bn Coldstream Guards.
1st Bn Irish Guards.

Tools and sandbags to be carried by assaulting troops on Z day can be drawn as follows :-

	Sandbags.	Tools.
2/Gren.Gds. 1/Irish Gds.	Divl. Dump near CARNOY A.13.d.9.1	Battn. tools. All tools that can be salvaged. Remainder will be made up on application to Bde.H.Q.
2/Cold.Gds. 3/Cold.Gds.	Dump T 8 c Central.	Those now in possession.

WBS

Captain.
23/9/1916. Brigade Major, 1st Guards Brigade.

"A" Form.

Army Form C.2121
(in pads of 100).
No. of Message

MESSAGES AND SIGNALS.

Prefix ...... Code ...... m. | Words | Charge | This message is on a/c of: ...... Service. | Recd. at ...... m.

Office of Origin and Service Instructions.

Sent
At ...... m.
To ......
By ......

(Signature of "Franking Officer.")

Date ......
From ......
By ......

TO 2nd Ger Fus
1st Irish Fus

Sender's Number.	Day of Month.	In reply to Number.	AAA
* B.M. 652	23rd		

Ref attached amendment to 1st Fus Bde Order No 77 para 11. The Brigadier considers that this will give Battalion Commanders latitude to carry out the assault according to their suggestions –

From 1st Fus Bde
Place
Time 7 pm

The above may be forwarded as now corrected. (Z) [signature] Capt

Censor. Signature of Addressor or person authorised to telegraph in his name.

* This line should be erased if not required.

750,000. W 2186—M509. H. W. & V., Ld. 6/16.

SECRET.

Amendmnts to 1st Guards Brigade Order No 77.

Para 11. insert.

Waves for assaulting Battalions.

To prevent overcrowding two waves will attack the 1st objective, subsequent waves being sent forward to thicken up the line as required.

Battalion Headquarters will therefore not leave the assaulting trench with the leading waves but will control the progress of the attack by sending up such support as is required and will follow on when they consider the time is suitable to do so.

Para 25 add.

PIGEONS.

It is not necessary to send more than one pigeon at a time with messages.

W B Smith

Captain.

23/9/1916. Brigade Major, 1st Guards Brigade.

S E C R E T. Copy No. 15

1st Guards Brigade Order No 78.

Ref. Map. 57.c. 1/20,000. 24th Sept. 1916.

1 . The Brigade will move to its assembly positions for the attack on Sept. 25th. in accordance with attached march table.

2. The march must be carried out in absolute silence and there must be no smoking.

3. Arrival in assembly positions must be at once reported by all Units to this Office.

4. After arrival in assembly positions no fires of any kind may be lighted, and there must be as little movement as possible before ZERO.

5. Bayonets will not be fixed except by a percentage of the leading Battns. representing the normal garrison, until 2 minutes before ZERO and the greatest care will be taken then to prevent the enemy observing this movement.

6. Owing to the impassable state of the communication trench T 8 b - T 3 c assembly areas for 2nd Bn Coldstream Guards and M.G.Coy. have been altered.

(a) The 2nd Bn Coldstream Guards will assemble in the trench which runs from T 3 c 2.7 to T 9 a 2.7. The 2nd Bn Coldstream Guards will arrange to place police at the entrance to this trench about T 3 c 2.7 to prevent it being used by other Units for assembly purposes. This trench will be completed by 75th Field Coy. R.E. and a working party tonight from T 9 a 2.7 to the present reserve line. The 3rd Bn Coldstream Guards will use this trench or the trench from T 8 b to T 3 c ~~trench~~ for moving up to the front line. The 3rd Bn Coldstream Guards can also use the latter for forming up if required.

(b) The Machine Gun Coy. will assemble as follows:-

(1) The section detailed for the final objective will dig in tonight behind the centre of the present front line.

(2) Two guns will each assemble and dig in on the right and left respectively of the present front line.

(3) Four guns will then be in reserve and will assemble in the trench T 8 b 2.8.

A C K N O W L E D G E.

W B Smith
Captain.
Brigade Major, 1st Guards Brigade.

Issued through signals at :- 2 p.m.

Copy No 1. 2nd Bn Grenadier Guards.
2. 2nd Bn Coldstream Guards.
3. 3rd Bn Coldstream Guards.
4. 1st Bn Irish Guards.
5. Bde. Machine Gun Coy.
6. 1st Guards T.M.Battery.
7. 75th Field Coy. R.E.
8. 3rd Guards Brigade.
9. Guards Division.
10. Right Group. G.D.A.
11. Staff Captain.
12. Signals.
13.)
14.)
15.) Retained.
16.)

M A R C H   T A B L E.

Unit.	Starting point.	Time.	Route.	Remarks.
2/Gren. Gds.	S 22 d 9.1.	8 p.m.	Tracks N. of GINCHY.	(a) 8 guides from 2/Cold.Gds. front line Coy. will meet Battn. at the TANK just N. of Bde. H.Q. at 8.15 p.m. (b) To move by Coys. at 200 yards interval. (c) To assemble in present front line or new assembly trench 150 yards in rear.
2/Cold. Gds.	-	Direct on relief.		(a) To detail 8 guides who know the way to the front line to be occupied by 2/Gren. Gds. to be at Bde. H.Q. at 7.30 p.m.
3/Cold.Gds.	-	" "	"	(a) To detail 8 guides who know the way to the front line to be occupied by 1/Irish Gds. to be at Bde. H.Q. at 8 p.m.
1/Irish Gds.	S 24 c 2.2	9 p.m.	Tracks N. of GINCHY.	(a) 8 guides from 3rd Bn Cold.Gds. will meet Battn. at TANK just N. of Brigade H.Q. (b) To move by Coys. at 200 yards interval. (c) To assemble in present front line and new assembly trench 150 yards in rear.
M.Gun Coy.	Present bivouacs.	9.45 p.m.	" " "	
T.M.Battery.	" "	10 p.m.	" " "	
75th Field Coy. R.E.	" "	7 p.m.	" " "	

S E C R E T. Copy No.

Communications for attack on Sept. 25th.

1. Brigade Headquarters as already announced will be at T 19 a 0.1½ It is possible that if the attack is successful they may move forward to about T 8 b 1.8.

2. An advanced visual and runners post will be established tonight in the communication trench just off the road at T 3 c 0.5. All messages from Battalions East of this point will be directed there. It will be marked by signal flags and by a board. It is essential that when a Battan. H.Q. moves it should notify this post of its new position as soon as possible in order that communications may be opened up to their new position.

3. Units in support before they move East of T 3 c 0.5 should send all messages to T 8 b 1.3 where there is another 1st Guards Brigade REPORT CENTRE.

4. Pigeons will be supplied to Battalions tonight as follows :-

2nd Bn Grenadier Guards.	4.
1st Bn Irish Guards.	4.
3rd Bn Coldstream Guards.	8.

Not more than one pigeon will be sent with any one message unless the message in very urgent or the weather conditions are very bad.

5. No. 9 Squadron R.F.C., propose having a special Control Patrol machine out during Z day to keep Brigade H.Q. informed of the position of Battalion Headquarters. It is therefore of the utmost importance that Battalions should put out their numerals and panels at ZERO but not before.
Battalions should use every available means for communication with this aeroplane and must persevere until an answer is received.

Ver B Smith
Captain.
Brigade Major, 1st Guards Brigade.

Copy No 1. 2nd Bn Grenadier Guards.
2. 2nd Bn Coldstream Guards.
3. 3rd Bn Coldstream Guards.
4. 1st Bn Irish Guards.
5. Bde. Machine Gun Coy.
6. 1st Guards T.M.Battery.
7. Right Group. G.D.A.
8. 2nd Guards Brigade.
9. 3rd Guards Brigade.
10. Guards Division.
11. 18th Infantry Brigade.
12. Staff Captain.
13. Signals.
14.)
15.) Retained.
16.)

"A" Form. Army Form C. 2121.

MESSAGES AND SIGNALS. No. of Message

Prefix ... Code ... m.	Words	Charge	This message is on a/c of:	Recd. at ... m.
Office of Origin and Service Instructions.	Sent At ... m. To ... By ...		... Service. (Signature of "Franking Officer.")	Date ... From ... By ...

TO All Bns.

Sender's Number.	Day of Month	In reply to Number	AAA
* BM 738	26th		

Ref para 6 of Bde Order 79 Sallant & Five will proceed to CITADEL aaa

From [illegible]
Place
Time 7.25 pm

The above may be forwarded as now corrected. (Z) [signature] Capt

Censor. Signature of Addressor or person authorised to telegraph in his name.

* This line should be erased if not required.

(4199) Wt. W14042—M14. 300000 Pads. 12/15. Sir J. C. & S

"C" Form.

MESSAGES AND SIGNALS.

Prefix .... Code .... m.	Words	Charge	This message is on a/c of:	Recd. at ....
Office of Origin and Service Instructions.	Sent		.... Service.	Date ....
	At .... m.			From ....
	To			
	By		(Signature of "Franking Officer.")	By ....

TO: all Bns, M.G. Coy, T.M. By — 75th Coy RE

Sender's Number.	Day of Month.	In reply to Number.	AAA
* B.M. 726	26th		

The Bde will be relieved tonight by the Gauntlet aaa M.G. Coy will remain in the line until tomorrow night & first & work platoons will carry on work on present sector tonight aaa work platoons will rejoin Bde on completion of nights work aaa details later aaa

From: Firm

Place

Time: 12.15 pm

The above may be forwarded as now corrected. (Z)

Censor. — [illegible] Capt

Signature of Addressor or person authorised to telegraph in his name.

* This line should be erased if not required.

225,000 W 14042—M 44. H. W. & V., Ld. 12/15

SECRET. Copy No. 16

1st Guards Brigade Order No 79.

Ref. Map. 57 c S.W. 1/20,000. 26th September 1916.

1. The whole of the front occupied by the 1st Guards Brigade will be relieved by 2nd Bn Irish Guards of 2nd Guards Brigade tonight.

2. 2nd Bn Irish Guards will take over the line as follows :-

1 Coy. in BLUE LINE in area of 1st Bn Irish Gds.

1. Coy. in BLUE LINE in area of 2nd Bn Grenadier Guards.

1 Coy. in support in LES BOEUFS and BROWN LINE.

1 Coy. in reserve in GREEN LINE. Bn. H.Q. at 1st Bn Irish Gds Headquarters.

3. Guides will be provided as follows and will report to Staff Officer, 1st Guards Brigade at advanced Brigade dump T 3 c central at 7.30 p.m. tonight.

1st Irish Gds.	4 guides for BLUE LINE in their area and 2 for Battalion H.Q.
2/Gren.Gds.	4 guides for BLUE LINE in their area.
2/Cold. Gds.)	4 guides for LES BOEUFS and BROWN LINE.
3/Cold. Gds.)	4 guides for GREEN LINE.

4. Machine Gun Coy. will remain in its present position. O.C. Machine Gun Coy. will report and remain at Brigade H.Q. from 8 p.m. tonight.

5. T.M.Battery will withdraw from the line as soon as it is dark O.C. will report position of his ammunition dumps to these H.Q.

6. On completion of relief Brigade will be bivouaced at CARNOY. and guides will meet Battalions at S 28 d 3.0, from which point they will move as Battalions.

7. 1st Line Transport will remain in its present bivouacs.

8. 75th Field Coy. and work platoons will continue consolidation of the line after dark tonight.
On completion of this work, work platoons will rejoin their Battns. at CARNOY.

9. Completion of relief will be reported by wire to these H.Q.

10. Brigade Headquarters will move to CARNOY on completion of relief.

M B Smith
Captain.
Brigade Major, 1st Guards Brigade.

Issued through Signals at :- 3.30 pm

Copy No
1. 2nd Bn Gren. Gds.
2. 2nd Bn Cold. Gds.
3. 3rd Bn Cold. Gds.
4. 1st Bn Irish Gds.
5. Bde. M.Gun Coy.
6. 1st Gds. T.M.Bty.
7. Guards Division.
8. 75th Field Coy. R.E.
9. 2nd Guards Bde.
10. 3rd Guards Bde.
11. Right Group. G.D.A.
12. Staff Captain.
13. Signals.
14.) 15.) 16.) Retained.

"A" Form.

MESSAGES AND SIGNALS.

Army Form C.2121
(in pads of 100).
No. of Message...........

Prefix ....Code..........m. Office of Origin and Service Instructions.	Words	Charge	*This message is on a/c of:*	Recd. at..............m.
	Sent		....................*Service.*	Date....................
	At..............m.			From....................
	To..................			
	By..................		(Signature of "Franking Officer.")	By......................

TO

Sender's Number.	Day of Month.	In reply to Number.	AAA
*			

From

Place

Time

The above may be forwarded as now corrected. (Z)

Censor. Signature of Addressor or person authorised to telegraph in his name.

* This line should be erased if not required.

750,000. W 2186—M509. H. W. & V., Ld. 6/16.

"A" Form.

Army Form C.2121
(in pads of 100).

MESSAGES AND SIGNALS.

No. of Message ....

Prefix .... Code .... m.	Words	Charge	*This message is on a/c of:*	Recd. at .... m.
Office of Origin and Service Instructions.	Sent		.... *Service.*	Date ....
	At .... m.			From ....
	To			
	By		(Signature of "Franking Officer.")	By ....

TO [illegible]

Sender's Number.	Day of Month.	In reply to Number.	AAA
*	[illegible]		

[illegible handwritten message]

From [illegible]

Place

Time 11.30 am

The above may be forwarded as now corrected.

(Z) [illegible signature]

Censor.

Signature of Addressor or person authorised to telegraph in his name.

* This line should be erased if not required.

750,000. W 2186—M509. H. W. & V., Ld. 6/16.

S E C R E T. Copy No. 12

1st Guards Brigade Order No. 80.

Ref. Map - ALBERT 1/40,000. 27th Sept., 1916.

1. 2nd and 3rd Bn's Coldstream Guards will move to-day to bivouacs at F.13 Central.

2.

	Starting Point.	Time.	Route.
2/Cold.Gds.,	Cross-roads F.18.c.5.2.	6-45 PM.	Cross country tracks.
3/Cold.Gds.,	" "	7-0 PM.	" "

3. 1st Line Transport will move in rear of Battalions.

4. Billeting parties will report to Brigade H.Q., for instructions as soon as possible.

5. An Officer should be sent in advance to reconnoitre the route.

Acknowledge.

for [signature]

Captain,

Brigade Major, 1st Guards Brigade.

Issued to Signals at 5-0 P.M.

Copy No. 1 2nd Bn. Gren.Gds.,
2 2nd Bn. Cold.Gds.,
3 3rd Bn. Cold.Gds.,
4 1st Bn. Irish Gds.,
5 Bde., Transport Officer.
6 Bde., Supply Officer.

Copy No. 7 Town Major, CARNOY.
8 Guards Division.
9 O.C., Signals.
10 Staff Captain.
11)
12) Retained.

S E C R E T.   Copy No.

1st Guards Brigade Order No. 81.

Ref. Map - ALBERT. 1/40,000.   2[illegible]th Sept., 1916.

1. Brigade H.Q., and 2nd and 3rd Bn's. Coldstream Guards will move to [illegible] Camps E.12.d. to-day.

2. 2nd Bn. Coldstream Guards will move by Companies to be clear of present Area by 4 P.M.

   3rd Bn. Coldstream Guards will march from present Area at 4 P.M.

   Brigade H.Q., will move at 4-15 P.M.

3. 1st Line Transport will accompany Units.

4. Billeting parties of Units will report to Acting Staff Captain at 12 noon at Brigade H.Q., E.12.d.

   Acknowledge.

Captain,
Brigade Major, 1st Guards Brigade.

Issued to Signals at 10-45 A.M.

Copy No.1 2nd Bn. Grenadier Gds.,
2 2nd Bn. Coldstream Gds.,
3 3rd Bn. Coldstream Gds.,
4 1st Bn. Irish Gds.,
5 Bde., Machine Gun Coy.,
6 1st Guards T.M.Battery.

S E C R E T.   Copy No. 13.

1st Guards Brigade Order No. 82.

Ref. Maps - ALBERT. 1/40,000. &
AMIENS. 1/100,000.   29th Sept., 1916.

1. The Brigade will move to billets at MORLANCOURT tomorrow Sept., 30th.

2.

Order of March.	Starting Point.	Time.	Route.
Brigade H.Q.,	Junc. of ~~roads~~ TRACKS E.24.a.7.0.		Cross country tracks.
2nd Cold.Gds.,	" "	9-30 A.M.	" "
3rd Cold.Gds.,	" "	9-35 A.M.	" "
1st Irish Gds.,	" "	9-40 A.M.	" "
2nd Gren.Gds.,	" "	9-45 A.M.	" "
M.G.Company.	" "	9-50 A.M.	" "
T.M.Battery.	" "	9-55 A.M.	" "
75th Coy.R.E.	" "	9-55 A.M.	" "

3. 1st Line Transport will move by road under the Bde., Transport Officer as follows :-

(a) Sept. 30th - to Bivouacs at DAOURS Via MORLANCOURT and CORBIE - head of column to pass cross-roads E.18.a. at 9 A.M. Order of march as for Battalions.

(b) Oct. 1st - to AILLY and PICQUIGNY Via VECQUEMONT and AMIENS - thence South of SOMME - to be clear of VELQUEMONT by 8-30 A.M. - Can march to Area 4 if required passing through Area 3.

4. Billeting parties will report to Staff Captain at Town Majors Office MORLANCOURT at 8-0 A.M. tomorrow.

5. Lorries have been asked for - one per Battalion - one for Machine Gun Company and Trench Mortar Battery - one for Brigade H.Q.,

6. (a) On Oct. 1st the Brigade (less transport and mounted personnel) will move to No.4 Area 10th Corps which from Divnl. Orders appears to be AILLY and PICQUIGNY. Buses will be at E.20.b.3.9. at 10-30 A.M.

(b) Lewis Guns, Handcarts and a minimum of personnel will be left behind at MORLANCOURT - they will proceed by Tactical Train with the 2nd Guards Brigade on Oct., 2nd.

(c) Billeting Area will be notified later and detailed orders for embarkation in buses.

ACKNOWLEDGE.

[signature]
Captain,
Brigade Major, 1st Guards Brigade.

Issued to Signals at 6-45 P.M.

Copy No.1 2nd Gren.Gds.,
2 2nd Cold.Gds.,
3 3rd Cold.Gds.,
4 1st Irish Gds.,
5 Bde. M.G.Coy. & T.M.Btty.,
6 75th Fld. Coy.,R.E.

Copy No.7 Bde., Transport Officer.
8 Bde., Supply Officer.
9 Guards Division.
10 Staff Captain.
11 O.C., Signals.
12 & 13 Retained.

Amendment to 1st Guards Brigade Order No. 82.

29th Sept., 1916.

Para. 2.	for	9-30	A.M.	read	2-30	P.M.
	"	9-35	"	"	2-35	"
	"	9-40	"	"	2-40	"
	"	9-45	"	"	2-45	"
	"	9-50	"	"	2-50	"
	"	9-55	"	"	2-55	"
	"	9-55	"	"	2-55	"

Para. 4. for 8 A.M. read 12 noon.

W B Smith

Captain,
Brigade Major, 1st Guards Brigade.

Operation orders

2nd Guards Brigade

SECRET. Copy No........

Operation Order No. 63
by
Lieutenant-Colonel B.N.S. Brooke, D.S.O.
Commanding 2nd. Guards Brigade.
-:o0o:-

Reference Map 1/40000 Albert Sheet.
1/10000 Longueval Trench Map.

1. 2nd. Guards Brigade will relieve part of 3rd. Guards Brigade on the night of September 12th/13th. Relief to be complete by 5.0 a.m.

2. 2nd. Bn. Irish Guards will hold the front line from T.14.d.0.5. to T.14.a.2.3.
1st. Bn.Scots Guards will be in support.
3rd. Bn. Grenadier Guards and 1st. Bn. Coldstream Guards will be in reserve.

3. 2nd. Bn. Irish Guards and 1st. Bn. Scots Guards will march after dinners and halt north of CARNOY for teas.
2nd. Bn. Irish Guards will march 2.0 p.m., 1st. Bn. Scots Guards at 2.30. p.m. Relief will be carried out at night.
1st. Bn. Coldstream Guards will take over billets of 1st. Irish Guards at CARNOY.
3rd. Bn. Grenadier Guards will take over billets of 2nd. Grenadier Guards at CARNOY.
These Battalions will march at an hour to be notified later, not earlier than 5.30 p.m.

4. M.G. Coy will send forward one section with 2nd. Irish Guards and one section with 1st. Scots Guards.
Remaining two sections will be in reserve and will take over reserve billets of two sections 1st. Guards Brigade M.G. Coy at CARNOY. Company to march at 3.0 p.m.

5. T.M. Battery will be in reserve at CARNOY. To march at an hour to be notified later not earlier than 3.15 p.m.

6. All units will march to CARNOY by cross country tracks.
Route from CARNOY for 2nd. Irish Guards, 1st. Scots Guards and two sections M.G. Coy will be MONTAUBAN Road to western exit of MONTAUBAN, where guides from 3rd. Guards Brigade will meet them.

7. Separate orders will be issued regarding rations and dumping of surplus kit.

8. 1st. Line transport will remain in its present lines.

9. Brigade Headquarters will close at HAPPY VALLEY at 6.0 p.m. and reopen at BERNAFAY WOOD S.28.b.central at an hour to be notified later.

ACKNOWLEDGE. FMG

[signature]
Captain.
Brigade Major.

12/9/16.

Copies to:-

No. 1	3rd. Grenadier Guards	No. 9	Bde. Supply Officer
No. 2	1st. Coldstream Guards	No.10	Guards Division.
No. 3	1st. Scots Guards	No.11	1st. Guards Brigade
No. 4	2nd. Irish Guards	No.12	3rd. Guards Brigade
No. 5	Bde. M.G. Company	No.13	Left Bde. 6th Div
No. 6	Bde. T.M. Battery	No.14)	
No. 7	Bde. Transport Officer	No.15)	Office
No. 8	Bde. Signalling Officer	No.16)	

SECRET. Copy No....10...

Operation Order No.65
by
Brigadier-General J. Ponsonby, C.M.G., D.S.O.
Commanding 2nd. Guards Brigade.

-:*****:-

Reference 1/20,000 Sheet 57 C. S.W.

1. (a). The Fourth Army will renew the attack on Z day in combination with attacks by the French to the south and the Reserve Army to the north.

   (b). The objectives of the XIVth. Corps include MORVAL and LESBOEUFS and those of the XVth. Corps GUEUDICOURT.

   (c). The attack of the XIVth. Corps will be carried out by the 5th. Division, on the right, the 6th. Division in the centre, and the Guards Division on the left.
   The 56th. Division will form a defensive flank to the south of the 5th. Division.
   The 21st. Division will be attacking on the left of Guards Division.

2. 1st. Guards Brigade will attack on the right, 3rd. Guards Brigade on the left.
   2nd. Guards Brigade (less 3rd. Battalion Grenadier Guards) will be in Divisional Reserve.
   3rd. Battalion Grenadier Guards will be in Corps Reserve.

3. A steady bombardment of hostile positions will be opened at 7 a.m. on Y day and will be continued till 6.30 p.m. It will be renewed at 6.30 a.m. on Z day. There will be no intensive fire before the hour of zero.
   Night firing will be carried out nightly between 6.30 p.m. and 6.30 a.m.

4. The objectives allotted to Guards Brigades and neighbouring Divisions, the boundaries, and the forming up areas are shewn on the attached map.

First Objective - GREEN LINE.

Second Objective - BROWN LINE.

Third Objective - BLUE LINE.

5. The Infantry will advance to the attack of the successive objectives as follows :-

GREEN LINE at zero.

BROWN LINE at zero plus 1 hour.

BLUE LINE at zero plus 2 hours.

6. 50 % of the Field Artillery of the Division will be used for creeping barrage and 50 % for stationary barrage. The creeping barrage will advance at 50 yards per minute.

7. The task of the two leading Guards Brigades is to press the attack through to the Blue Line by all means available. They will garrison and consolidate the Brown Line with a portion of their reserves when the attack goes forward.to the Blue Line.

On gaining the Blue Line, patrols will be pushed out and any ground from which good observation can be gained will be occupied. Such points will be consolidated and eventually joined up with our line.

8. One contact aeroplane will be in the air from zero till 6.30 p.m. on Z day. Flares will be lit by leading lines on reaching each objective, and also at 6 p.m. on Z day.

9. Watches will be synchronized at 6 p.m. on Y day and at 8 a.m. on Z day by telephone from this office.

10. Prisoners will be collected under Battalion arrangements and sent back to Divisional Collecting Station, CRATER POST, A.8.a.6.3., when possible.

11. Supplementary orders will be issued later on the following points :-

(a). Movement of 2nd. Guards Brigade to Reserve Brigade forming-up area.

(b). Rations and water.

(c). S.A.A., Bombs, Stokes and other ammunition.

12. Ammunition portions of 1st. Line Transport will be collected on the southwest side of BERNAFAY WOOD - to the south of the GUILLEMONT - MONTAUBAN road - by 12 noon on Z day.

Remainder of 1st. Line Transport will bo in the neighbourhood of MINDEN POST.by 12 noon on Z day.

An orderly from each Brigade Transport will be in waiting at Advancod Divisional Headquartors, BERNAFAY WOOD, (S.28.b.4.4) by 12 noon on Z day.

An officor from each Brigade Transport will be at Divisional Headquarters, MINDEN POST, by 12 noon on Z day.

13. Advanced Brigade Headquarters will be at DUMMY TRENCH, S.23.b.5.2.

14. Three tanks will be in reserve on Z day at T.13.central.

15. Z day will be September 25th.

The hour of zero will be notified later. It will probably be in tho afternoon.

ACKNOWLEDGE. Lmg

Issued to Signals at:- 2.15 p.m.

22/9/16.

E W M Grigg.
Captain.
Brigade Major.

Distribution:-

1. 3rd. Bn. Grenadier Guards.
2. 1st. Bn. Coldstream Guards.
3. 1st. Bn. Scots Guards.
4. 2nd. Bn. Irish Guards.
5. M.G.Company.
6. T.M.Battery.
7. Bde. Signal Officer.
8. Bde. Transport Officer. } Map not attached.
9. Guards Division.
10. 1st. Guards Brigade.
11. 3rd. Guards Brigade.
12. Staff Captain.
13. War Diary.
14. } Office.
15. }

-:*:-

Supplementary Orders to 2nd. Guards Brigade Order No.65.

Reference 1/20,000 Sheet 57 C. S.W.

1. 2nd. Guards Brigade will be disposed as follows on Z day:-

1st. Bn. Scots Guards) 2nd. Bn. Irish Guards) Bde. M.G.Company.) Bde. T.M.Battery.)	TRONES WOOD area.
3rd. Bn. Grenadier Guards) 1st. Bn. Coldstream Guards)	CARNOY.

2. Units detailed for TRONES WOOD area will move up on the morning of Z day.

The area will be divided as follows:-

1st. Bn. Scots Guards -	East of the wood, and south of the railway.
2nd. Bn. Irish Guards -	East of the wood and north of the railway.
M. G. Company -	West of tho wood and north of the railway.
T. M. Battery -	West of the wood and south of the railway.

Each of these units will reconnoitre its area tomorrow and arrange for the disposal of its troops so that single companies or sections, or the whole unit, may move on receipt of orders as rapidly as possible.

All the TRONES WOOD area will have been vacated by troops of 1st. and 3rd. Guards Brigades by the morning of Z day.

3. In the event of 2nd. Guards Brigade being called upon to reinforce the attacking Brigades, it will probably be ordered to move in the first instance to the area T.7.d. or to the reserve line in T.8.a. & b.

Units will carry out tomorrow the reconnaissance necessary to ensure that they reach these areas without delay by the most covered route available.

Commanding Officers will consider the advisability of moving across GINCHY ridge in artillery formation, if ordered to advance by daylight.

It may be noted that on the 15th. and 16th. the enemy barrage along the GINCHY - DELVILLE WOOD crest was always more intense in the neighbourhood of GINCHY.

4. M.G.Company will take its gun limbers up to TRONES WOOD and park them clear of the railway track in its own area.

5. Units detailed for TRONES WOOD will take their cookers up with them. These cookers will carry rations for Z plus 1 day. Units will carry both this ration and their iron ration on them, if ordered to advance.

ACKNOWLEDGE.

Issued to Signals at:- 8.10 pm

E.W.M. Grigg.

Captain.
Brigade Major.

23/9/16.

Distribution.

1. 3rd. Bn. Grenadier Guards.
2. 1st. Bn. Coldstream Guards.
3. 1st. Bn. Scots Guards.
4. 2nd. Bn. Irish Guards.
5. Bde. M.G.Company.
6. Bde. T.M.Battery.
7. Bde. Signal Officer.
8. Bde. Transport Officer.
9. Guards Division.
10. 1st. Guards Brigade.
11. 3rd. Guards Brigade.
12. Staff Captain.
13. War Diary.
14.) Office.
15.)

-:*:-

SECRET.   Copy No...12...

Supplementary Orders to 2nd. Guards Brigade Order No.65.

Reference 1/20,000. Sheet 57 C. S.W.

1. a. Units detailed for TRONES WOOD area will move tomorrow as follows :-

1st. Bn. Scots Guards - 6 a.m.

2nd. Bn. Irish Guards - 6.30 a.m.

M.G.Company.) - 7 a.m.
T.M.Battery.)

Bde. Headquarters - 8.15 a.m.

Battalions will move by companies at 5 minutes interval. Companies will move across country.
M.G.Coy, T.M.Battery and cookers will move by road.

b. 3rd. Bn. Grenadier Guards will move to CRATER POST (A.8.a.6.3) at 8.30 a.m. To move by companies at 5 minutes interval.

O.C., Battalion will report his arrival there to 6th. Division Advanced Headquarters at A.3.c.1.6. Any orders for movement of this Battalion will be issued by XIVth. Corps through 6th. Division Advanced Headquarters, where and officer of the Battalion will remain in waiting.

c. 1st. Bn. Coldstream Guards will await further orders at CARNOY.

2. All units, including 3rd. Bn. Grenadier Guards and 1st. Bn. Coldstream Guards, will be ready to move at a moment's notice by 11 a.m.

3. a. All O.R. will be ready supplied with the following by 11 a.m. :-

I. Haversack ration for remainder of Z day.
Full ration for Z plus 1 day.
Iron ration.
Full waterbottle.
II. Four bombs per man (except M.G.Coy & T.M.Battery).

b. 400 tins of water will be available at Brigade Headqrs, DUMMY TRENCH, S.23.b.5.2. Units will draw on this while at TRONES WOOD and keep their waterbottles full.

c. If ration for Z plus 1 day is not available when units march off, it will be brought up by cookers as soon as possible afterwards.

4. Units will send an orderly to Brigade Headquarters, DUMMY TRENCH, immediately on arrival in TRONES WOOD area. He will remain there and act as guide to Headquarters of units when required.

5. Battalions will be supplied with two pigeons each tonight. It is not necessary to send more than 1 bird at a time. Each bird will be issued in a separate basket. Each basket should be given to a separate pigeon man.

Two more pigeon men will be sent to Brigade Headquarters on the evening of Z day to collect more pigeons for the following day.

Pigeons may be kept for 48 hours before being released.

6. All surplus kits will be dumped tomorrow under arrangements to be communicated by the Staff Captain.

7. Brigade Headquarters will close at BRICK TRENCH at 8 a.m. and open at DUBBY TRENCH (S.23.b.5.2) at the same hour.

ACKNOWLEDGE.

Issued to Signals at:- 3.0pm

24/9/16.

Captain.
Brigade Major.

Distribution.

1. 3rd. Bn. Grenadier Guards.
2. 1st. Bn. Coldstream Guards.
3. 1st. Bn. Scots Guards.
4. 2nd. Bn. Irish Guards.
5. Bde. M.G.Company.
6. Bde. T.M.Battery.
7. Bde. Signal Officer.
8. Bde. Transport Officer.
9. Bde. Supply Officer.
10. Bde. Bombing Officer.
11. Guards Division.
12. 1st. Guards Brigade.
13. 3rd. Guards Brigade.
14. Staff Captain.
15. War Diary.
16.) Office.
17.)

-:0:-

Operation Order No. 68
by
Brigadier-General J. Ponsonby C.M.G. D.S.O.
Commanding 2nd. Guards Brigade.

-:*:-

1. 2nd. Guards Brigade will move to No. 4 Training Area, S.W. of AMIENS, on October 2nd. under orders to be issued later. Movement will be by tactical train.

2. 1st. Line Transport will move to the same area by road on October 1st. as follows:-

October 1st.	-	to DAOURS.
Route	-	MORLANCOURT - CORBIE Not to enter DAOURS before 4 p.m.
October 2nd.	-	to AILLY and PICQUIGNY
Route	-	Main road to AMIENS.
October 3rd.	-	to No. 4 Area.

Transport of all units will move under orders from Brigade Transport Officer.

3. 1st. Line Transport of Pioneer Bn (4th. Coldstream Guards) will move with 2nd. Guards Brigade Transport under orders from 2nd. Guards Brigade Transport Officer.

4. (a) No. 4 Coy Train will move to DAOURS on October 1st. and to AILLY on October 2nd. It will not enter DAOURS before 4 p.m. on October 1st. It will arrange to move in advance of 1st. Line Transport.

(b) One supply wagon will remain with each unit for carriage of supplies for men and horses proceeding by road.

(c) On arrival at AILLY on October 2nd. supplies for transport for October 3rd. will be picked up at Church.

5. If possible, one lorry will be provided for each battalion on October 2nd. so that a certain amount of kit may be kept in bivouacs after 1st. Line Transport has moved.
One lorry will also be provided for Bde. Hqrs. and two lorries for the joint use of M.G. Coy and T.M. Battery. These two lorries will carry the guns, gun equipment, hand carts and camp kettles of T.M. Battery and in addition the officers' kits and mess kits of M.G. Company and T.M. Battery.

6. Bde. Transport Officer will report to this Office tonight his arrangements for the move.

ACKNOWLEDGE

Issued to Signals at:- 5 p.m.

E.W.M. Grigg
Captain.
Brigade Major.

30/9/16

Copies to:-

No. 1	3rd. Bn. Grenadier Guards	No. 10	Pioneer Bn (4/C.G.)
No. 2	1st. Bn. Coldstream Guards	No. 11	No. 4 Coy Train
No. 3	1st. Bn. Scots Guards	No. 12	Guards Division "G"
No. 4	2nd. Bn. Irish Guards	No. 13	Guards Division "Q"
No. 5	Bde. M.G. Company	No. 14	Staff Captain
No. 6	Bde. T.M. Battery	No. 15	76th. Field Coy R.E.
No. 7	Bde. Transport Officer	No. 16	No. 9 Field Ambulance
No. 8	Bde. Signal Officer	No. 17	War Diary
No. 9	Bde. Supply Officer	No. 18	Office

2 G.B. No. 187/G

Supplementary Order to 2nd. Guards Brigade Order No. 68

-:--:-

1. 1st. Line Transport of 76th. Field Coy R.E. and of No. 9 Field Ambulance will move tomorrow with Transport of 2nd. Guards Brigade Group under orders from Bde. Transport Officer.

2. Personnel of both units will move by tactical train with personnel of 2nd. Guards Brigade Group on October 2nd. Orders will be issued later for this.

ACKNOWLEDGE

30/9/16

Captain.
Brigade Major.

Same distribution as O.O. No. 68.

3rd. Grenadier Guards.
1st. Coldstream Guards.
1st. Scots Guards.
2nd. Irish Guards.
Bde. M.G.Company.
Bde. Signal Officer.
Bde. Transport Officer.
Guards Division.
1st. Guards Brigade.
3rd. Guards Brigade.
71st. Infantry Brigade.

2nd.G.B.No.129/G.

Appendix "A" and Map not attached.

[signature]

Captain.
Brigade Major.

13/9/16.

SECRET. 2nd.Gds.Bde.No.129/G.

Reference Map Sheet 57 C. S.W.

1. The Fourth Army will attack enemy's defences between COMBLES RAVINE and MARTINPUICH on Z day with the object of seizing MORVAL - LES BOEUFS - GUEUDECOURT - FLERS.

The French will attack simultaneously on the right, and the Reserve Army on the left.

The attack is to be pushed with the utmost vigour all along the line until the most distant objectives are reached. The failure of a unit on the flank is not to prevent other units from pushing on to their final objective.

As soon as the final objectives have been captured by the Infantry, the Cavalry will advance and will seize the high ground ROCQUIGNY - VILLERS AU FLOS - RIENCOURT LES BAPAUME - BAPAUME.

The Guards Division is to be prepared to support the Cavalry on the above line at the earliest possible moment.

2. The objectives allotted to Guards Brigades are marked on the attached map as follows:-

First objective	-	Green	(X Line).
Second objective	-	Brown	(Xa Line).
Third objective	-	Blue	(Y Line).
Fourth objective	-	Red	(Z Line).

2nd. Guards Brigade will be on the right. 1st. Guards Brigade will be on the left. 3rd. Guards Brigade will be in reserve. 71st. Infantry Brigade will be on the right of 2nd. Guards Brigade.

3. The Brigade will attack with two Battalions in front, and two Battalions in support.
3rd. Grenadier Guards will be right front Battalion.
1st. Coldstream Guards will be left front Battalion.
1st. Scots Guards will be right support Battalion.
2nd. Irish Guards will be left support Battalion.

4. Battalions will be formed up on a company front in column of half companies. Troops will be in single rank. Each Battalione will therefore advance in four waves.

5. 2nd. Guards Brigade Machine Gun Company will detail guns as follows :-

I. Two guns to advance with 3/G.G. and two guns with 1/C.G. These guns will take position in the third wave on the inner flank of the right and left flank platoons respectively.

II. Four guns to advance with 1/S.G. and four guns with 2/I.G. Four of these guns will take position in the sixth wave on the inner flank of the right and left platoons respectively. The other four will take the same position in the eight wave. The remaining three guns will advance in the centre of the ninth wave.

6. Four Stokes Guns will be detailed to advance on the flanks of the ninth wave.

1/S.G. and 2/I.G. will find carrying parties of 1 Officer and 50 men each to advance with these guns.

Remaining guns will be in Brigade Reserve with 76th. Field Company, R.E.

7. The formation for attack will accordingly be as follows:-

	1/C.G.				3/G.G.			
	B Coy.		A Coy		B Coy.		A Coy	
First Wave	6	5	2	1	6	5	2	1
Second Wave	8	7	4	3	8	7	4	3
	D Coy.		C Coy		D Coy.		C Coy.	
Third Wave	14 (2 MG's)	13	10	9	14	13	10	9 (2 MG's)
Fourth Wave	16	15	12	11	16	15	12	11

	2/I.G.				1/S.G.			
	~~A Coy.~~				~~A Coy.~~			
	B Coy		A Coy		B Coy		A Coy	
Fifth Wave	6	5	2	1	6	5	2	1
Sixth Wave	8 (2 MG's)	7	4	3	8	7	4	3 (2 MG's)
	D Coy	~~D Coy.~~	C Coy		D Coy	~~C Coy~~	C Coy	
Seventh Wave	14	13	10	9	14	13	10	9
Eighth Wave	16 (2 MG's)	15	12	11	16	15	12	11 (2 MG's)
Ninth Wave	SG	SG	4 M.G's. and carrying parties.		SG	SG		

Sapping Platoons will be formed up in rear of Battalion Headquarters which will move in the centre of the fourth and eighth waves. The distance between waves will be 50 yards.

8. Details of Artillery barrage are given in Appendix A.

9. Nine tanks will advance from Guards Division front. They will probably start from each successive line well in advance of the attacking troops.

The actions of the troops will be entirely independent of the action of the tanks, and will be carried out as ordered, whether the tanks are held up or not.

10. The assaults on successive objectives will be delivered at the following times :-

Attack on X Line at zero.
Attack on Xa Line at zero plus 1 Hour.
(This second assault is limited to 1st. Guards Brigade. 2nd. Guards Brigade will not move till time for third assault).
Attack on Y Line at zero plus 2 Hours.
Attack on Z Line at zero plus 4 Hours and 30 minutes.

11. The action of the waves of attack will be as follows :-

a. First four waves will pass over X line, and lie down close in rear of the barrage, which will halt till zero plus 1 hour and 10 minutes at X plus 200 yards.
Fifth and Sixth waves will clear up X line.
Seventh and Eighth waves will pass over X line and lie down in rear of fourth wave.
Ninth wave will lie down short of X line.

b. At zero plus 2 hours all waves will advance to the Y line. Seventh and Eighth waves will advance in front of Fifth and Sixth waves.
Ninth wave will be in rear, as before.

c. On reaching Y line, first four waves will pass over Y line and lie down close in rear of barrage as before.
Seventh and Eighth waves will clear up Y line.
Fifth and Sixth waves will pass over Y line and lie down in rear of fourth wave.
Ninth wave will lie down short of Y line.

d. Half an hour after reaching Y line all Commanding Officers will meet at Battalion Headquarters, 3rd. Battalion Grenadier Guards, and will confer on attack on Z line.
Lieutenant-Colonel Brooke, D.S.O., 3rd. Bn. Grenadier Guards, if present will command the attack on Y line.
In the absence of Lt.Colonel Brooke senior officer present will command .
Stokes Gun Sections will act in accordance with orders of O.C., attack.

12. Itbis the object of these dispositions to ensure a steady flow of troops so as to press the strongest possible attack against each successive objective.

Rear lines will reinforce leading lines wherever they appear thin.
No troops will be left in any objective when the attack goes on.

The task of the two leading Guards Brigades is to drive the attack through LES BOEUFS to the ultimate objective by every means in their power.

3rd. Guards Brigade will be in close reserve to carry out any of the following duties, as may be required :-

a. To pass through Z and press the attack behind the Cavalry.

b. To make a defensive flank, if the attack on our flanks is held up.
c. To support the attack of the leading Guards Brigades, if held up anywhere.

13. 76th. Field Company, R.E. will be in Brigade Reserve.
It will be formed up in a place to be notified later, and will await orders from the Brigade.

14. Ninth Squadron, R.F.C. will have ~~two~~ one contact aeroplane in the air from zero to dark on Z day and again from 6.30 a.m. to 9.0 a.m. on Z plus 1 day.
Flares will be lit as follows :-

i. On obtaining each objective.

ii. At 12 noon and 5 p.m. on Z day.

iii. At 6.30 a.m. on Z plus 1 day.

Red flares will be used by Infantry, Green flares by Cavalry.

15. All transport will be packed up and ready to move forward at 1 hour's notice after zero plus 4 hours.

Brigade Transport Officer will report at Divisional Headquarters, MINDEN POST, at zero plus 2 hours, and await orders there.

16. Separate orders will be issued regarding :-

I. Supply of Rations.
" " water.
" " S.A.A.
" " Stokes ammunition.
" " bombs.

II. Disposal of Prisoners.

III. Medical arrangements.

17. Watches will be synchronised at 12.30 p.m. and 6.30 p.m. on Y day by telephone from this Office.

18. Brigade Headquarters will close at BERNAFAY WOOD at 5.0 p.m. tomorrow and open at T.19.a.½.3½. at the same hour.

ACKNOWLEDGE.

[signature]

Captain.
Brigade Major.

13/9/16.

Copies to:-

No.1. 3rd. Grenadier Guards.
No.2. 1st. Coldstream Guards.
No.3. 1st. Scots Guards.
No.4. 2nd. Irish Guards.
No.5. Bde. M.G.Company.
No.6. Bde. T.M.Battery.
No.7. Bde. Signal Officer.
No.8. Bde. Transport Officer.
No.9. Guards Division.
No.10. 1st. Guards Brigade.
No.11. 3rd. Guards Brigade.
No.12. 71st. Infantry Brigade.
No.13.)
No.14.) Office.
No.15.)
No.16.)

-:*:-

3rd Brigade Operation Orders

SECRET. Copy No 8....

3RD GUARDS BRIGADE.

Operation Order No. 59.

Reference Maps: Sheet 57c S.W. 1/20,000.

---

1. The Fourth Army will attack the enemy's defences between COMBLES RAVINE and MARTINPUICH on the 15th September, with the object of seizing MORVAL, LES BOEUFS, GUEUDECOURT and FLERS, and of breaking the enemy's system of defence. The French are attacking simultaneously on the South and the Reserve Army in the North.

The 6th Division are attacking on the right og the Guards Division and the 14th Division on the left.

The Division is attacking with the 2nd Guards Brigade on the right and the 1st Guards Brigade on the left - objectives and forming up areas are shown on map issued to C.Os.

Tanks will be employed to cooperate with the attack - information regarding their employment is forwarded.

2. The 3rd Guards Brigade will be in Divisional Reserve and will be formed up on the night 14th/15th September in and East of TRONES WOOD as follows :-

4th Bn. Grenadier Guards - East of the WOOD between the railway and the MONTAUBAN - GUILLEMONT ROAD.

2nd Bn. Scots Guards. - North of the Railway in S.24.c.

1st Bn. Grenadier Guards - About the trench running N and S through the centre of the WOOD.

1st Bn. Welsh Guards and Machine Gun Compnay less 4 guns along W edge of the WOOD.

Trench Mortar Battery - In the vicinity of the Copse S.24.c.5.0.

A separate order is issued regarding the move to those positions.

3. At Zero plus 1 hour and 30 minutes the Brigade will advance in the following order:-

4th Bn. Grenadier Guards - To T.19.b. astride the GUILLEMONT - [illegible] GINCHY RD.

2nd Bn. Scots Guards - To T.13.c.

These 2 Battalions will halt when the leading troops reach the S.W. outskirts of GINCHY.

1st Bn. Grenadier Guards - To the vicinity of GUILLEMONT STATION.

1st Bn. Welsh Guards - N.W. of 1st Bn. Grenadier Guards with their Left about WATERLOT FARM.

Brigade M. G. Company. - To S.24.a.

Brigade T. M. Battery will not move.

Battalions will be formed up in depth.

4. (a) If the attack is completely successful the role of the Brigade will be to pass through the 1st and 2nd Guards Brigades and support the Cavalry beyond the 4th objective. The Cavalry will not enter villages.

(b) Should the attack be partially successful and the 4th objective reached in face of determined resistance the Brigade might be required to relieve the 1st and 2nd Brigades in the line of the 4th objective or to move into a position of reserve in T.8.c. and T.7.d.

As soon as the situation permits Officers Commanding 4th Bn. Grenadier Guards and 2nd Bn. Scots Guards will send forward Officers to reconnoitre this reserve position and lines of approach to it. Reports from these Officers will be at once forwarded to Brigade Headquarters.
(c) Should the advance be held up the Brigade might be ordered to press home a fresh attack, passing through 1st and 2nd Brigades.
(d) If the attack on either flank be held up the Brigade might be required to secure the flank of the Division, probably by offensive action.
(e) Detailed information regarding Artillery support will form part of the orders for any of these movements.
(f) The direction of the attack is N.E. Officers must know the compass bearing to prominent points.

5. Brigade Machine Gun Company less 4 guns will be held in Brigade reserve. 2 guns Brigade M.G. Company will attached to 4th Bn. Grenadier Guards and 2 guns to 2nd Bn. Scots Guards and will report to Officers Commanding these Battalions East of TRONES WOOD on the night 14th/15th September.

6. Brigade Trench Mortar Battery will be held in Brigade reserve. Battalions will each detail a carrying party of 1 N.C.O. and 10 men to be attached to Brigade T.M. Battery; these parties will report to Headquarters of the Battery at 2.30 p.m. 14th September in fighting order as many cartridges as possible must be carried.

7. No. 9 Squadron R.F.C. will have a contact patrol aeroplane in the air from Zero to dark on the 15th inst., and from 6.30 a.m. to 9 a.m. on the 16th inst. In the event of any troops of the Brigade being in the leading line of the attack at 12 noon or 5 p.m. the 15th, or 6.30 a.m. the 16th they will light flares and make every endeavour to indicate their position by flashing mirrors and tin discs etc. Red flares will be used by Infantry blue by Cavalry.
Pigeons will be issued to Battalion Headquarters. 4 pigeon men per Battalion will report at Brigade Headquarters at 2.30 p.m. 14th.
Brigade report centres will be established S.30.a.5.9. on arrival of the Brigade at the TRONES WOOD position, at S.24.b.6.1½. at Zero plus 1 hour and 30 minutes, and in GINCHY when the Brigade moves forward from the position detailed in para 3.
Orderlies will be detailed by units as under to report to Brigade Headquarters at 2.30 p.m. 14th inst. in fighting order:-

Battalions.	1 N.C.O. and 8 O.R.	
Machine Gun Coy.	-	2 O.R.
Trench Mortar Battery.	-	1 O.R.

Headquarters of preceding units will be taken over whenever possible in order to facilitate communication.

8. Pack animals, 2 S.A.A. limbers per Battalion, and 3 limbers of Machine Gun Company will be parked at the S. end of TRONES WOOD where they will remain under the orders Lieut. BARLOW, Brigade Machine Gun Company who will report at Brigade Headquarters at 2 p.m. 14th inst. for instruction. They will not be moved without a Brigade order. The remainder of 1st Line Transport will remain in its present position and will be packed up today to move at 1 hours notice after Zero plus 4 hours. No transport of any description will move without a Brigade or Divisional order; Lieut. FARMER, 2nd Bn. Scots Guards will report to Divisional Headquarters at Zero plus 2 hours and will remain there to convey orders to the transport. In the event of a considerable advance units will send guides at dusk to Brigade Headquarters to conduct

transport to their carrying parties.
Traffic moving Westwards from GUILLEMONT STATION will not use the road through TRONES WOOD but will be diverted Southwards onto the GUILLEMONT - MONTAUBAN ROAD.

9. Prisoners will be sent to Crater Post A.8.a.6.3. Escorts will obtain receipts and return to their units. Documents will be sent with prisoners.

10. Battalion Sapping Platoons will be held in Brigade Reserve and will assemble in TRONES WOOD near the point where the railway enters the WOOD and will draw 80 boxes of Mills Rifle bombs at the above point during the night 14th/15th. Orders regarding the disposal of these bombs will be issued by Brigade Headquarters.

11. Fighting order will be:-
1 days rations.
1 iron ration.
A ration of OXO and chewing gum.
3 bombs.
1 Mills rifle bomb.
200 rounds S.A.A. 1 Haversack ration

At least 50 per cent of tools will be carried by Battalions. Signallers, Orderlies and carrying parties will not carry bombs or full compliment of S.A.A. Machine Gun Company and Trench Mortar Battery will carry rations as detailed above and ammunition and tools as ordered by Officers Commanding.

12. Officers Commanding 4th Bn. Grenadier Guards and 2nd Bn. Scots Guards will each detail a Liaison Officer to report to Brigade Headquarters on arrival at CARNOY on the evening of the 14th inst.

13. (a) Aid Posts - T.14.c.4.9. and T.25.b.1.5.
AdvancedbBearer Post - S.24.d.9.5.
Ambulance Posts - S.28.d.9.1.
BRIQUETERIE A.4.b.
S.30.a.8.4.
Advanced dressing station - CARNOY.

(b) When the attack reaches the 3rd objective casualties will be conveyed to advanced dressing station at S.30.b.5.6.
(c) When the attack reaches 4th objective a Divisional Collecting Station will be established at GINCHY.
(d) Walking wounded will be directed to A.14.c.6.1 near CARNOY.
Bearer Divisions will pauh forward stretcher squads and maintain touch with Battalion Medical Officers as the attack progresses.

14. A dump of S.A.A., Bombs, Stokes Mortar Ammunition and R.E. Material has been established on the West edge of BERNAFAY WOOD. Forwar R.E. dumps are at S.24.b.9.8. and T.19.c.2.4.
Each Battalion will carry 125 petrol tins full of water and on arrival at the position detailed in para 3 will dump them as follows:-
1st Bn. Grenadier Guards & - At GINCHY BRICK FIELD T.13.d.9.1.
2nd Bn. Scots Guards.

4th Bn. Grenadier Guards & - At GUILLEMONT STATION.
1st Bn. Welsh Guards.

These tins will be drawn at the cross roads N.W. corner of BERNAFAY WOOD during the night 14/15th September. 1st Bn. Grenadier Guards and 4th Bn. Grenadier Guards will leave guards at the station and Brickfield respectively when their Battalions move forward.

15. Watches will be synchronised at 3 p.m. by telephone and before leaving CARNOY by an Orderly sent with a watch from Brigade Headquarters.

16. Brigade Headquarters will be at DUMMY TRENCH S.23.c.5.2. at 10 p.m. 14th September and may advance to S.24.b.6.1½. when the Brigade moves from the position detailed in para 3. Further movements depend on the situation but will probably be to GINCHY and the German trench in T.8.d.

C B Warner

B.H.Q.
14/9/16.

Captain,
Brigade Major, 3rd Guards Brigade.

Copies issued to:-

1. 1st Bn. Grenadier Guards.
2. 4th Bn. Grenadier Guards.
3. 2nd Bn. Scots Guards.
4. 1st Bn. Welsh Guards.
5. Machine Gun Company.
6. Trench Mortar Battery.
7. Guards Division.
8. 1st Guards Brigade.
9. 2nd Guards Brigade.
10. Reserve Brigade, 6th Division.
11. " " 14th Division.
12. No. 4 Signal Section.
13. Brigade Transport Officer.
14. Staff Captain.
15. No. 2 Company Guards Divnl. Train.
16.) Retained.
17.)

SECRET. Copy No...

3RD GUARDS BRIGADE.

Operation Order No. 66.

Reference Map: 57c S.W. 1/20,000.

1. The Fourth Army will renew the attack on the 25th September, in combination with attacks by the French in the South and the Reserve Army in the North.
The Guards Division will capture LES BOEUFS. The 1st Guards Brigade will attack on the right and the 3rd Guards Brigade on the left. The 5th Division will attack MORVAL on the right and the 21st Division (62nd Brigade) will attack GUEUDECOURT on the left of the Guards Division.

2. OBJECTIVES.
Objectives, Assembly trenches and dividing lines between Brigades and Divisions are marked on attached maps:-
1st Objective. GREEN.
2nd Objective. BROWN.
3rd Objective. BLUE.
2nd Bn. Scots Guards and 4th Bn. Grenadier Guards will capture the 1st and 2nd objectives, and will advance in two waves on a front of 2 Companies each. 2nd Bn. Scots Guards will attack on the right and 4th Bn. Grenadier Guards on the left.
1st Bn. Grenadier Guards will pass through the 2 leading Battalions and capture the 3rd objective. 1st Bn. Welsh Guards less 2 Companies will be held in Brigade Reserve in T.8.a.

3. ASSAULT.
2nd Bn. Scots Guards and 4th Bn. Grenadier Guards will be formed up in X and Y trenches, and will advance to the attack on the 1st objective at Zero hour close up to their barrage. There are 2 hostile lines to cross before the objective is reached, the first being from T.2.b.9.7. to T.2.b.3.10. and the second the main German front line.
These 2 Battalions will reorganise in the 1st objective and advance to the attack on the 2nd objective at Zero plus 1 hour.
She left of the 2nd Bn. Scots Guards will direct. 1st Bn. Grenadier Guards will be formed up in Z trench and will advance so as to reach the 1st objective at Zero plus 1 hour. The Battalion will advance to the attack of the 3rd objective so as to reach their barrage 200 yards beyond the 2nd objective at Zero plus 2 hours.
2 Companies 1st Bn. Welsh Guards will be formed up in T.8.a. and will move into the X line so as to be ready to occupy the 1st objective as soon as the 1st Bn. Grenadier Guards leave that line. In timing their advance to the X line these 2 Companies will seize opportunities offered by any slackening of the hostile barrage.

4. CONSOLIDATION.
1st Bn. Grenadier Guards will consolidate the 3rd objective with strong points on the flanks. 4th Bn. Grenadier Gds and 2nd Bn. Scots Gds will consolidate the 2nd objective. At Zero plus 2 hours 4th Bn. Grenadier Gds will push a unit forward up the SUNKEN ROAD in N.33.b.& d. and consolidate a strong point at the Northern end, obtaining touch with the 62nd Inf.Bde. The Battn will also consolidate a strong point on the left flank of the 2nd objective.
Officer Commanding, 2nd Bn. Scots Guards will detail 1 Company to push forward at Zero plus 2 hours on his right flank and consolidate a strong point to protect the right rear of the 1st Bn. Grenadier Guards against attack from the South.
2 Companies, 1st Bn. Welsh Guards will consolidate the 1st objective, making strong points on the left flank of that objective, and at N.32.d.3.3. and maintaining touch with 62nd Inf. Brigade.
In the event of Brigades on our right and left being held up defensive flanks must be formed.
As soon as the situation permits fighting patrols will be advanced to the SUNKEN ROADS in N.34.a. and d.

5. ARTILLERY SUPPORT.
A deliberate bombardment of the enemy2 positions will be carried

out on the 24th and 25th September. There will be no intensive fire before the hour of Zero. At Zero the creeping barrage will commence 100 yards in front of our line and advance to 200 yards beyond the GREEN LINE where it will remain till Zero plus 1 hour.

At Zero plus 1 hour the creeping barrage will commence 200 yds in front of the GREEN LINE and advance to 200 yards beyond the BROWN LINE where it will remain till Zero plus 2 hours.

At Zero plus 2 hours the creeping barrage will commence 200 yds in front of the BROWN LINE and advance to 200 yards beyond the BLUE LINE where it will remain.

The stationary barrage will lift to the next objective when the creeping barrage reaches it. The creeping barrage will advance at the rate of 50 yards per minute.

6. ROYAL ENGINEERS.

The 55th Field Coy.R.E. will be attached to the Brigade for the operation and will be held in Brigade Reserve in T.7.d.

O.C., 1st Bn. Welsh Guards will hold 1 Company in readiness to act as a carrying party for the R.E. on receipt of orders.

7. PRELIMINARY MOVEMENT.

Battalions will move up to assembly positions on the night 24/25 September. 1st Bn. Grenadier Guards will not move before 10 p.m.

Assaulting Battalions will cut any wire in front of our trenches on the night 24/25 September. Wire cutters can be drawn at GUILLEMONT STATION if required.

Units will report when they have reached their assembly positions as detailed above on the night 24/25 September. Relief of 1st Bn. Welsh Gds will be arranged direct between Os.C., 4th Bn. Grenadier Gds, 2nd Bn. Scots Gds and 1st Bn. Welsh Gds.

8. MACHINE GUNS.

2 Machine Guns will be attached to the 1st Bn. Grenadier Gds to advance with that Battn, to assist in consolidation of the 3rd objective. 2 Machine Guns will be attached to the 2nd Bn. Scots Gds and 4th Bn. Grenadier Gds to assist in consolidation of the 2nd objective.

2 Machine Guns will advance with the 4th Bn. Grenadier Gds as far as the 1st objective and will be placed to guard the left flank; these 2 guns will remain in the 1st objective and assist the 1st Bn. Welsh Gds to consolidate there. They will report to O.C., 4th Bn. Grenadier Gds at Battn Hqrs T.8.a. at 11 p.m. 24th inst.

Bde Machine Gun Coy less 8 guns will be held in Brigade Reserve and will move to T.8.a. at 12 midnight on the 24th inst. The Company will be used for the consolidation of strong points in the 2nd & 3rd objectives and possibly to protect the flanks of the Brigade.

9. TRENCH MORTARS.

2 guns Bde T.M.Bty will be attached to 4th Bn. Grenadier Gds and 2 to 2nd Bn. Scots Gds. Bde T.M.Bty less 4 guns will be held in Brigade Reserve and will move to T.7.d. at 12 midnight on the 24th inst. Battalions to which guns are attached are responsible for detailing carrying parties of 1 N.C.O. & 10 men per gun.

1st Bn. Welsh Gds will detail a carrying party of 3 N.C.Os and 25 men to report at Hqrs, T.M.Bty, T.7.d. at 12 midnight 24th inst.

10. SAPPING PLATOONS.

1st Bn. Welsh Gds Sapping platoon will be held in Brigade Reserve. Other Sapping platoons will be at the disposal of Battn Commanders..

11. TRANSPORT.

Ammunition portions of 1st Line Transport will report at the S.W. side of BERNAFAY WOOD, South of the GUILLEMONT-MONTAUBAN ROAD at 12 noon on 25th September. Remainder of 1st Line Transport will report at MINDEN POST at 12 noon 25th inst. Lieut. FARMER will remain at Divisional Hqrs, MINDEN POST, from 12 noon 25th inst.

A Brigade Orderly will be at Divisional Hqrs, BERNAFAY WOOD from 12 noon 25th September.

12. DUMP.

A Battle Dump is established at T.8.a.6.4. Units will report to Bde Hqrs when they draw from this Dump. Empty petrol tins must be returned to GUILLEMONT STATION or to T.8.a.6.4.

13. MEDICAL.
Detailed Medical arrangements will be notified.

14. PRISONERS.
Prisoners will be sent to the Craters, A.8.a. Officers will be searched and effects forwarded with the escort. Other ranks will not be searched.

15. COMMUNICATION.
Battalion Hqrs of all Battalions will be established about T.8.a.central and in the event of moving forward Battalions will establish report centres at this point. Pigeons will be issued to Battn and Company Hqrs.

No.9 Squadron R.F.C. will have a contact machine in the air from Zero till 6.30 p.m. 25th inst. Flares will be lit by the leading lines on obtaining each objective and at 6 p.m. 25th September and every effort will be made by the leading troops to indicate their positions.

Orderlies will be detailed by Units as follows:-

Battalions 8 each.
Machine Gun Coy 2.
Trench Mortar Bty. 1.
55th Coy. R.E. 1.

To report at Bde Hqrs at 8 pm 24th inst.

A Brigade Observation Post will be established at T.8.b.2.8.

Watches will be synchronised at 8 p.m. 24th inst and 8 a.m. 25th inst by telephone from Brigade Headquarters.

16. EQUIPMENT.
Each man will carry :-

1 day's rations
1 iron ration
1 haversack ration
4 bombs
200 rounds S.A.A.
1 pick or shovel

17. BRIGADE HEADQUARTERS.
Brigade Headquarters will be at GUILLEMONT STATION and might move forward to T.8.a.6.4.

ACKNOWLEDGE.

B.H.Q.
22.9.16

C.C. Warner
Captain,
Brigade Major, 3rd Guards Brigade.

Copies issued to :-

1. 1st Bn. Grenadier Guards.
2. 4th Bn. Grenadier Guards.
3. 2nd Bn. Scots Guards.
4. 1st Bn. Welsh Guards.
5. Machine Gun Company.
6. Trench Mortar Battery.
7. Guards Division. (Map not attached).
8. 1st Guards Brigade. " "
9. 2nd Guards Brigade. " "
10. 62nd Inf. Brigade. " "
11. 55th Field Coy. R.E. " "
12. Left Group, G.D.A. " "
13. No. 3 Field Ambulance. " "
14. Staff Captain. " "
15. No. 4 Signal Section. " "
16. Brigade Transport Officer.
17.)Retained.
18.)

OPERATION ORDERS FROM OTHER

BRIGADES

<u>S E C R E T</u> Copy No.______.

18th INFANTRY BRIGADE OPERATION ORDER No 87.

Ref. Trench Map 1/20,000 Sh 57c S.W.
GUILLEMONT.
Special Map attached.

<u>Septr 22nd 1916.</u>

1. The 4th Army will renew the attack on 25th Septr, in combination with the attacks of the French to South and Reserve Army to North.

2. The objectives of XIV Corps include capture of MORVAL and LES BOEUFS.
The attack of XIV Corps will be made by Guards Div on left, 6th Div in the centre and 5th Div. on the right, the 56th Div will form a protective flank facing South.

3. The attack of the 6th Division will be carried out by the 16th Inf. Bde on the right and the 18th Infy Brigade on the left.
x 71st Inf Bde. (less 1 Battalion) will be in Divisional Reserve.

4. The dividing line between the 18th Inf. Bde and the Guards Division is the GINCHY-LES BOEUFS Road inclusive to Guards Div.
The dividing line between the 18th Inf. Bde and 16th Inf. Bde is T 9.B.6.2 - T.10.A.7.6 - [illegible] T.4.D.6.0 - T.5.C.8½.2 all inclusive to 16th Infantry Brigade.

5. The attack of the 18th Infantry Brigade will be carried out by the 11th Essex Regt on the left and the 2nd D.L.I. on the right against the 1st objective (BROWN LINE)
The West Yorks will be in support and after the capture of the 1st objective, will pass through the Essex and 2nd D.L.I. and attack second objective (BLUE LINE)
The 14th D.L.I. will be in Brigade Reserve.

6. The dividing line between the Essex and 2nd D.L.I. during the attack on the first objective will be an imaginary line from T.9.B.4.7 to T.4.C.6.2 all inclusive to 2nd D.L.I.

7. The objectives allotted to Battalions are as follows :-

(a) 2nd D.L.I. to capture consolidate and hold the line of road from T.10.A.7.6 (exclusive) to T.4.C.6.2 (inclusive)
(b) 11th Essex to capture consolidate and hold the line of road from T.4.C.6.2 (exclusive) to Cross Roads T.4.C.4.7½ (exclusive)
(c) 1st West Yorks to capture consolidate and hold the line of road T.4.D.6.0 (exclusive) to T.4.B.4.5. (inclusive)

8. On reaching their objective the West Yorks will at once construct strong points at T.4.D.5.3 and T.4.B.4.3.

9 (a) Throughout the attack Battalions will detail special parties to keep close touch with the troops on their flanks.

(b) On reaching their objective the West Yorks will push forward strong patrols to seize vantage or observation points along the ridge running North from MORVAL MILL as soon as our barrage permits, through T 5 Central, from whence Lewis and Machine gun ~~fix~~ fire can be brought to bear across the front of the 16th Inf. Bde. and Guards Division who will be pushing out similar patrols.

10. The objectives allotted to the Division and the boundaries required to be known are as shewn on the attached Map A.

11 (a) A steady bombardment of the hostile positions will be commenced at 7. .a.m. 24th Septr and continued until 6-30 p.m. It will be recommenced at 6.30 a.m. 25th Septr.

The ground in front and rear of the bombarded position will be searched occasionally with Shrapnel and H.E.

There will be no intensive fire previous to the hour of Zero

Night ~~firing~~ firing will be carried out nightly between the hours of 6-30 p.m. and 6.30 a.m.

The attack in each stage will be carried out under cover of a creeping and a stationary barrage.

(b) The field Artillery supporting the 6th Division in the attack will be :-

24th Div. Artillery.)
1 Bde 6th Div. Arty.) C.R.A. Brig-Genl H.C. Sheppard.
1 Bde 20th " ")

An Artillery Liason Officer will be attached to the Head Qrs of the 11th Essex Regt and one to the 2nd D.L.I. and one to West Yorks.

12. ZERO hour will be notified later

13 (a) At Zero hour the 5th Div (on our right) and the Guards Div (on our left) will advance to the attack of their first objective (GREEN LINE) <u>During this stage the 18th Infantry Brigade STANDS FAST and will act as ordered in para 14</u>.

(b) At Zero plus 1 hour the Essex and 2nd D.L.I. will advance to the attack of the second objective (BROWN LINE)

(c) At Zero plus 2 hours the West Yorks will advance to the attack of the third objective (BLUE LINE)

(d) As the 6th Division is already in a portion of the green line, the remainder of which forms the 1st objective of the other Divisions; it follows that the Brown and Blue lines referred to as the second and third objectives are really the 1st and 2nd objectives for the 6th Division.

14 (a) Owing to the difficulty of bombarding the GREEN line (first objective of 5th and Guards Division) in the immediate vicinity of our own positions in it the troops of the 18th Brigade will take the following action to assist the advance of the Guards Division.

At Zero ~~xxxx~~ hour a heavy Machine gun and Stokes mortar fire will be opened on to the enemy trench running North West from Sunken road at T.3.D.4.1. and along Sunken roads running N.E. from that point.

This fire will be continued until stopped by gds Bde

(b) O.C. 11th Essex will take such action as he considers necessary in withdrawing troops from vicinity of T.3.D. 4.9 during our bombardment of GREEN LINE

15. During the advance of the 6th Division, Field Artillery barrages will be as follows :-

(1) At Zero plus 5 minutes, a barrage will be placed ~~xxxx~~ 200 yards in front of the GREEN line on the 6th Division front, and will remain stationary while the 5th and Guards Divisions are consolidating their first objective. (GREEN LINE)

(2). (a) At Zero plus 1 hour, a stationary barrage will commence on the BROWN line and a creeping barrage will commence to roll forward at the rate of 50 yards a minute from 200 yards in front of the GREEN Line until it has passed 150 yards beyond the BROWN line, when it will become stationary.

As soon as the creeping barrage reaches the stationary barrage on the BROWN line, the latter will lift to the line T.10.b.6.1.- junction of roads T.10.b.7.5. and thence along road to T.4.c.8.9.

(b). At Zero plus 2 hours, the creeping barrage will again commence to go forward at the rate of 50 yards a minute from 150 yards beyond the BROWN line until it has passed 200 yards beyond the BLUE line, when it will become stationary. The stationary barrage will lift to the BLUE line.

As soon as the creeping barrage reaches the stationary barrage on the BLUE line, the latter will lift to the line MORVAL MILL - T.5.Central - Cross roads T.5.b.0.6½.

(c), The creeping barrage will remain 200 yards East of the BLUE line and the stationary barrage on the line MORVAL MILL - T.5.Central - Cross roads T.5.b.0.6½. until ordered by Divisional Headquarters to lift, in order to permit of the advance of patrols.

Battalion Commanders concerned will inform Brigade Head Quarters when they wish these barrages to lift.

16. O.C. 12th Coy. R.E. will place two sections at the disposal of O.C. West Yorks, these Sections will not move further forward than BROWN LINE (1st objective) until orders are sent them by O.C. West Yorks.

17. A Contact Aeroplane will be in the air from Zero till 6-30 p.m. Flares will be lit on gaining each objective and also at 6 p.m. 25 th September.

18. Instructions as to Medical arrangements will be made known when received.

19. Prisoners of war will be sent under Battalion arrangements to advanced Brigade Head Quarters.

20. O.C. Signals will notify correct time to all concerned at 6 p.m. 24th Septr. and 6 a.m. 25th Septr.

21. Brigade Head Qrs will close at BRIQUETERIE at 6 p.m. Septr 24th and open at the same hour at the QUARRIES GUILLEMONT (T.19.A. 1.3) to which place reports on the situation should be sent as frequently as possible.

22. Acknowledge.

[signature]

Capt.
Brigade-Major 18th Infantry Bde.

Issued at p.m.

No 1. 1st West Yorks.
2. 11th Essex.
3. 2nd D.L.I.
4. 14th D.L.I.
5. 18th M.G. Coy.
6. 18th L.T.M.Btty.
7. Signals.
8. B.T.O.
9. 1st Guards Brigade.
10. 16th Inf. Bde.
11. 71st Inf. Bde.
12. 6th Div "G"
13. 6th Div "Q"
14. 18th Field Ambulance.
15. A.D.M.S.
16. 12th Coy R.E.
17. Staff Capt 18th Inf. Bde.
18. Left Group R.F.A.
19 & 20. Office.

NOTE Owing to shortage of maps the special Map referred to is only issued to those directly concerned.

S E C R E T. Copy No 8.

18th INFANTRY BRIGADE OPERATION ORDER No 88.

Ref. Trench Map GUILLEMONT. Septr 23rd 1916.

1. 14/D.L.I. will take over present front and support lines from 11/Essex and 2/D.L.I. tonight, placing 2 companies in front line and 2 Companies in support line.

2. The 1/West Yorks will send 2 Companies tonight to dig themselves in about T.8.D. as arranged direct between Brigadier and O.C.West Yorks.
The remaining 2 Companies will be at disposal of Staff Captain 18th I.B. for carrying parties up till 3 a.m., after which they will proceed and occupy the trenches near Battalion Head Qrs T.8.D. at present held by Essex and 2/D.L.I.

3 (a) On relief 2/D.L.I. will bivouac in area at present occupied by West Yorks.

(b) On relief Essex will bivouac in area at present occupied by 14/D.L.I.

4. All details to be arranged direct between C.Os. concerned.

5. Completion of relief to be reported to Brigade Head Qrs.

6. Acknowledge.

Grenville Garnier
Capt.
Brigade Major 18th Inf Bde.

Copy No 1. West Yorks.
2. Essex.
3. 2/D.L.I.
4. 14/D.L.I.
5. 18. M.G.Coy.
6. 18. T.M.Btty.
7. Signals.
8. 1st Guards Bde.
9. 16th I.B.
10. 6th Div "G"
11. Left Group R.F.A.
12. Office.

SECRET. Copy No. 13

41st INFANTRY BRIGADE ORDER No. 102.

13th September, 1916.

Refce: 1/20,000 Sheet 57c S.W.

1. For the last two and a half months the Allied Armies have been gradually gaining ground and wearing down the enemy. The enemy's moral is now shaken, he has few, if any, fresh reserves available, and there is every probability that a combined and determined effort will result in decisive victory.

2. (a) The Fourth Army is to attack the enemy's defences between MORVAL and MARTINPUICH with the object of seizing MORVAL, LES BOEUFS, GUEUDECOURT and FLERS, and breaking through the enemy's system of defence.

(b) The French and Reserve Armies are attacking simultaneously on our right and left.

3. It is to be impressed on all ranks that a special effort is required, and that the attack is to be pushed home with the utmost vigour all along the line until the most distant objectives have been captured.

4. A new engine of war "The Tank" is to be used for the first time. A separate memorandum in the use of this weapon is being issued, and is to be carefully explained to all ranks.

5. The objectives allotted to the Division, together with their sub-allotment to Infantry Brigades, are shown in Appendix "A" and on map issued with starred copies of Operations Orders.

6. The attack will be made at Zero on Z day. Date and hour will be notified separately to all concerned.

7. The attack will be preceded by a bombardment of the hostile defensive system, which will take place daily from 6 a.m. to 8.30 p.m.. This bombardment commenced on the 12th inst.

8. (a) At Zero on Z day, an intense barrage of field artillery will be opened all along the line.

(b) The Infantry detailed to capture the "first objective" will leave their positions of assembly and advance as close behind the barrage as possible. The barrage will move in front of them at the rate of 50 yards a minute.

(c) No pause will be made on the line PINT TRENCH - TEA SUPPORT, which are to be dealt with by "mopping up" parties specially detailed.

(d) On reaching the "first obejctive," the Infantry will not advance further until sixty minutes after Zero.

(e) At sixty minutes after Zero, the barrage will start creeping back to the "second objective." The Infantry detailed for this objective will advance as close as possible to the barrage and will regulate their pace by that of the barrage and not by the pace of any tanks that may be accompanying them.

(f) At two hours after Zero the Infantry detailed to capture the "third objective" will advance as far as the blue line.

(g) At four hours, thirty minutes after Zero, the Infantry for the capture of the "third objective" closely followed by the Infantry detailed for the capture of the "fourth objective" will leave the blue line and advance on their objectives.

(h) Time and table of attack is attached, Appendix "C".

9. Objectives, when gained, will at once be consolidated.

10. (a) Weather permitting, two contact aeroplanes will be continuously in the air from Zero on "Z" day until dark, and one aeroplane will be up from 6.30 a.m. to 8.30 a.m. on the day after "Z" day.

(b) Red flares will be used and will be lit -

(i) On reaching each objective.
(ii) At 2 p.m. and 5 p.m. on "Z" day.
(iii) At 7 a.m. on the day following "Z" day.
(iv) When called for by contact plane.
(v) On the initiative of the troops when contact plane is over them.

(c) Full use is to be made of signalling to aeroplanes from battalion and Brigade H.Q. by signalling panels and ground sheets.

11. C.R.E. will arrange for a mobile reserve of R.E. material to be packed on wagons and held ready to advance if required.

12. The 14th Divl. Signal Co. will arrange to send out the time on "X" day at 11 a.m. and 5 p.m. All watches to be carefully synchronised.

13. No orders, sketches, letters or papers likely to be of use to the enemy to be taken into action.

14. Attacking Infantry battalions will report situation to Brigade H.Q. every two hours on "Z" day, and oftener as necessary. Negative reports will be rendered.

15. 43rd Inf. Bde. will place two Companies at disposal of 41st Inf.Bde. in order to assist the 41st Inf. Bde. to carry out the attack on the preliminary objective. Details to be arranged between Brigadier.

16. On the afternoon of 14th inst. the following moves will take place.
(i) Advanced 41st Inf. Bde.H.Q. to new advanced Brigade H.Q. in YORK TRENCH, S.23.a. 7.4.

(ii) Advanced H.Q., 42nd Inf. Bde. to present H.Q. of 41st Inf.Bde.
(iii) 42nd Inf. Bde. to bivouac South of POMMIERS Redoubt.
(iv) 43rd " " to camp, F.13.c.

17. Divl.H.Q. remains at FRICOURT Chateau.

18. The 41st Inf.Bde. attack as follows:-
In front line - 8th Rifle Bde. on the right - 8th K.R.R.C. on the left.
This line will assault and consolidate first objective.
In second line - 7th Rifle Bde. on the right - 7th K.R.R.C. on the left.
This line will assault and consolidate the second objective.

19. Officers Commanding Battns. in the first line will each detail the necessary "mopping up" parties referred to in para 8(e).

20. Assaulting troops will be armed and equipped as laid down in this office letter No.33/10, dated 13/8/16.

21. Further more detailed orders on certain points, including Appendix "B" for the movement of tanks, will be issued later.

Issued at 9 a.m. 14th inst.

Copies (attached)

[signature] Captain,
Brigade Major,
41st Infantry Brigade.

Copies to:

1. 7th K.R.R.C.
2. 8th K.R.R.C.
3. 7th R.B.
4. 8th "
5. 41st B.M.G.Co.
6. 41st T.M.Bty.
7. 89th Field Co.,R.E.
8. 42nd Field Amblce.
9. 14th Division (2 copies).
10. 42nd Inf.Bde.
11. 43rd " "
12. 123rd " "
13. 1st Guards Bde.
14. N.Z.Bde., R.F.A.
15. 35th " "
16. 22nd " "
17. 14th " R.H.A.
18. 7th Divl.Artillery.
19. B.G.C.
20. B.M.
21. S.C.
22. A/S.C.
23. B.T.O.
24. B.S.O.
25. B.I.O.
26. File.
27. Diary.

SECRET.

APPENDIX "A" to accompamy 41st Inf. Bde. Order No.102.

The objectives allotted to the Division and their sub-allotment to Infantry Brigades are:-

	Objective.	Allotted to:
Preliminary Objective.	HOP ALLEY and ALE ALLEY to junction with PINT TRENCH.	41st Infantry Bde.
First Objective.	SWITCH LINE from junction with LAGER LANE T.8.a.3.5 (exclusive) to junction with COCOA LANE T.1.d.0.2 (inclusive).	41st Infantry Bde.
Second Objective.	Third line defences from T.2.d. 2.5 to road at T.1.b. 1.2 (inclusive).	41st Infantry Bde.
Third Objective.	GIRD SUPPORT from N.33.c. 4.2 to N.26.c. 6.9	42nd Infantry Bde.
Fourth Objective.	Capture GUEUDECOURT and establish the approximate line of N.33.central in touch with XIV Corps - Northern outskirts of GUEUDECOURT to N.20.d.5.0 in touch with 41st Div.	42nd Infantry Bde.

SECRET.

APPENDIX "C" to 41st Inf. Bde. Order No.102.

TIME TABLE OF ATTACK.

- 0.53 Left Tank Group starts.

- 0.30 ALE ALLEY Tank starts.

- 0.24 HOP ALLEY tanks start.

0.00 (Zero) Tank and bombing attack on HOP and ALE ALLEY starts.

0.00 " Infantry leave their trenches and advance close up to the barrage which will begin creeping back in front of them at 0.6 minutes. Creeping barrage will go back steadily at 50 yards per minute until it joins stationary barrage on first objective (green line).

0.25 minutes. Tanks reach positions on first objective East of FLERS ROAD.

(i) 0.20 min. (i). Barrage lifts from green line West of FLERS ROAD.
(ii) 0.30 min.(ii). Barrage lifts from green line East of FLERS ROAD - Infantry capture first objective as the barrage lifts in each case. Creeping barrage halts 300 yards beyond green line.

1 hour 00 min. Infantry and tanks advance together behind creeping barrage. Creeping barrage goes back 100 yards in three minutes, and on arrival at FLERS LINE joins stationary barrage.

1 hour 25 min. Barrage lifts from second objective. 41st Inf. Bde. capture brown line.

1 hour 45 min. Covering barrage goes back to allow tanks to advance from brown line.

2 hours 00 min. Infantry advance and establish the blue line.

4 hours 15 min. Covering barrage taken off to allow tanks to go forward.

(i) 4 hrs.30 min.	) barrage lifts from	((i) Right boundary and road N.32.b.3.8
(ii) 4 hrs.55 min.	) GIRD TRENCH & GIRD	((ii) Road N.32.b.3.8 and track N.26.c. 4.5.
(iii) 5 hrs.00 min.	) SUPPORT between	((iii) Track N.26.c. 4.5 and left boundary.

5 hrs. 30 minutes. Bombardment of GUEUDECOURT ceases - Tanks push forward, and Infantry complete capture of fourth objective.

S E C R E T.   AFTER ORDER TO:-   Copy No.14.

41st INFANTRY BRIGADE ORDER No.102.

14th September, 1916.

1. In continuation of Brigade Order No. 102 -
The 41st Infantry Brigade will in addition to other objectives clear the enemy from the area - BEER TRENCH - BITTER TRENCH - East edge of DELVILLE WOOD - HAYMARKET - HOP ALLEY - ALE ALLEY as far East as T.13.a. 5.9 and the new trench running from T.13.a. 5.9 to about T.13.b. 0.5. This is referred to in previous orders as the Preliminary Objective.

2. This attack will be made in conjunction with two tanks allotted to 14th Division and one tank furnished by the Guards Division.

3. Twp Coys., 6th K.O.Y.L.I., will relieve the 8th Rifle Bde. in the Sector from T.13.a.central to junction of JAMES STREET with EDGE STREET to-night.

4. These two Coys., 6th K.O.Y.L.I., will carry out the above attack. The O.C. will detail not less than two bombing squads to escort and assist the tank furnished by the Guards Division, and will get into touch with the 3rd Coldstream Guards on his right, and locate the tank which is due to start from T.13.b. 3.0 at 5.30 a.m.

5. The O.C., two Coys., 6th K.O.Y.L.I. will report the result of the above attack at once to Brigade H.Q., to the O.C. 8th R.B. in BROWN STREET, and the O.C. 7th Div. Medium Trench Mortars in the Eastern portion of DELVILLE WOOD. The O.C. 8th R.B. will inform the O.C. 41st Stokes Mortar Bty. in GREEN TRENCH.

6. The 14th Div. tanks are due to arrive at their respective objectives HOP ALLEY - ALE ALLEY ~~from T.13.c. 5.9 to T.13.b. 0.5~~ at 5.30 a.m. at which hour the attack on these trenches will start.

7. At Zero, the 6th K.O.Y.L.I. holding PILSEN LANE will advance in touch with the 3rd Coldstream Guards on their right.

8. Zero hour is 6.20 a.m. on the 15/9/16.

9. For the attack on the other objectives, the first line 8th R.B. and the 8th K.R.R.C. will be formed up in BROWN STREET - GREEN STREET and adjoining trenches: the second line, the 7th R.B. & 7th K.R.R.C., in DELVILLE WOOD in artillery formation. All troops to be in position by 4.30 a.m. The 7th R.B. & 7th K.R.R.C. will be North of YORK TRENCH by 1 a.m.

10. At Zero, the 7th R.B. and 7th K.R.R.C. will advance through DELVILLE WOOD, and will remain in artillery formation or deploy into extended lines as is most suitable. They will be careful to cover the whole front allotted to the Brigade.

11. The second line will avoid merging into the first line, but if the first line fails to secure its objective, then the second line must capture it instead.
The great point being that the attack must be pushed forward with as much energy as possible.

12. All units or parties penetrating an objective will consolidate at once, and form defensive flanks, as necessary.

13. Four guns, Bde.M.G.Coy., will be held in DELVILLE WOOD ready to consolidate in first objective, and two machine guns will follow in rear of each of the battalions in second line, those behind the 7th K.R.R.C. to assist in forming a defensive flank from the second objective towards FLERS.

14. Runner posts are to be established where WATLING STREET crosses the first and second objectives.

15. Separate instructions have been issued with regard to Signalling and Medical arrangements.

16. The battalions in second line will make every effort to keep the 42nd Brigade in rear of them informed of the situation.

17. In the event of the attack on the preliminary objective being unsuccessful, the attack on the other objectives will be carried out nevertheless as planned, but the Os.C. Medium Trench Mortar and Stokes Batteries will at Zero open a steady barrage on HOP & ALE ALLEYS.

18. A Stragglers Post of 1 Sergt. and four men will be established by the O.C. 7th K.R.R.C. at the QUARRY Dump. A reserve officer will be detailed by the Staff Captain to take charge of this post.

19. Prisoners will be sent back to Advanced Brigade H.Q. under minimum escort.

20. O.C., Brigade Signals, will arrange to send the time to all combatant units of the Brigade at 10 p.m., 14th inst.

21. The general magnetic bearing of the advance to the first objective is 53°.

22. Brigade H.Q. will remain at its present Advanced H.Q. until otherwise notified.

Issued at 8 p.m.
Copy to:
1. 7th K.R.R.C.
2. 8th "
3. 7th R.B.
4. 8th "
5. 41st B.M.G.Co.
6. 41st T.M.Bty.
7. 89th Field Coy.
8. 42nd Field Amb.
9. Maj.CHARLESWORTH,6th K.O.Y.L.I. att. 8th R.B.
10. 14th Div.
11. 42nd Inf.Bde.
12. 43rd " "
13. 123rd " "
14. 1st Guards Bde.
15. N.Z.Bde.,R.F.A.
16. 35th " "
17. 22nd " "
18. 14th " R.H.A.
19. 14th Div.Artillery.
20. O.C.Nos. 1 & 2 Tanks.
21. B.G.C.
22. B.M.
23. S.C.
24. A/S.C.
25. B.T.O.
26. B.S.O.
27. B.I.O.
28. File.
29. Diary.

G E R Prior
Captain,
Brigade Major,
41st Infantry Brigade.

S E C R E T.

APPENDIX "B"
to 41st Inf. Bde. Order No. 102.

ORDERS FOR USE OF TANKS.

1. Two male and two female tanks have been allotted to the Division from the commencement of the attack.

2. On the night of XY the tanks allotted to the Division will move to positions of assembly as follows:-

(i) Two male and one female tanks to GREEN Dump, S.18.c. 8.2.
(ii) One female tank to S.23.c. 1.6.

3. On night YZ tanks move to positions of departure as under:-

(i) Tanks from GREEN Dump to point just East of COCOA LANE about S.12.d. 5.5.
(ii) Tank from S.23.c. 1.6 to point about T.13.c. 2.8.

4. Arrangements for the provision of guides, taping of routes and reconnaissance by Heavy Machine Gun Section Officers have been made under separate instructions.

5. The tanks are allotted to objectives as follows:-

(i) Female tank at T.13.c. 2.8 under Capt. MORTIMER (No. 1 Tank) and one male tank at S.12.d. 5.5 (No.2 tank) under Lieut. BLOWERS, are allotted to deal with HOP ALLEY and ALE ALLEY respectively.
(ii) One male and one female tank at S.12.d. 5.5 to form No. 1 Tank Group for the attack on the first, second, third and fourth objectives.

6. At the times laid down in Appendix "C" the tanks will start for their respective objectives and by the routes shown in the attached map.

7. Attack on preliminary objective.

(a) The points to be attacked in the first instance are:-
(i) By tank from T.13.c. 2.8 (No. 1 tank) to junction of HOP ALLEY and East edge of DELVILLE WOOD.
(ii) By tank from S.12.d. 5.5 (No. 2 tank) to junction of ALE ALLEY and EDGE TRENCH.

(b) It is most important that these important junctions are thoroughly dealt with and cleared.

(c) After dealing with these points No. 1 Tank will work along HOP ALLEY. No. 2 Tank will work along ALE ALLEY. No. 1 Tank on arriving at the junction of HOP ALLEY and BEER TRENCH about T.13.a. 5.4 will turn to the North and follow No. 2 Tank. The two tanks will then proceed in line ahead along red route as rapidly as possible and endeavour to catch up with the advance.

(d) On reaching the green line No. 2 Tank is to proceed via WATLING STREET so as to get on to blue route and join No. 1 Tank Group.

(e) Simultaneously with the attack on HOP and ALE ALLEYS, the 41st Inf. Bde. will organise an attack to -
(i) Prevent any enemy breaking West into DELVILLE WOOD.
(ii) To bomb down HOP and ALE ALLEYS and assist the tanks in clearing out these alleys.

8. Attack on first objective

(a) No. 1 Group of tanks will move by the blue route starting just East of COCOA LANE.

(b) On reaching TEA SUPPORT one tank is to halt and assist Infantry in clearing this trench. It will then push on rapidly to the first objective.

(c) The tanks to assist the Infantry who may be held up by uncut wire, machine guns, etc. One tank to deal with trench junction at T.1.c. 9.3.

9. Attack on Second Objective.

(a) Tanks and Infantry will advance together under the creeping barrage. Infantry must not however wait for any tanks that may drop behind.

(b) Action as in para 8(c).

10. In order to prevent accidents to the wounded, small guards of an N.C.O. and six men to each tank will be detailed and will accompany tanks as under:-

(i) By 8th R.B. to accompany tanks Nos. 1 & 2 up as far as the Second Objectives. These guards are not to be with the tanks till they have reached and cleared the edge of DELVILLE WOOD.

(ii) By 8th K.R.R.C. to accompany tank dropped at TEA SUPPORT from that point to first objective.

(iii) By 8th K.R.R.C. to accompany No. 1 Tank Group from First to Second Objectives.

(iv) By the nearest unit whenever a tank unaccompanied by a guard falls behind the Infantry but is still capable of movement.

11. If tanks get behind time table or get out of action Infantry must on no account wait for them.

12. The following signals will be used from tanks to Infantry and aircraft:-

Flag Signals.

Red flag = Out of action.
Green flag = Am on objective.
Other Flags = Are inter-tank signals.

Lamp Signals.

Series of "Ts." = Out of action.
Series of "Hs." = Am on objective.

A proportion of the tanks will carry pigeons.

13. If Infantry wish to speak to tanks the best way of attracting attention is to knock loudly on doors on the rear side of the SPONSONS.

"A" Form.

Army Form C. 2121.

MESSAGES AND SIGNALS.

No. of Message

Prefix .... Code .... m. | Words | Charge

Office of Origin and Service Instructions.

This message is on a/c of .... Service.

Sent At .... m. To .... By ....

(Signature of "Franking Officer.")

Recd. at .... m. Date .... From .... By ....

SECRET

TO Gain

Sender's Number.	Day of Month	In reply to Number	AAA
* G.470	14		

Herewith Operation Order No. 76 Copy No. 19 of 42nd Infantry Brigade AAA Acknowledge by wire AAA.

From Great

Place

Time 12/30 pm

C Maynard Lt Col

The above may be forwarded as now corrected.

(Z)

Censor.

Signature of Addressor or person authorised to telegraph in his name.

* This line should be erased if not required.

(174-5) —McC. & Co. Ltd., London.— W 1789/1402. 150,000. 8/15. Forms C 2121/10.

S E C R E T

Copy No. 19

42nd Inf Bde Operation Order No. 76

Reference, 1/20,000 Sheet 57c S.W.

14/9/16

1. For the last two and a half months the Allied Armies have been gradually gaining ground and wearing down the enemy. The enemy's moral is now shaken, he has few, if any, fresh reserves available, and there is every probability that a combined and determined effort will result in a decisive victory.

2. (a) The Fourth Army is to attack the enemy's defences between MORVAL and MARTINPUICH with the object of seizing MORVAL, LES BOEUFS, GUEUDECOURT and FLERS and breaking through the enemy's system of defence.

(b) The French and Reserve Armies are attacking simultaneously on our Right and Left.

3. To the 14th (Light) Division is allotted the task of capturing GUEUDECOURT, and establishing a line to the North and East of it, which includes the capture of four definite objectives, the first and second being allotted to the 41st Inf Bde, the third and fourth to the 42nd Inf Bde.

4. The objectives allotted to the Division, their sub-allotment to the 41st and 42nd Inf Bdes, and Battalions of the latter are given in Appendix "A", and also shown on xxxx map to be issued to units today.

5. There are four enemy lines of defence between us and our final objective, viz:-

(a) Enemy third line
(b) GAP trench
(c) GIRD trench
(d) GIRD Support

(a) and (b) are allotted to the 41st Inf Bde.
(c) and (d) are allotted to 9th Rif Brig and 5th Shrops L.I., 9th Rif Brig on the right.

(d) ~~This~~ objective is about 1800 yards long, and from 3500 to 4000 yards distant from the North edge of DELVILLE WOOD, and about $3\frac{1}{2}$ miles in a straight line from the CHECK line.

The final objective is allotted to 9th K.R.Rif C. and 5th Oxf & Bucks L.I., 9th K.R.Rif C. on the right.

It is about 2200 yards long, and from 3500 to 4500 yards distant from the North edge of DELVILLE WOOD, and about 4 miles in a straight line from the CHECK line.

6. The XIV Corps will be on our Right and the 41st Division on our left, and they will establish their left and right flanks respectively on the right and left flanks of the final objective of 42nd Inf Bde.

7. It is to be impressed on all ranks that a special effort is required and that the attack is to be pushed home with the utmost vigour all along the line until the most distant objectives have been captured.

8. A new engine of war "The Tank" is to be used for the first time. A separate memorandum in the use of this weapon is being issued, and is to be carefully explained to all ranks.

9. O.C. 42nd Brigade Machine Gun Company will detail two machine guns and personnel to proceed with each Battalion under the orders of O.C. Battalion, and similarly O.C. 42nd Brigade Trench Mortar Battery will detail two mortars and personnel to each Battalion. These mortars will not be placed in the front line.

10. The remaining guns and personnel of the 42nd Bde Machine Gun Company will be distributed as follows :-

(a) 6 guns will follow about 400 yards in rear of the last line of the 9th K.R.Rif C. and 5th Oxf & Bucks L.I., and will take up positions in the 3rd objective, until a reconnaissance has been made of GUEUDECOURT, and the final objective under arrangements to be made by O.C. Machine Gun Company, when these 6 guns will move forward to positions selected.

(b) 2 guns will remain in Brigade Reserve and move as ordered by Brigade H.Q.

11. All battalions of the Brigade will carry Tables "A" and "E" of this Office B.M. 14/576 of 13th inst, and also Stokes Mortar bombs to the scale laid down in Table "C".

12. The positions of the troops of the 42nd Inf Bde at ZERO will be as follows :-

(a) 9th Rif Brig and 5th Shrops L.I. in YORK ALLEY and the CHECK line between TRONES Wood and CRUCIFIX ALLEY.
(b) 9th K.R.Rif C. in MONTAUBAN ALLEY between BERNAFAY WOOD and S.27.b.central.
(c) 5th Oxf & Bucks L.I. in MONTAUBAN defences.
(d) Machine guns and Stokes mortars as detailed in para. 9 will be with their respective battalions.
(e) Machine guns in Brigade Reserve in MONTAUBAN Defences.

13. An Advanced Transport Camp will be established South West of MONTAUBAN, the exact position will be notified later.
Convoys, loaded with S.A.A., bombs, food, water and stores will be parked here under the B.T.O., and sent forward under Brigade arrangements.
Details of the Transport arrangements will be issued separately.

14. The Brigade Dump will be in the quarry at the N.W. corner of BERNAFAY WOOD.

15. The attack will be made at ZERO on Z day. Date and hour will be notified separately to all concerned.

16. The attack will be preceded by a bombardment of the hostile defensive system, which will take place daily from 6 a.m. to 6.30 p.m. This bombardment commenced on 12th instant.

17. At ZERO on Z day an intense barrage of field artillery will be opened all along the line.

18. The following are the movements of the 41st Inf Bde from ZERO :-
(a) The Infantry detailed to capture the "first objective" will leave their positions of assembly and advance as close behind the barrage as possible. The barrage will move ~~xxxxxx~~ in front of them at the rate of 50 yards a minute.
(b) No pause will be made on the line PINT TRENCH - TEA SUPPORT, which are to be dealt with by "mopping up" parties specially detailed.
(c) On reaching the first objective the infantry will not advance further until 60 minutes after Zero.
(d) At 60 minutes after ZERO, the barrage will start creeping back to the "second objective". The infantry detailed for this objective will advance as close as possible to the barrage and will regulate their pace by that of the barrage and not by the pace of any tanks that may be accompanying them.

19. The following are the movements of 42nd Inf Bde :-
(a) At Zero the 9th Rif Brig and 5th Shrops L.I. will advance, and

The 9th K.R.Rif C, and 5th Oxf & Bucks L.I. will move up into YORK ALLEY and the CHECK LINE.

(b) At one hour forty five minutes after Zero the 9th Rif Brig and 5th Shrops L.I. will be formed up immediately in rear of the second objective ready for a further advance, and the 9th K.R.Rif C. and 5th Oxf & Bucks L.I. will be formed up clear and N.E. of DELVILLE WOOD.

(c) At two hours after Zero the 9th Rif Brig and 5th Shrops L.I. will advance, keeping as close as possible to the Artillery barrage until they reach the line of the road from N.33.c.2.0 to N.31.b.4.0, where they will establish themselves and reform preparatory to the capture of the Third Objective. The 9th K.R.Rif C. and 5th Oxf & Bucks L.I. will form up in rear of them, with their leading lines about 400 yards in rear of the rear lines of 9th Rif Brig and 5th Shrops L.I.

(d) At four hours thirty minutes after Zero the 9th Rif Brig and 5th Shrops L.I. will advance and, following the barrage as closely as possible, will capture the Third Objective, after which the 9th K.R.Rif C, and 5th Oxf & Bucks L.I. will push on close behind the barrage and capture the final objective.

(e) The bombardment of GUEUDECOURT ceases at 5 hours, 30 minutes after Zero.

20. For detailed Time Table of Attack see Appendix "C".

21. As soon as each objective is gained the work of consolidating it will be proceeded with at once.

22. The troops allotted to the Third Objective will commence consolidating it as soon as captured and will not advance further.

The troops allotted to the final objective will commence to dig in as soon as the position has been gained, covered by machine and Lewis guns. A special garrison will be told off by O.C. 5th Oxf & Bucks L.I. for the defence of GUEUDECOURT.

Attention is directed to Fourth Army Tactical Notes, page 18, para. 44.

23. Special "mopping up" parties will be told off

(a) to clear any dugouts there may be in GIRD TRENCH and GIRD SUPPORT.

(b) to clear out dugouts and cellars in GUEUDECOURT and guard the entrances.

24. It is very important to ensure that assaulting battalions keep their direction and occupy the whole of the objective allotted to them.

Leading battalions will arrange beforehand to mark the line of march of their flanks through DELVILLE WOOD by means of tapes, and will also during the advance lay a paper trail through the Wood.

Direction will be frequently checked by compass bearing, carefully worked out beforehand. Care must be taken that the steel helmet does not affect the compass needle.

25. Every opportunity will be taken to reform under cover of the Artillery barrage, and to gain touch with the flanks.

26. The protection of the flanks of each unit and formation, however small, is of vital importance.

27. (a) Weather permitting, two contact aeroplanes will be continuously in the air from Zero on "Z" day until dark and one aeroplane will be up from 6.30 a.m. to 8.30 a.m. on the day after "Z" day.

(b) Red flares will be used and will be lit -

i. On reaching each objective.
ii. At 2 p.m. and 5 p.m. on "Z" day.
iii. At 7 a.m. on the day following "Z" day.
iv. When called for by contact aeroplane.
v. On the initiative of the troops when the contact plane is over them.

(c) Full use is to be made of signalling to aeroplanes from Battalion and Brigade H.Q. by signalling panels and ground sheets.

27. O.C. Brigade Signals will arrange to send out the time to all combatant units of the Brigade at 11.30 a.m. and 5.30 p.m. on Y day. Watches to be carefully synchronised.

28. No orders, sketches, letters or papers likely to be of use to the enemy to be taken into action.

29. Information of the situation will be sent back to Brigade H.Q. as frequently as possible.

30. Attention is directed to the 42nd Inf Bde instructions for forthcoming [illegible], copies of which are being issued separately. *operations*

31. Not more than 20 officers per Battalion will accompany it into action, the remaining officers and details of the Bde will be at the Advanced Transport Camp South West of MONTAUBAN.

The details of each Battalion will send an orderly to report at Brigade H.Q. in MONTAUBAN Defences one hour before ZERO on Z day.

32. Medical arrangements will be notified later.

33. All ranks will be warned against the danger of drinking any water in the enemy lines until passed fit for drinking by a Medical Officer.

34. Battle police posts will be established as follows, each post consisting of 1 officer, 1 N.C.O. and 4 men :-

(a) S.22.d.7.0 found by 5th Oxf & Bucks L.I.
(B) S.28.a.0.3 found by 5th Shrops L.I.
(c) S.27.c.2.2 found by 9th K.R.Rif C.

These posts will be in position one hour before Zero on Z day.

Stragglers will be collected and sent up to their units again in a formed body.

The names and units of all stragglers will be taken, and a special mark made against those without rifle or equipment.

Officers in charge of posts will report at Brigade H.Q. with these lists at the conclusion of the operations.

The 9th K.R.Rif C. and 5th Oxf & Bucks L.I. will place guards at th junction of ANGLE trench and LONGUEVAL ALLEY, and of YORK trench and CRUCIFIX ALLEY respectively to turn back any stragglers.

35. Battalion H.Q. will mark their position for runners by means of small red flags.

36. The S.O.S. is three blue rockets fired in quick succession. Attention is directed to S 1/284 L.I. of yesterday.

37. Brigade H.Q. will move on night of 14/15th to MONTAUBAN defences.

On Z day Brigade H.Q. will move forward about two hours after Zero to new advanced Brigade H.Q. in YORK trench.

Any further forward move of Brigade H.Q. will be notified in advance to all concerned.

After Zero all runners from units to Brigade H.Q. will report at Advanced Bde H.Q. in YORK trench, which will be marked by a small red flag.

38. Signalling arrangements will be notified later.

B T Paget

Capt.
Bde Major,
42nd Inf Bde.

Issued at 9.15 a.m.

Copy No. 1 to 5th Oxf & Bucks L.I.
2 5th Shrops L.I.
3 9th K.R.Rif C.
4 9th Rif Brig.
5 Bde Machine Gun Company
6 Bde Trench Mortar Battery
7 No. 3 Section Signals
8 Staff Captain
9 A/Staff Captain
10.
11. 14th Division
12. 41st Inf Bde
13. 43rd Inf Bde
14. 7th Div'l Artillery
15, 16 & 17 for issue to Artillery Bdes.
18. 41st Division
19. Guards Division
20. 62nd Field Company R.E.
21. 11th King's Regt.
22. 42nd Field Ambulance.
23,24,25 Filed

S E C R E T

APPENDIX "A" to accompany 42nd Inf Bde
Operation Order No. 76
=*=*=*=*=*=*=*

The objectives allotted to the Division and their sub-allotment to the 41st and 42nd Inf Bdes, and Battalions of the latter :-

Objective		Allotted to
Preliminary objective	HOP ALLEY and ALE ALLEY to junction with PINT TRENCH	41st Inf Bde.
First objective	SWITCH LINE from junction with LAGER LANE T.8.a.35 (exclusive) to junction with COCOA LANE T.1.d.02 (inclusive)	-do-
Second objective	Third line defences from T.2.d.25 to road at T.1.b.12 (inclusive	-do-
Third objective	GIRD SUPPORT	
	(a) from N.33.c.4.2 to N.32.b.3¼.8	9th Rif Brig.
	(b) from N.32.b.3¼.8 to N.26.c.8.9	5th Shrops L.I.
Fourth objective	(a) Establishing approximate line from N.33.central in touch with XIV Corps to road junction N.27.a.5.0 in touch with 5th Oxf & Bucks L.I.	9th K.R.Rif C.
x N.20.d.5.0	(b) Capture of GUEUDECOURT and establishing approximate line from road junction N.27.a.5.0 in touch with 9th K.R.Rif C. to x ~~N.[illegible]0.d.5.0~~ in touch with 41st Division.	5th Oxf & Bucks L.I.

S E C R E T APPENDIX B

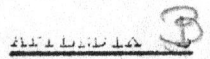

ORDERS FOR USE OF "TANKS"

1. Two male and two female tanks have been allotted to the Division from the commencement of the attack.

2. On the night of X/Y the tanks allotted to the Division will move to positions of assembly as follows :-

(i) 2 male and 1 female tanks to Green Dump S.16.c.8.2
(ii) 1 female tank to S.23.c.1.6

3. On night Y/Z tanks move to positions of departure as under -

(i) tanks from Green Dump to point just East of COCOA LANE about S.12.d.5.5.
(ii) tank from S.23.c.1.6 to point about T.13.c.2.8.

4. Arrangements for the provision of guides, taping of routes and reconnaissance by Heavy Machine Gun Section officers have been made under separate instructions.

5. The tanks are allotted to objectives as follows :-

(i) Female tank at T.13.c.2.8 under Captain MORTIMER (No. 1 Tank) and one Male Tank at S.12.d.5.5 (No. 2 Tank) under Lieut BLOWERS are allotted to deal with HOP ALLEY and ALE ALLEY respectively.

(ii) One male and one Female Tank at S.12.d.5.5 to form No. 1 Tank Group for the attack on the First, Second, Third and Fourth Objectives.

6. At the times laid down in Appendix "C" the tanks will start for their respective objectives and by the routes shown in the attached map.

7. Attack on Preliminary Objective

(a) The points to be attacked in the first instance are :-

(i) By tank from T.13.c.2.8 (No. 1 Tank) the junction of HOP ALLEY and East edge of DELVILLE WOOD.
(ii) By tank from S.12.d.5.5 (No. 2 Tank) the junction of ALE ALLEY and EDGE TRENCH.

(b) It is most important that these important junctions are thoroughly dealt with and cleared.

(c) After dealing with these points No. 1 tank will work along HOP ALLEY, No. 2 Tank will work along ALE ALLEY. No. 1 Tank on arriving at the junction of HOP ALLEY and BEER TRENCH about T.13.a.5.4 will turn to the North and follow No. 2 Tank. The two tanks will then proceed in line ahead along red route as rapidly as possible and endeavor to catch up with the advance.

(d) On reaching the Green line No. 2 Tank is to proceed via WATLING STREET so as to get on to blue route and join No. 1 Tank Group.

(e) Simultaneously with the tank attack on HOP and ALE ALLEYS, the 41st Inf Bde will organise an attack to -

(i) prevent any enemy breaking West into DELVILLE WOOD.
(ii) to bomb down HOP and ALE ALLEYS and assist the tanks in clearing out these alleys.

8. Attack on First Objective.

(a) No. 1 Group of Tanks will move by the blue route starting just East of COCOA LANE.

(b) On reaching TEA SUPPORT one tank to halt and assist Infantry in clearing this trench. It will then push on rapidly to the First objective.

(c) The tanks to assist the infantry who may be held up by uncut wire, machine guns, etc. One tank to deal with trench junction at T.1.c.9.3.

9. Attack on Second Objective.

(a) Tanks and Infantry will advance together under the creeping barrage. Infantry must not however wait for any tanks that may drop behind.

(b) Action as in para. 8 (c)

10. Attack on Third and Fourth Objectives.

(a) No. 2 Single Tank from 41st Division Area now comes into 14th Division Area.

(b) Tanks advance 15 minutes in advance of the Infantry up to blue line where they halt till 4 hrs. 15 minutes after ZERO. During this halt No. 1 Single Tank ought to have got up in line and No.2 Tank ought to have joined No. 1 Tank Group.

(c) At 4 hrs. 15 minutes after Zero the tanks advance in advance of the Infantry and deal with any wire or machine guns that may be found.

(d) During this advance Nos. 2 and 3 Groups of tanks from the 41st Division Area pass into 14th Division Area.

(e) At 5 hrs. 30 minutes after Zero the tanks, on whose route the village is, can enter GUEUDECOURT.

(f) Many of the houses in GUEUDECOURT have cellars, tanks will endeavor to blow in any loopholes discovered.

(g) There is reported to be an underground passage between the Church N.26.b.3.2 and a small quarry about N.26.b.6.3. No. 2 Group of tanks will try and locate and deal with this passage.

(h) No. 2 Group of tanks assisted by No. 2 Single Tank will deal with large farm N.26.b.9.6 which is reported to have a very good cellar.

11. As soon as the Infantry has reached the final objective and battalion commanders on the spot are satisfied that there is no strong point left in GUEUDECOURT which cannot be dealt with by the infantry, the battalion commander on whose front the tanks happen to be will order them back to a position of assembly South of LONGUEVAL. It is of the utmost important not to keep the tanks out (and particularly stationary) longer than can be avoided.

12. In order to prevent accidents to the wounded small guards of a N.C.O. and 6 men to each tank will be detailed and will accompany tanks as under:-

(i) By 41st Inf Bde to accompany Tanks Nos 1 and 2 up as far as the Second objective. These guards are not to be with the tanks till they have reached and cleared the edge of DELVILLE WOOD.

(ii) By 41st Inf Bde to accompany Tank halted at TEA SUPPORT from that point to First objective.

(iii) By 41st Inf Bde to accompany No. 1 Tank Group from First to Second Objective.

(iv) By the nearest unit whenever a tank unaccompanied by a guard falls behind the Infantry but is still capable of movement.

13. If Tanks get behind time table or get out of action infantry must on no account wait for them.

14. The following signals will be used from tanks to infantry and aircraft :-

Flag Signals

Red flag	=	Out of action
Green flag	=	Am on objective.
Other flags	=	Are inter-tank signals.

Lamp signals

Series of T's	=	Out of action
Series of H's	=	Am on objective.

A proportion of the tanks will carry pigeons.

15. If infantry wish to speak to tanks the best way of attracting attention is to knock loudly on doors on the rear side of the sponsons.

SECRET

APPENDIX "C" to 42nd Inf Bde Operation Order No. 76

TIME TABLE OF ATTACK

- 0.53 Left Tank group starts

- 0.30 ALE ALLEY tank starts

- 0.24 HOP ALLEY tank starts.

0.00 (Zero) Tank and bombing attack on HOP and ALE ALLEY starts.

0.00 " Infantry leave their trenches and advance close up to the barrage which will begin creeping back in front of them at 0.6 minutes.
Creeping barrage will go back steadily at 50 yards per minute until it joins stationary barrage on first objective (green line)

0.25 minutes. Tanks reach positions on first objective East of FLERS Road.

(i) 0.20 min. (i) Barrage lifts from green line West of FLERS ROAD
(ii)0.30 min. (ii) Barrage lifts from green line East of FLERS ROAD - Infantry capture first objective as the barrage lifts in each case. Creeping barrage halts 300 yards beyond green line.

1 hour 00 min. Infantry and tanks advance together behind creeping barrage. Creeping barrage goes back 100 yards in three minutes, and on arrival at FLERS LINE joins stationary barrage.

1 hour 25 min. Barrage lifts from second objective. 41st Inf Bde capture brown line.

1 hour 45 min. Covering barrage goes back to allow tanks to advance from brown line.

2 hours 00 min. Infantry advance and establish the blue line.

4 hours 15 min. Covering barrage taken off to allow tanks to go forward.

(i) 4 hrs.30 min.	) barrage lifts from	((i)	Right boundary and Road N.32.b.38
(ii) 4 hrs.55 min.	) GIRD TRENCH and GIRD	((ii)	Road N.32.b.38 and track N.26.c.45.
(iii) 5 hrs.00 min.	) SUPPORT between	((iii)	Track N.26.c.45 and left boundary.

5 hrs. 30 minutes. Bombardment of GUEUDECOURT ceases - Tanks push forward, and infantry complete capture of fourth objective.

SUGGESTIONS FOR THE ATTACK

Hd: Qrs: 1st Guards Brigade

Consider that it would be best to attack in 3 waves. The leading wave consisting of 2 Coys the 2nd & 3rd of one Coy each.

The 2nd wave would move forward at a distance of 75 yards & the 3rd would advance with Batt. Hd: Quarters at the discretion of the C.O.

This would ensure that the whole of the Battn was not on top of the ground at the same time & would leave a Company at the disposal of the C.O. in case anything unforeseen should occur –

23.9.16.

C. Corkran Lt Col
2nd Bn Grenadier Gds

"A" Form.
MESSAGES AND SIGNALS.

Army Form C.2121
(in pads of 100).
No. of Message ....

Prefix .... Code .... m. | Words | Charge | This message is on a/c of: | Recd. at .... m.
Office of Origin and Service Instructions.
Sent
At .... m.
To ....
By ....
.... Service.
(Signature of "Franking Officer.")
Date ....
From ....
By ....

TO 1st Gds Bde

Sender's Number.	Day of Month.	In reply to Number.	AAA
MC 211	22nd	1st G Bde 265	

I fully concur AAA This will presumably mean that the Battalion may assault its objective in more than the 2 waves ordered AAA Suggest that the amendment to para 25 should be made quite clear to the pigeon-MEN who have strong views on the subject

From 1 Irish Gds
Place
Time 9.40 pm

The above may be forwarded as now corrected. (Z)
....
Censor. Signature of Addressor or person authorised to telegraph in his name.

* This line should be erased if not required.

750,000. W 2186—M509. H. W. & V., Ld. 6/16.

SECRET

1 Gd/C/74/16

1st Guard Brigade.

In view of your supplementary note to O.O.77, issued last night, I feel bound to put on record my view that the task allotted to the Battn. under my command – viz – an attack on 3 separate & successive objectives – is one beyond the powers of a single Battn., under-officered & inexperienced as all Battns. now are.

I only do so because I see that in neither of the Brigades on our flanks is a Battn. expected to take more than 2 objectives. At the same time I shall of course do my utmost to ensure that my Battn. does reach its final objective.

My reasons for writing thus, are founded on experience of 15th inst, when: –

(i). Two Battns. were allotted 3 objectives each, out of 4.
(ii). Neither Battn. reached its 2nd objective without very considerable support.
(iii). The only further advance beyond the 2nd objective was made by parties from a supporting Battn.
(iv). It was obviously not easy to lead troops which had suffered losses, from one objective to a further one.
(v). The casualty lists of all 4 Battns. were very similar.

I may add that I have not consulted OC 2nd Bn Gren Gds before writing, and I fully appreciate that his task is a still greater one.

R. McCalmont
Lt Col
Comdg 1st Irish Guards

24.9.16

O.C. 1st [illegible] Irish Guards

In reply to your IG/10/7416

In continuation of my conversation this morning, the following is the reason for my drawing up the attack orders.

1) In order to ensure success I have kept the two battalions which are to carry out the attack (2nd G.G. & 1st I.G.) entirely clear of trenches in order to have them as fresh as possible.

The 2nd & 3rd Coldstream have been long time & have had a very great amount of digging to do.

2) The Brigade orders distinctly states that they are to provide what support is required.

3) My conviction is that the Brigade will gain enormously by keeping assaulting troops & support troops apart as long as possible to avoid disorganization, then as soon as the assaulting battalions have come to end of their ~~tour~~ tether the support battalions are still organised & ready to carry on the task.

The OC 2nd Grenadiers agrees with the orders for the assault.

I am glad that you raised the question so that I can assure

that I am convinced that the present form of attack gives a maximum chance of success & that I think that the attack of the 15th Sept differs radically from that which the Brigade is now called on to do.

H J Perceval
Brig Genl
Comdg 1st Guards B.

24/4/16.

NARRATIVE OF OPERATIONS

1st Guards Brigade

during AUGUST & SEPTEMBER

1916

Operations carried out by 1st Guards Brigade
during August and September 1916.

On August 20th the 1st Guards Brigade was relieved in the trenches opposite Serre by the 5th Infantry Brigade of the 2nd Division. Between August 20th and August 25th the Brigade was on the move almost every day. Three short marches were done under excellent weather conditions, which helped to shake Battalions and the whole Brigade together.

By August 25th the whole Brigade including 75th Company Royal Engineers and 4th Field Ambulance was concentrated and billeted in MEAULTE. It was not known for certain how long the Brigade was to be in this area but it was thought that it would be there for about a week or ten days.

The day after the arrival of the Brigade a conference of Commanding Officers was held. The general programme of training was discussed and training areas were allotted. On the following day a conference of all Commanding Officers and Company Commanders was held and many details of the attack were gone into. Such points as the dress and equipment of troops in the assault; distinguishing badges for carriers; runners and clearing up parties; the frontage to be allotted to a Company in the assault; the number of waves and the interval between them; the method of advance; consolidation of ground gained and the bold handling of patrols and lewis guns to gain ground after the capture of the final objective, were all discussed and laid down. Copies of the minutes of this conference were sent to units to allow of distribution on the scale of one per company and to prevent a repetition of orders on these subjects. Only one subsequent alteration was necessary - the addition of either a pick or a shovel to the equipment to be carried by every man in the attack.

Throughout/

Throughout this period it was generally known that the Brigade would be called upon at no very distant date to take it's part in the Battle of the Somme - but little was known beyond this.

From August 25th to September 10th the Brigade remained in billets at Meaulte. Training was carried on almost contin:uously during this period, in spite of moderate weather conditions, and the fact that the crops in the neighbourhood were only partially cut. On August 31st, 2nd Bn. Grenadier Guards were sent up to Carnoy to dig under orders of 20th Division. They rejoined the Brigade on September 3rd.

At 7 P.M. on September 5th the Brigade was warned to be ready to move at short notice from 5 A.M. the following day but during the night these orders were cancelled and training continued as usual.

The training area allotted to the Brigade was sub-allotted to the four Battalions. Included in the training area was a good bombing ground on which the Brigade Bombing Officer daily instructed two Companies from the Brigade in the general principles of bombs, rifle grenades, and bombing attacks. Every Company in the Brigade underwent this training and it was hoped that this would enable Companies in the future to do their own elementary training and allow of more advanced training to be done by the Brigade Bombing Officer. Owing to casualties during subsequent operations this hope would appear to have been false. Live bombing during this period was carried out under Battalion arrangements.

In the training area, in addition to the bombing ground there was a system of trenches which was allotted to Battalions for practising companies in the assault. There was also ground for practising open fighting.

For/

For the first ten days (up to September 4th) training was carried out more or less by Companies, except on one day when 3rd Bn. Coldstream Guards carried out a practice attack with a contact aeroplane. Several useful lessons were learnt by signallers on this day, and the accuracy with which the contact patrol could follow the movements of our troops was made clear to all.

From September 5th Battalion training was carried out, Battalions practising the assault of a first objective from an imaginary line of trenches and then pushing on to the attack of a second objective, a thousand yards or more distant.

Although the exact task of the Brigade in the near future had not yet been indicated, it now became generally known that the task which the Brigade would have to carry out would be an ambitious one, and for this reason great attention was paid during the whole of this period to training in open fighting. The pushing forward of patrols, moving in artillery formation, deploying from artillery formation were practised freely every day.

In addition to the above training a class of all Signallers under the Brigade Signalling Officer was carried on throughout. Every form of visual signalling except helio was practised and extra runners up to 8 per Battalion were also trained by the Brigade Signalling Officer. It was decided in all future operations to try and establish one main trunk line to a point as far forward and as central as possible, rather than to try and get a number of bad lines to each Unit. This trunk line was to be either telephone, visual or relay posts - if possible, all three.

Work platoons 30 strong under an Officer were formed in each Battalion and were trained daily under 75th Coy., R.E. Extra men from Battalions were also trained by the Trench Mortar Battery in order to replace casualties in that Battery in the event of heavy casualties.

On/

On September 3rd a Conference was held at Divisional Head-Quarters and the general outline of the task to be carried out by the Brigade was made known, and communicated subsequently to Commanding Officers only. As has already been stated the attack was to be a more ambitious one than any other that had taken place up to that date. Owing to the fact that operations were still in progress to capture what was to be our jumping off line it was impossible to lay down any details of the plan of attack.

For this reason from September 4th all efforts were centred in Battalion training. Points, which received special attention, were how to get most men across "No Man's Land" in the shortest time, how to keep close under barrage, formation for attacks on various objectives, communications. Finally on September 8th a Brigade field day was held.

At 12 noon on September 9th Orders were received for the Brigade to move on the following day to bivouacs about Carnoy. Arrangements had previously been made for the storage of all surplus kits, equipment, etc., in one larege Brigade Store at MEAULTE, and as soon as this order was received the storing began. Caps, greatcoats and packs were left in this Store in charge of a small party.

On 10th September after arrival at Carnoy two Companies of the 1st Bn. Irish Guards were sent up to support the 3rd Guards Brigade and on September 11th the remaining two Companies of this Battalion were also sent up, the whole Battalion re-:joining the Brigade on September 12th about 8 A.M.

At 4 P.M. on September 11th Orders were received for the Brigade to relieve half the 3rd Guards Brigade in the front line - 2nd Guards Brigade were to relieve the other half - on September 12th and at the same hour a Conference was held at Divisional Head-Quarters to explain the detailed orders for the forthcoming attack. These Orders were in turn communicated to Commanding Officers at a Conference held at Brigade Head-Quarters at 6 P.M. The chief points were :-

(1) assembly trenches out of the question owing to

want of time.

(2) The attack to be at or just before dawn.

(3) Tanks to be used and the attack would therefore not be a surprise.

(4) Distance to first objective 700 or 800 yards, which eventually proved an under-estimation of the distance which in reality was over 1,200 yds.; extension to be two pacer between men and 50 yards between waves.

(5) Flow of waves to be continuous.

(6) Frontage of Brigade 500 yards.

(7) Forming up areas must be reconnoitred and direction of attack carefully laid out beforehand.

On September 10th and 11th Battalions drew all equipment for the attack such as bombs, extra S.A.A., sandbags, distinguishing armbands; rockets, flares, very lights, wirecutters. The principle was that Battalions were to move up complete in everything but tools, relying on finding ~~on finding~~ nothing in the line except tools.

During the time the Brigade was in Meaulte the Brigade Bombing Officer had been busily employed in making Mills Rifle Grenades so that Battalions were now all issued with an ample supply of these Grenades.

Thus by September 12th the Brigade was fully equipped and nothing but the issuing of the final definite orders for the attack remained to be done.

This proved to be a wise precaution as the written orders for the attack were not received from the Division until 9 P.M. on the 12th when the Brigade was in process of relieving the 3rd Guards Brigade. The left half of the 3rd Guards Brigade front was taken over during the night of Sept.,12/13th by the 2nd Bn. Grenadier Guards while the 1st Bn. Irish Guards moved up in support in Trones and Bernafay Woods.

The/

The 2nd and 3rd Bn's. Coldstream Guards who were to carry out the assault remained resting at Carnoy till the last possible moment. Brigade Head-Quarters moved up to Dummy Trench between Trones and Bernafay Woods.

Nearly the whole of September 13th was occupied in drafting the written orders for the attack on September 15th, and were not finally issued until 8 P.M. that evening.

Four successive objectives had been allotted to the Brigade. The first was distant about 1,200 yards, the second 1,500 yards, but concerned only the left Battalion of the Brigade, the third 2,500 yards while the final objective which included the northern outskirts of Les Boeufs was no less than 3,500 yards distant.

The Infantry were to advance to the attack of the first objective at 6-20 A.M., to the second objective at 7-30 A.M., to the third objective at 8-20 A.M. and to the final objective at 10-50 A.M.

The front allotted to the Brigade was about 500 yards, from about T 14 a 2.2 to T 13 b 3.0. On September 14th the Brigade was holding rather more than it's battle front but this was taken over by the 14th Division on our left during daylight on September 14th. The jumping off line was an irregular semi-circle and the left flank held by the 14th Division was turned back and faced N. The Germans held the point of the GINCHY Orchard and had Machine Guns in the GINCHY - FLERS Sunken Road about 400 yards North of GINCHY. With a view to clearing away these posts which might seriously hold up the attack at its very start the 2nd Bn. Grenadier Guards made an attack on the night of the 13/14th Sept., They were successful in advancing our line to the point of the Orchard in the face of very determined opposition, but could not get up the Sunken Road. However great their success might have been the left flank of the Brigade was bound to have been in the air.

This/

This attack helped to show the the Germans were in considerable strength between us and our first objective and that the Sunken Road from GINCHY to FLERS was defended by Machine Guns. The supposed position of these Machine Guns was bombarded by heavies both on September 13th and September 14th and a Tank was specially detailed to deal with this point on Sept., 15th.

The general plan of attack for September 15th was then formulated as follows :-

The 2nd Coldstream Guards on the right and the 3rd Coldstream Guards on the left were to attack and capture the 1st, 2nd and 3rd objectives. The 1st Irish Guards, passing through the Coldstream Guards at the 3rd objective were to attack and capture the 4th objective and if possible push out patrols beyond. The 2nd Grenadier Guards who had already been 3 day's in the line, had been heavily shelled and carried out a small attack, were given what was thought to be, the easiest task. They were to follow up the two Coldstream Battalions and be prepared to form a defensive flank especially to the North (or left flank) where trouble was anticipated. When the first objective was clear of the Coldstream the 2nd Grenadier Guards were to occupy it and allow the 1st Irish Guards to go through them there. Then when the 1st Irish Guards had gone through, the 2nd Grenadier Guards were to move forward in support and be prepared to support the Irish Guards in their attack on the fourth objective. Failing support from the Grenadier Guards the Irish Guards were to call on the two Coldstream Battn's. for any support required. One Section of Machine Guns was sent with each Battalion and four Stokes Guns were sent with 2nd Grenadier Guards, with orders not to advance beyond the 2nd objective.

The 75th Field Coy., R.E. and Work Platoons were to remain in Reserve near Brigade H.Q., until ordered up. Brigade H.Q., were to be close to GUILLEMONT Stn. where some old German dug-outs had been found and made habitable by the R.E.

The/

The forming up areas of the two leading Battalions were reconnoitred beforehand by the Battalions concerned. Those of the two support Battalions were marked out by the R.E., and the general line of their advance was also marked by posts.

Dumps of R.E. material, S.A.A., Bombs, etc., had been made under Brigade arrangements on the WATERLOT Farm - GUILLEMONT Road, and the rations of the 2nd Grenadier Guards for the 15th had been dumped in their assembly positions. A water dump had been made at Brigade H.Q., containing 200 gallons of water.
For list of stores in these dumps see APPENDIX "A".

Before passing to the execution of the attack the following points must be borne in mind :-

(1) The weather had been fine and the going was good but the ground in the neighbourhood of GINCHY was one succession of shell holes.

(2) Owing to continual shelling it was impossible to get by day to the front line which was merely a single line of connected trench.

(3) The position of the nearest enemy was obscure.

(4) Owing to the fact that we were on the top and not over the top of the ridge, there was little or no Artillery observation of fire.

(5) There was no track or road of any kind est of the WATERLOT Farm - GUILLEMONT Road by which to bring up supplies.

(6) It was impossible to see any of our objectives from any part of our line.

(7) GINCHY was a shell-trap.

(8) Our left flank was a serious danger as the enemy were very strong there and our line bent back; a Tank and two Companies of King's Own Yorkshire Light Infantry had been specially detailed to deal with this at Zero - 50 mins.

Zero/

Zero on September 15th was at 6-20 A.M. The situation up to this hour was perfectly normal. The assembly march was carried out without a hitch and Units were all in position by 1 A.M. on the 15th. Arrangements had been made to give the men a meat sandwich before the attack started and also hot tea but the latter was somewhat outweighed by the necessity for keeping down the number of lights and fires before Zero, in order not to give away the concentration of troops for the attack.

At 5-30 A.M. the Tanks were seen moving forward on the left flank of the Brigade, but apparently they did not attract any fire, nor did they arouse suspicion. What happened to the Tank which was to clear up the situation immediately on our left flank is not known but it appears to have accomplished it's task, judging from the slight opposition which the Infantry met in that neighbourhood.

General Feilding Sep 18 did not

At 6-20 A.M. the leading Infantry went forward and our barrage started. Almost immediately the two Coldstream Battn's. who were leading came under the most terrific machine gun fire from the FLERS - GINCHY Sunken Road - about 400 yards North of GINCHY. The first waves of the assault were literally mown down. Major Vaughan, 2nd in Command and Captain Cubitt Adjutant of the 3rd Bn. Coldstream Guards were killed before they had gone 100 yards, while almost at the same time, Captain G. R. Lane, Adjutant of the 2nd Bn. Coldstream Guards was killed and Major Bentinck 2nd in Command of that Battalion wounded.

Captain Longueville who Commanded one of the leading Coy's. of the 3rd Coldstream, arrived at a point [illegible]0 yards from the Sunken Road with only four men of his Company. For a moment there was a slight check; Lt-Col., Campbell, Comdg., the 3rd Bn. Coldstream realised that at all costs the attack must be pressed home. One note from his hunting horn was sufficient to rally the leading waves by this time dangerously thinned and to carry the whole attack forward in one headlong and irresistable rush. Of waves there were none - The fourth wave was striving to beat the remnants of the first in the race for the FLERS - GINCHY Rd.

Within/

Within a few moments of that first note, Coldstreamers and Irishmen (from the leading Company of the 1st Irish Guards) had got to work with the bayonet. Large numbers of Germans were either killed or taken prisoner and no less than 4 Machine Guns were captured at one point alone besides a number of Trench Mortars. But the line did not halt here - On over the road it swept - down the valley and over another entirely unexpected German Line - up the slope the other side and on into a third German trench. Here again a large number of Germans were either killed or taken prisoner and it was only with the greatest difficulty that the line, which by this time was a mixture of men from all three Coldstream Battn's., from the 3rd Grenadier Guards and from the 1st Irish Guards, was halted.
Casualties had been very heavy especially amongst Officers. The 2nd Coldstream had only two Officers in addition to the Commdg; Officer left with the Battalion. The result of that check in the first stages of the attack had been to draw the 3rd Bn. Coldstream and the 2nd Bn. Coldstream on their right towards the point of the check so that when the attack went forward after capturing the GINCHY - FLERS Road it went in too northerly a direction.

But in spite of this the attack had now reached and penetrated the German line of defence which previous to July 1st had constituted their third main line and which in this part of the battle-field ran along the Eastern and last slopes of the high ground. Before September 15th the British line had been established on the high ground about DELVILLE Wood, and the Villages of GINCHY, and GUILLEMONT, this ground being as high as any ground occupied by the Germans. The Germans were still clinging and fighting desperately for the most easterly high ground, which even though it did not command our position, at any rate prevented us from occupying ground which commanded the whole country for miles both to the East towards LE TRANSLOY and to the North towards BAPAUME.

The/

The ground which the attack had to pass over in order to reach this third main German line (1st objective) sloped gently down for five or six hundred yards into a valley running almost due North to FLERS. Beyond the dip of the valley it again sloped glacis-like up to the German line, which had been cleverly constructed so as to sweep the whole of the 1,200 yards over which our attack had to pass, not only with frontal but also with enfilade fire. The line was a continuous one, well traversed and with deep dug-outs for the entire garrison. It was protected by three rows of barbed wire, which had been well cut by our artillery fire.

This then was the trench which our leading Infantry captured at 7-15 A.M. on September 15th. As they entered it the barrage could be seen playing on the ground 200 yards beyond. Still the country to the North and East remained hidden from view.

A Conference was held by the Officers Commanding the three Coldstream Battalions and it was decided that the third objective had been reached and that it was impossible to advance further until a certain strong point on the right flank about 500 yards away (T.8.d.4.5) had been captured. This was accomplished by the troops on that flank about 11 A.M. Meanwhile Lt-Col., Campbell, who as senior Officer present had taken charge of all troops in the neighbourhood, discovered that the line captured was not our third objective but our first. He again realised that another advance, cost what it might, was imperative and gave orders for the 2nd and 3rd Battalions of the Coldstream to push forward at once while all men of the 2nd Guards Brigade were ordered to sideslip to the right in order to assist in clearing the strong point which was holding up the attack from that direction. It must be remembered that at this time the trench held by our troops was crowded with men from almost every Battn., of the 1st and 2nd Guards Brigades all mixed and with only a very small percentage of Officers amongst them.

For/

For this reason alone the movement would have been a difficult one to effect but in addition to this the difficulties were greatly increased by the heavy sniping and continual barrage which the enemy kept on the trench - by the number of wounded with whom the trench was blocked and by the necessity for the immediate consolidation of the position.

Nevertheless the movement was carried out though unfortunately it was in it's execution that Lt-Col., Baring, Commdg., the 1st Bn. Coldstream was killed.

About 11 A.M. the 2nd and 3rd Coldstream with some parties of 1st Irish Guards on the extreme left in touch with 14th Division pushed forward to attack the 2nd objective. Again almost immediately they came under a very heavy barrage and also under Machine Gun fire from the right. Again too the attack seemed to wither up under the intense fire that was brought to bear on it but with another note from his hunting horn Lt-Col., Campbell led the attack forward in a second irresistable rush. The second objective was carried and Posts were pushed forward about 600 yards. Consolidation was begun and a message sent back to the 1st Irish Guards to move up in Support.

Meanwhile the other two Battalions of the Brigade had not been idle. At Zero the 2nd Grenadier Guards moved forward by platoons in Artillery formation. This Battalion started some 350 yards in rear of the two Coldstream Battalions and by the time they reached GINCHY a heavy German barrage had come down. Luckily the barrage was chiefly on the South side of the Village and this Battalion moving by the North end of the Village halted in and just North of the Village till about 7 A.M. and then passed through the barrage with very few casualties. The ground was very soft and the numerous shell holes afforded excellent cover.

About 7-20 A.M. the Battalion emerged on the Eastern side of GINCHY with it's right on the GINCHY to LES BOEUFS Road, but nothing could be seen of the two Coldstream Battalions.

The/

The left of the Battalion came under fire almost at once from the first objective at about T 8 d 3.8 to T 8 a 8.4. The right of the Battalion was however able to get into the 1st objective and there got into touch with some of the 3rd Grenadier Guards of the 2nd Guards Brigade on their right. The attack of the Division on the right had apparently failed with the result that the right flank was dangerously in the air and that our troops were suffering very heavy casualties by Machine Gun and Rifle fire from that direction.

Meanwhile the left of the 2nd Grenadier Guards was still held up outside the wire of the 1st objective and in addition that part of the Battalion in the 1st objective was gradually being pressed back by a German bombing attack which was coming down the trench from the North. The supply of bombs gave out and at this critical stage Company Sergt.-Major Norton led a bayonet attack from outside the wire against the bombing attack which was crossing his front.

This momentarily relieved the pressure but the Germans organised another bombing attack and when the situation was again critical Captain Harcourt Vernon organized and led a second bayonet charge from out of the trench which was being bombed, with the result that many Germans were killed and driven back, while 40 or 50 more surrendered.

Soon after this about 3-30 P.M. the situation in the 1st objective was finally cleared up and the 2nd Grenadier Guards were then in touch with a mixture of British Troops on their left as well as with the 3rd Grenadier Guards on their right.

It must not be forgotten that Captain Cuninghame's Coy. of this Battalion (2nd Grenadier Guards) had pushed forward and was in line with the 3rd Coldstream Guards, some 500 yards to the left front of the remainder of the Battalion.

During the day three carrying parties with bombs, S.A.A., were sent up and reached the 2nd Grenadier Guards in time to be of great assistance.

As/

As has already been mentioned the Irish Guards were the rear Battalion of the Brigade. They were formed up in two lines about 150 yards in rear of the 2nd Grenadier Guards with 100 yards between their two lines. At Zero they moved forward in this formation. The Irish Guards followed the line of the attack of the two Coldstream Battalions and when the 3rd Coldstream experienced their first check about one Company of the 1st Irish Guards came up and went on with the leading Coldstream waves. The remainder of the Battalion followed in support of the attack and by 7-30 A.M. were all gathered in the 1st objective which was crowded with men of all Regiments, including some of the 14th Division on our left.

The Irish Guards remained in the 1st objective with the exception of the parties already mentioned until about 11-15 A.M. when in response to a message from the Officer Commanding 3rd Coldstream Guards they moved forward about 500 yards into line with the 2nd and 3rd Coldstream Guards with every available man. A covering party was pushed out 300 yards in front of the line occupied by the main body of Coldstream and Irish Guards and a message sent to Brigade H.Q., to say that it was impossible to push the attack any further owing to the very heavy casualties and the consequent scarcity of Officers and Men.

Up to this point the position reached by the two Coldstream Battalions has not been mentioned for the reason that there was great uncertainty throughout as to their exact position. At 7-15 A.M. Lt-Col., Campbell reported he had captured the 3rd objective. This was seen to be impossible on account of our own barrage and the time table and it was taken to mean that the first objective had been captured. This surmise turned out to be correct. From 2-30 P.M. and throughout the remainder of the day Lt-Col., Campbell and Lt-Col., McCalmont both reported their position as being in our 3rd objective just North West of LES BOEUFS, while Aeroplanes reported that nowhere were troops of the Guards Division in their third objective. At that time the value of the Aeroplane reports were not realised with the result/

result that when at 3-45 P.M. the 2nd Bn. Scots Guards of the 3rd Guards Brigade were sent up to support the two Coldstream Battn's. who had reported that they were hung up and unable to advance, they were ordered to move to the third objective just North West of LES BOEUFS in T.3.a.

The result was that only one Company of this Battalion with 2 Lewis Guns arrived to support the Coldstream Guards about 5 P.M. and further that throughout the whole operation communications with the Coldstream and Irish Guards were never properly established.

During the afternoon the Corps had issued Orders for our third objective to be bombarded by the Heavy Artillery. On hearing of this a strong protest was sent in by the Brigadier, as at that time it was firmly believed that our troops were occupying the third objective. The Corps however, were so satisfied by the Aeroplane reports that the protest was over-ruled, and the bombardment took place.

About 6-30 P.M. and again at 7-15 P.M. the enemy attempted two counter attacks from the right and right rear of the troops holding the second objective. Both these Attacks were driven off though at times it looked as if the enemy would succeed in turning this flank.

At dusk on Sept., 15th the position was actually as follows :-

(1) The remnants of 2nd and 3rd Coldstream Guards, 1st Irish Guards with the remains of one Company of 2nd Grenadier Guards and one Company of 2nd Scots Guards were holding the second objective from about T.2.c.2.8. to about T.2.d.central. The total number of rifles in this line was 250 to 300.

(2) The 2nd Grenadier Guards were holding the first objective with their right on the GINCHY - LES BOEUFS Road, in touch with the 3rd Grenadier Guards on their right and with their left about T.8.a.9.4. where there was a mixture of Coldstream and Scots Guards of the 2nd Guards Brigade. Troops of the 2nd Guards Brigade which had reached the 3rd objective due West of LES. BOEUFS had been driven back and a counter attack from/

from this direction appeared imminent to both the Coldstream Guards and 2nd Grenadier Guards, but the enemy did not come on.

(3) The 2nd Grenadier Guards were not in touch with the Coldstream Guards to their left front but they were in touch with Brigade Head Quarters.

(4) The enemy were still keeping up an intermittent barrage on the GINCHY - DELVILLE WOOD ridge and also on GINCHY Village.

At 8 P.M. a convoy consisting of the 75th Field Coy., R.E., Work Platoons with S.A.A. and material, and mules loaded with water and extra rations such as rum; and parties to form relay posts, were all sent off to H.Q., 2nd Grenadier Guards. The 75th Field Coy., R.E. had Orders to push on and consolidate the line held by the Coldstream and Irish Guards.

The water and rations were to go to H.Q., 2nd Grenadier Guards who were to distribute it among troops of the Brigade at that time under the Command of the O.C., 2nd Grenadier Guards and send a proportion up to the troops of the Brigade in the second objective. The Brigade Transport Officer, Captain Shaw Stewart, actually managed to get water and rations direct to H.Q., of the 2nd and 3rd Coldstream, while 1st Irish Guards sent for their's to H.Q., 2nd Grenadier Guards, but the R.E. failed to reach their destination partly owing to the fact that the R.E. Officer who had reconnoitred the position by day and was acting as guide was wounded on the way up. The work of the R.E. was therefore expended on strengthening the position of the 2nd Grenadier Guards.

The Relay Posts also failed to find the position of the H.Q., of the 2nd and 3rd Coldstream, with the result that Brigade H.Q., was never properly in touch with these Battalions throughout the 16th September.

The night of Sept., 15/16th passed without any event of importance. The enemy shelled the first objective freely as well as GINCHY Village and the GINCHY - DELVILLE WOOD ridge throughout the night. He also put up a barrage just behind the line held by the two Coldstream Battalions and the 1st Irish Guards, but this did not prevent these Battalions from working hard at the consolidation

of/

of their position. Before dawn on Sept., 16th these Battn's. withdrew the posts which, it may be remembered, they had thrown forward.

During Sept., 16th the Brigade remained in the same positions. The enemy shelled our positions very heavily at times especially that of the 2nd Grenadier Guards but casualties were comparatively slight in spite of the fact that all lines were greatly overcrowded.

At 4-30 P.M. Orders were received that the Brigade was to be relieved. The troops in the first objective were relieved by the 59th Brigade, 20th Division, while those in the second objective were relieved by two Companies of the 62nd Brigade, 21st Division. The relief of the last mentioned was not completed until after daylight on the 17th, and outgoing troops were subjected to somewhat heavy shell fire. Information had been received that the enemy intended to counter attack at 2 A.M. Battalions were warned and considerable suspense ensued but the attack never developed.

Battalions collected at the South West end of BERNAFAY WOOD where Cookers with a hot meal were awaiting Battalions. The Brigade marched out 970 strong and went into Camp at the CITADEL about 1½ miles South of FRICOURT.

Casualties during this Action were as follows :-

Unit.	Killed. O.	Killed. O.R.	Wounded. O.	Wounded. O.R.	Missing. O.	Missing. O.R.	Total.
2nd Bn. Gren. Gds.,	3	118	11	225	-	12	- 369.
2nd Bn. Cold. Gds.,	7	128	9	271	-	46	- 461.
3rd Bn. Cold.Gds.,	3	84	8	293	-	32	- 420.
1st Bn. Irish Gds.,	5	74	10	302	-	31	- 422.
Bde., M.G.Company.	-	24	3	60	1	5	- 93.
1st Gds. T.M.Btty.,	-	4	1	6	-	-	- 11.
Total :-	18	432	42	1157	1	126	- 1776.

In criticising this action in the light of after events the first point noticed is the loss of direction of the attack. As has already been mentioned the first reason for this was probably the fact of the attack being checked momentarily from about T.13.b.4.8. and in order to overcome this resistance, closing in on the place which was causing the trouble.

On the other hand the attack of the 2nd Guards Brigade on our right was driven from the line of its attack by the failure of the attack of the Division on their right and the consequent very heavy barrage and Machine Gun fire, which the enemy were able to bring to bear on that flank from the right. This also tended to drive our attack further to the left in too northerly a direction. Another reason for the loss of direction was the unevenness of the jumping off line along the whole front. These combined with the facts that the whole country was an unrecognisable desert of shell holes and that it was impossible to obtain a view of the country in front of our jumping off line, owing to the position of that line just on and not over the crest, contributed to the loss of direction in the attack. Precautions had been taken beforehand to lay out direction stakes for the Grenadier and Irish Guards, but this was not possible for the leading Battalions.

The feasibility of withdrawing the line in order to improve the jumping off line is doubted seeing that this line had been advanced to the point of the Orchard at the North East corner of GINCHY and that this Orchard was a place of considerable recrimination. The front line was only partially dug and free movement was difficult. An enterprising enemy might have noticed the withdrawal and the fruits of seizing the point of the Orchard would have been lost.

An important fact which considerably increased our casualties is that a Tank should have passed over the point T.3.b.2.9. where a Machine Gun was known to be and where afterwards, as has already been mentioned, four Machine Guns and some Trench Mortars were captured. Not only did the Tank never reach it's objective but a gap a 100 yards broad was left in it's

intended/

intended track so that the barrage never touched the vital point and these Machine Guns opened fire as soon as our troops left their trenches. Of the four captured Machine Guns one was allotted to each Battalion of the Brigade, to be retained as trophies by them after the War.

Immediately North of our Area on our left flank there was a German Salient that was dealt with by a special Tank just before Zero. It can be seen therefore, that the conditions for the launching of our attack could not have been worse and it would seem worth while always carrying out minor operations before hand in order to give troops a straight run at their objective and to have a straight and not a semi-circular creeping barrage put down in front of the leading troops.

Another point of some importance was that the attack in it's earliest stages was considerably helped by the enormous number of shell holes which allowed our troops to make short rushes over a distance of 400 yards right up to the very mouths of the Machine Guns in the GINCHY - FLERS Road.

Practically the only other point that calls for criticism is that of Communication, and the failure of Communication was also largely due to the loss of direction in the Attack, since it was thought up to a late hour on the 15th inst., both by Battalions and Brigade Head Quarters that the 2nd and 3rd Coldstream had established themselves in the third objective <u>in the Brigade Area</u>. The result of this was that every message and messenger from Brigade H.Q., was sent via the 2nd Grenadier Guards H.Q., in the 1st objective since it was thought that this Battalion was bound to be in touch with the two Coldstream Battalions presumed to be immediately to their front. As it was, however,,the 2nd Grenadier Guards were unaware of the position of the two Coldstream Battalions although these Battalions were fully aware of the position of the 2nd Grenadier Guards. Pigeons proved to be of the greatest use, but owing to haze, smoke, and the shelling of the various Stations Visual broke down altogether. As soon as the H.Q., of the 2nd Grenadier Guards was fixed a wire was laid to them but maintained with

some/

some difficulty. Runners got through every time but it should be noted that the first two or three runners sent back by Battn's. should be kept at Brigade Report Centres and sent back accompanied by as many Brigade Runners as possible.

Again the R.E. failed to reach their destination owing to the one guide they had being wounded. Parties in future should therefore have at least two guides.

Artillery Liaison Officers were sent forward with Battn., H.Q., which in this ambitious attack had to move forward with their Battalions. These Liaison Officers turned out to be of little use in sending back information to their Group and it would have been better to keep them and send them forward with lines to establish forward Observation Posts as soon as the situation in front had become clear.

Seconds in Commands went into action with their Battalions. A proportion of all other ranks of Officers and N.C.O's. were left behind with the Transport which proved to be a wise precaution. As regards Seconds in Command, all four became casualties and it would seem essential in the future that either the Second in Command of a Battalion or the Commanding Officer should be left behind.

One Machine Gun Section had been detailed to each Battn., but the long distance over which the attack had to be carried out and the pace of the Infantry caused the various Sections to arrive quite disorganised and scattered. Machine Gun Sections must be allowed to get over the ground in their own time.

From Sept., 17th to 20th the Brigade remained at the CITADEL. The weather was wet and cold and the Brigade was busily employed in absorbing drafts and getting out recommendations and narratives of past events.

On Sept., 18th the Brigade was warned to be ready to relieve the 20th Division in the line on the following day, but the relief and consequent operations were postponed 24 hours on account of the weather.

A Conference was held at 2nd Guards Brigade H.Q., on the afternoon of Sept., 19th, at which the scheme of future operations/

operations was outlined. The frontage and objectives of the Brigade for an attack, which was to take place on Sept., 23rd in conjunction with attacks by the French to the South and Reserve Army to the North, were outlined. The weather was still very unsettled and it was announced that any further postponement of operations would be for 48 hour periods.

During the evening of Sept., 19th a Conference of Commdg., Officers was held at Brigade H.Q., and the Scheme explained to them. As the front allotted to the Brigade was about 700 yards it had been decided to attack with 3 Battn's. in front and one in Support and it was also decided to put the three attacking Battn's. into the line on their battle fronts as soon as the Brigade went into the line.

Time being short the greater part of Sept., 20th was spent in drafting the Orders for the Attack on the 23rd, although no written Orders had yet been received from the Division. About 3 P.M. on Sept. 20th intimation was received from the Division that our frontage had been considerably lessened, so at the last moment the Orders for the relief of the 61st Brigade were changed and only the two Coldstream Battn's. were put into the line that night. This shortening of the Brigade Battle Front (to 500 yds.) meant that the attack could be carried out by two Battn's. instead of three and since the two Coldstream Battn's. had been in front in the attack on Sept. 15th, the Grenadier and Irish Guards were to do the next attack. The intention then was to put the two Coldstream Battn's. into the line and keep the Grenadier and Irish Guards out until the last possible moment.

At 6 P.M. on Sept. 20th the Brigade began moving by Coy's. from the CITADEL to relieve the 61st Brigade. It was raining hard and had been for three days which had made life in the CITADEL Camps most uncomfortable and restless and the cross country tracks well nigh impassable. All the roads were blocked by transport and the track from BERNAFAY WOOD through TRONES WOOD and thence North of GINCHY was simply a sea of mud. It was hardly surprising then that the relief of the 61st Brigade

was/

was not complete until 6-30 A.M. on the 21st and that the two Coldstream Battn's. arrived in the line in an exhausted condition. On this occasion all Battn's. had decided to take up their greatcoats with them which proved to be a wise and most necessary precaution as the nights were now becoming colder. Other spare kit and equipment, such as packs and caps, had again been stored at MEAULTE. It should also be mentioned that at the Conference held at the CITADEL on Sept. 19th it had been decided that the equipment carried by the troops in the attack on Sept. 15th had proved most satisfactory so that it was determined to keep it the same for the forthcoming attack. No further Orders therefore were issued on this subject. The question of Battn's. keeping their greatcoats up to the last possible moment had been raised and concurred with. Units were made responsible for making their own arrangements to get them back into the MEAULTE store. It might also be mentioned here that from Sept. 10th to Sept. 27th the 1st Line Transport remained Brigaded in bivouacs just South of CARNOY, with the exception that during both the periods while the Brigade was in the Line, pack animals were brought up and remained in the vicinity of BERNAFAY WOOD so as to be handy for carrying up Stores to form advanced dumps.

From Sept. 20th to Sept. 24th the two Coldstream Battn's. remained in the line while the 2nd Bn. Grenadier Guards were bivouaced in BERNAFAY WOOD and the 1st Bn. Irish Guards in TRONES WOOD. On Sept. 21st Orders were received that operations had been postponed 48 hours, from Sept. 23rd till Sept. 25th, and at the same time Orders were received that the battle front of the Brigade had again been changed. This change of front entailed a somewhat complicated relief on the night of Sept. 21st/22nd. On Sept. 20th when the Brigade went into the line the front held was roughly from a point 500 yards South of the GINCHY - LES BOEUFS Road about 500 yards West of LES BOEUFS to a point 200 yards North of that Road and 800 yards W. of LES BOEUFS. The troops of the 2nd and 3rd Coldstream Guards South of the Road were relieved by three different Regiments of the 16th and/

and 18th Infantry Bde's. - troops of the two Coldstream Battn's. thus relieved taking over a piece of the line and extending our line 300 yards further to the left. This relief then put the Brigade on it's Battle Front and as the line was considerably shorter than that held on Sept. 20th, two Coy's. of the Coldstream were sent back into Reserve in BERNAFAY WOOD.

On Sept. 20th the weather became fine and throughout the period from Sept. 20th to 24th, preparations for the next attack were pushed forward. The 3rd Guards Brigade had started digging an assembly trench about 150 yards in rear of our front line and this was continued nightly by the 75th Field Coy. R.E. and Work Platoons which had again been attached to the R.E. as soon as the Brigade moved up from the CITADEL. This trench was actually completed on the night of Sept. 23rd, being continuous, well traversed and narrow from the GINCHY - LES BOEUFS Road, which marked the right flank of the Brigade, to the old German communication trench 500 yards N. of the Road, which marked the left flank of the Brigade.

In the plan of assembly for the attack it had been decided to form up one Battn. in the communication trench, which marked the left flank of the Brigade, and the 3rd Coldstream Guards were given Orders to work on it to this purpose. This trench, which was nearly 800 yards in length, was in a very bad state being well over the knees in mud and after two nights work there was little signs of any improvement.

On the morning of Sept. 24th another old German communication trench was found in the Brigade Area. This trench was in excellent order but it ended 500 yards short of the Reserve Line (SERPENTINE TRENCH) which it was essential that it should be joined to if it was to be of any use. It was finally decided that the R.E. and Work Platoons with a party of 350 from the two Coldstream Battn's. should dig it through on the night of Sept. 24th/25th, and that when completed the 2nd Coldstream Guards should use it as their assembly trench. This was actually done and the trench proved of the greatest value both

as/

as an assembly trench and as a communication trench on the day of the attack. The fact that it was not dug until the night before the attack prevented the enemy from registering on it and probably also prevented a large number of casualties. The other old German communication trench which marked the left flank of the Brigade was very heavily barraged on the day of the attack.

Meanwhile during these few days the Grenadier and Irish Guards had been employed in carrying and Salvage Work. An Advanced Brigade Dump of bombs, S.A.A., rations, water, R.E. material, was formed in the hollow about W.8.c.central. Most of this work was done by day with very little interruption from hostile shelling. The 2nd and 3rd Coldstream Guards were thus left free to carry out all the work needed on the front, support and reserve lines of trenches. The rations of the two Coldstream Battalions were when necessary carried up by the Grenadier or Irish Guards. All this work was considerably facilitated by the use of Brigaded pack animals, which as has already been mentioned, were kept well forward near Brigade H.Q. and used for carrying all kinds of Stores to the new forward Dumps as well as for carrying up rations.

About 8 P.M. on Sept. 21st, written Orders for an attack to be carried out on Sept. 23rd were received from Divnl. H.Q. Later on the same day the date of the attack was altered to Sept. 25th. These written Orders differed little from the verbal Orders issued at previous Divisional and Brigade Conferences The only question that as yet remained unsettled was the boundaries of the Brigade, but as this did not affect the general plan of attack Brigade Orders for the attack were issued about 11 P.M. on Sept. 21st.

The attack of the Guards Division was to be carried out in conjunction with attacks along a wide front both on the left and right of the Division. The 1st Guards Brigade were to attack on the right of the Guards Division - the 3rd Guards Brigade on the/

the left - while the 18th Brigade of the 6th Division were to attack on the right of the 1st Guards Brigade. The 2nd Guards Brigade were to be in Divisional Reserve. The attack of the 1st Guards Brigade was to be carried out by the 2nd Bn. Grenadier Guards on the right and 1st Bn. Irish Guards on the left. The 2nd Coldstream Guards were to support the attack of the 2nd Grenadier Guards on the right while the 3rd Coldstream Guards were to support that of the 1st Irish Guards on the left. The 2nd and 3rd Coldstream Guards were placed under the Command of Lt-Col. J.V.Campbell, D.S.O. 3rd Bn. Coldstream Guards.

Three distinct objectives were allotted to the Brigade :-

	Marked on the Map by -	Distance from Front Line -	Hour of advance to attack on -
1st objective -	Green Line.	350 yards.	12-35 P.M.
2nd objective -	Brown Line.	800 yards.	1-35 P.M.
3rd objective -	Blue Line.	1,400 yards.	2-35 P.M.

The assault of all three objectives was to be carried out by the two leading Battn's. i.e. the 2nd Grenadier Guards and 1st Irish Guards. The two Coldstream Battn's. were to move forward in support, moving via communication trenches to the front and support lines when these were clear and across the open to the Green and Brown Lines as soon as these were clear of the leading Battn's. The 2nd and 3rd Coldstream Guards were however each to send a Company up to shell holes just in rear of the Brown Line during the pause at that line by the leading Battn's. The task of these two Coy's. provided with a special supply of "P" Bombs and Mills Grenades, was to clear the dug-outs and cellars in LES BOEUFS in rear of the two leading Battn's. who would thus be left free to devote all their efforts to gaining and consolidating the final objective.

The supporting Battn's. were to be prepared :-

(i) to form a defensive flank either on the right or left.

(ii) to make good the 1st and 2nd objectives.

(iii) if necessary, to give any additional support required for the attack on the final objective.

The/

The Machine Gun Company which had suffered heavy casualties in the fighting on Sept. 15th and 16th, was formed into three sections of 4 guns each. Each of those Sections was given a definite task and was to move in its own time and by the best route available. As soon as possible after each of the three objectives had been captured one Section was to be sent forward to help in the consolidation of the captured line. When the final objective was reached there were to be 4 Guns in the final objective and 8 Guns in reserve in the Brown Line or second objective. There were always to be two Guns ready to form a defensive flank to the right.

The Trench Mortar Battery were ordered to place two Guns in position on the right of the Brigade Area previous to the attack, covering the Sunken Road which lead down into LES BOEUFS. These two Guns were to moveforward at the first available opportunity and establish themselves on the right of the 1st objective (Green Line). Two more Guns of the Battery were to remain in reserve in the front line and were only to move forward if ordered to do so by Lt-Col. Campbell or the Brigadier.

The 75th Field Coy. R.E. and Work Platoons were to remain in reserve in the reserve line (SERPENTINE TRENCH). An Officer and three orderlies were detailed to be in Liaison with Lt-Col. Campbell.

The Ammunition portion of 1st Line Transport was to be in position on the South side of BERNAFAY WOOD by 12 noon, while the remainder of the Transport remained in it's Lines near CARNOY. Pack animals were kept on the West side of TRONES WOOD ready for immediate use in carrying up rations, water or other necessaries.

The hour of the attack was not known until later, but it was previously made known that the attack would not take place until some time during the afternoon of Sept. 25th. This fact made the question of assembly for the attack a most important one. The assembly march was carried out on the night of Sept.

24th/25th without difficulty and by 1 A.M. all Units were in position as follows with the exception of the R.E., Work Platoons and 350 men of the 2nd and 3rd Coldstream Guards (all employed on digging the new communication trench already mentioned and finally completed by 3 A.M. on the 25th) :-

<u>2nd Gren.Gds.</u> - Battn.H.Q. and 2 Coy's. in front line, 2 Coy's. in new support line, Right of Battn. on the GINCHY - LES BOEUFS Road, Left of Battn. about 250 yards N. of the Road.

<u>1st Irish Gds.</u>- 2 Coy's. in front line, 2 Coy's. in new support line from Left of 2nd Gren.Gds. to an old German C.T. about 250 yards further North. Battn. H.Q. in a diagonal C.T. about the centre of the Line.

<u>2nd Cold.Gds.</u> - Partly in old C.T. and partly in newly dug C.T. about the centre of the Brigade Area.

<u>3rd Cold.Gds.</u>,- in Reserve Line or SERPENTINE TRENCH.

<u>M.G.Company.</u> - 1 Section behind centre of front line, 2 Guns on right and 2 Guns on left of the front line. 1 Section in Reserve in SERPENTINE TRENCH.

The Orders for the assembly march contained very strict instructions that no fires were to be lit and that there was to be as little movement as possible before ZERO, while bayonets were not to be fixed (except by a percentage of the leading Battn's. representing the normal garrison) until two minutes before the attack was timed to start.

Again, before passing to the execution of the attack, it is necessary to give some idea of the lie of the land and other points governing the carrying out of the assault. From our front line the ground sloped gradually down to LES BOEUFS which could be plainly seen about 1,000 yards away. Beyond LES BOEUFS the ground in front of the Brigade Area could not be seen, nor could it be seen to the South of the Brigade Area, but to the North it could be and appeared open though undulating and cultivated. The enemy's front line, which constituted our first objective about 350 yards away, was hidden from view on the right of the Brigade Area by a dip in the ground but otherwise most of the ground over which our attack had to pass was under good observation from our own O.P's. The enemy's front line appeared to be heavily wired but the Artillery reported that it

had/

had been well cut by the evening of Sept. 24th, except for a small portion on the right of the Brigade Front, where as already mentioned, no observation was possible from any point of our front. Nowhere was the ground very badly cut up by shell fire, in fact just behind the new support line there was a standing crop of wheat. Surrounding fields consisted for the most part of stubble or grass and the going had become excellent as the weather had been dry and fine since Sept. 21st.

Communication with the front line was always possible by day, via the old German C.T. which marked the left flank of the Brigade. In the actual attack, after leaving our front line, the left flank of the Brigade was not definitely marked by any natural feature of the ground, but the right flank throughout was marked by the GINCHY - LES BOEUFS Road which considerably assisted in the maintenance of direction both before and during the attack itself.

From the Map it appeared that the ground East of LES BOEUFS and in front of our final objective contained a decided hollow beyond which it rose again to about the same level as the ground where our final objective was to be/ The attention of C.O's. was drawn to this point in a special memo issued previous to the attack and the necessity for pushing out patrols to gain good ground for observation was again impressed on Battn's.

All the objectives allotted to the Brigade were recognisable on the ground and not merely lines drawn across the Map. Excellent photographs of the ground to be traversed were obtainable and as far as could be seen the enemy had only one real trench line with which to oppose our advance and that his front line, not 350 yards distant from our own front line. The other objectives were or followed closely the lines of roads. With regard to the objectives of the Brigade, there is only one other point to be borne in mind. As has been already mentioned the right flank of the Brigade was marked by the GINCHY - LES BOEUFS Road, South of which was the 18th Infantry Brigade of the 6th Division. Now their front line was not a continuation of

ours/

ours but was thrown forward about 350 yards and was a continuation to the South of the German trench which formed our first objective. Consequently, during the time of our advance to the 1st objective, the troops of the 18th Infantry Brigade were to remain stationary, making no advance until we moved forward to the attack of the 2nd objective, when they moved forward in line with us. A result of this feature in the line was that arrangements were made for a Machine Gun of the 18th Brigade to sweep our 1st objective with fire until our creeping barrage lifted from the 1st objective. This Machine Gun fire turned out subsequently to have been a great help in keeping enemy heads down along the right of our 1st objective, thereby allowing the 2nd Grenadier Guards to get to work with the bayonet with much less resistance than would otherwise have been possible.

Sept. 25th was a fine clear day and up to 12 noon had been fairly quiet. The attack was launched at 12-35 P.M. and subsequently from prisoners it was learnt that the hour of attack came as a complete surprise to the enemy though they expected an attack in the early morning or evening of the same day. At 12-35 P.M. the creeping barrage was put down 200 yards in front of our front line and at the same moment the 2nd Grenadier Guards and 1st Irish Guards advanced in two waves at 75 yards distance to the assault of the 1st objective. The 2nd Grenadier Guards on the right advanced in two waves with 2 Coy's. in each wave, while the 1st Irish Guards on the left sent forward their leading 2 Coy's. only to the assault of the 1st objective, keeping the remaining two in reserve with Orders to move into our front trench under cover as soon as the trench was clear of the leading two Coy's. Within about 1 minute of the launching of the attack the enemy put down a heavy barrage on our front, support and communication trenches and also on 'No Man's Land' immediately in front of our front line. The leading wave however was able to get close up under our creeping barrage within a minute - i.e. by 12-36 P.M. -

and/

and as soon as the barrage lefted off the first objective they captured it at the point of the bayonet. The 1st Irish Guards experienced very little difficulty in doing this but the 2nd Grenadier Guards were not so fortunate as the German wire on their front had been very little damaged by our Artillery fire. Captain A.K.S.CUNNINGHAME, Lieut., G.ARBUTHNOT, Lieut., IRVINE and other Officers at this stage set an excellent example by making their men lie down just outside the wire and themselves going forward to cut the wire. The result was that many Officers were unfortunately picked off by the enemy. In spite of this however, the wire was cut and the whole of the 1st objective was in our hands by 1-15 P.M. This first German line was very strongly held - Some hand-to-hand fighting took place but did not last long and a large number of Germans were killed and many more made prisoners. Three Machine Guns were also captured in this line. By 1-30 P.M. the whole of the two leading Battn's. were concentrated in the 1st objective. The rear two Coy's. of the 1st Irish Guards had experienced much difficulty owing to the hostile barrage in moving under cover from our support to our front line and eventually they gave this up and moved across the open to the front line and then on to the 1st objective.

At 1-35 P.M. the advance to the second objective began, close up under our creeping barrage. The opposition to this advance was feeble. Some more prisoners were made and some Dug-outs in the Sunken Roads on the right of the 2nd Grenadier Guards were bombed and a large number of casualties caused to the enemy. By 1-45 P.M. the second objective had been gained; the line held being that of the road which marks the Western edge of the Village of LES BOEUFS. Touch was gained between Battn's. and with Battn's. of Brigades on the right and left. During the pause at this objective the Company of the 2nd Coldstream Guards detailed for the clearing up of LES BOEUFS closed up in rear of the 2nd Grenadier Guards according to programme, and again according to programme at 2-35 P.M. the advance began on the 3rd objective through the Village of LES BOEUFS. It met with little opposition so that by 2-45 P.M. the two leading Battn's. were established on a line about 100 yards East of the Road which marksthe Eastern edge of LES BOEUFS Village. Consolidation was at once begun and was carried on until dark without any interference on the part of the enemy, except from a few snipers. The enemy were seen retiring in one's and two's over a ridge some 800 yards in front; small parties were also seen and patrols sent forward - some of these parties surrendering to the patrols. Touch was maintained between the two leading Battn's. and the 2nd Grenadier Guards were in touch with the 1st West Yorks. on their right who were also firmly established on the East of the Southern half of LES BOEUFS. The Irish Guards were by this time in touch with one weak Company of 1st Grenadier Guards on their left but as the situation on this flank appeared somewhat doubtful a Company of the 3rd Coldstream Gds. was moved up to secure and help in the consolidation of this flank. It was about this time that the only real hitch in the attack occurred. It had been arranged that the Artillery barrage should be put down 200 yards East of the final objective. The barrage was short, probably because the final objective was marked different-:ly on the Artillery and Infantry Maps and this caused a good many casualties amongst our own troops while they were digging in. It was nearly two hours before this mistake could be rectified and before the barrage could be lifted to a line about 400 yards in front of the line on which our troops were digging in. The shortness of the barrage prevented patrols pushing forward and establishing themselves on the best ground for observation purposes.

Meanwhile the 2nd and 3rd Coldstream Guards had been pushing forward in accordance with the plan of attack. Both these Battn's. moved up by the new communication trench to the support line, thence across the open to the 1st objective where by 2-15 P.M. they were concentrated. The movement up the communication trench was a slow and somewhat tedious one owing partly to congestion and partly to heavy enemy barrage about the front and support lines, but as the other communication trench marking the left flank of the Brigade was hravily barraged there can be little doubt that the digging and use of this new communication trench saved a large number of casualties. From the 1st objective, as has already been mentioned,

each/

each of these two Battn's. had sent on a Company to advance in close support in rear of the leading Battn's. as they advanced to the final objective, while the remainder of these Battn's. moved forward to the Brown Line (2nd objective) as soon as it was clear of the leading Battn's. They reached and began to consolidate this line shortly before 3 P.M. About 3-30 P.M. another Company of the 2nd Coldstream Guards was sent up to support the 2nd Grenadier Guards in the Blue Line and later in the afternoon the whole of the 3rd Coldstream Guards less half a Company, moved up and dug in in close support about 150 yards in rear of the line occupied by the 1st Irish Guards.

The movements of the Machine Gun Company and Trench Mortar Battery were executed according to programme with very few casualties Captain Meakin, Commanding Trench Mortar Battery, was unfortunately killed early during the day by a shell and one of the reserve guns buried. The reserve Guns of the T. M. Battery however were not required to come into action.

Thus at 6-45 P.M. when the Staff Captain returned from visiting the H.Q., of the Battn's. the situation appeared to be most satisfactory. All Battn's. were in the highest spirits. There was practically no hostile shelling East of the 1st objective and the hostile barrage about our old front line and 'No Man's Land' had died down considerably. The consolidation of the 2nd and 3rd objectives was well in hand the only difficulty apparently being that there was a shortage of shovels in the Irish Guards Sector. The R.E. and Work Platoons had already gone up with all available shovels to help in the consolidation of the Blue Line and at 7 P.M. 1 Company of the 4th Coldstream Guards and 2 Sections 76th Field Coy., R.E. were sent up to consolidate the Brown Line. A telephone wire was laid by 7 P.M. to H.Q., of 2nd Grenadier Guards, 3rd Coldstream Guards and 1st Irish Guards all of whose H.Q., had been established in the Brown Line in close proximity to each other. In fact throughout the day communication had worked almost without interruption. The wire to the most forward Brigade Report Centre which was in the communication trench marking the left of the

Brigade/

Brigade and just behind the front line was kept going practically throughout in spite of breaks. Relay Runner Posts were established at intervals between the most forward Report Centre and Brigade H.Q., and were useful in supplementing the wire.

Finally about 6 P.M. the 2nd Grenadier Guards reported that there appeared to be no enemy for some distance in front and suggested that Cavalry might be sent through. The Corps however, ruled that the general situation did not permit of this.

The night of Sept. 25th/26th was a quiet one and the Brigade Transport Officer - Captain W.G.SHAW STEWART, and Lieut. VEREKER - Transport Officer of the 2nd Grenadier Guards, experienced little difficulty in getting up water, rum, etc., to all Battn's. It should be mentioned that SERPENTINE Trench had been bridged during the attack in order to allow mule convoys to move Eastwards across country rather tan along the heavily shelled GINCHY - LES BOEUFS Road. During the night, Battn's. were ordered to thin out their line and hold the ground in depth as much as possible but in spite of this it was found that Battn's. were still far too crowded the next morning and it was not till about midday on Sept. 26th that the Brigade was properly distributed in depth. By daylight on the 26th four strong points had been made in or just in rear of the Blue Line, while other strong points had also been constructed in the Brown Line. R.E., Work Platoons and the Company of 4th Coldstream Guards withdrawing to their previous positions before daylight.

The early morning of the 26th was very quiet. Germans in two's and three's were seen running about apparently unarmed in front of our new front line and it was during this period of the operations that several good chances were missed by the Artillery owing to the F.O.O. having no means of communication with his Battery and not informing the Infantry Liaison Officer of his position.

It was only about this time that the importance of the ridge 800 yards East of LES BOEUFS was realised. The Maps did

not/

not show this ridge as being so clearly defined and consequently it had not been arranged for barrage to lift beyond it and allow patrols to get out onto it. About 11 A.M. on the 26th however, arrangements to this effect were made and the 2nd Grenadier Guards and 1st Irish Guards were instructed to try and push patrols forward at 1 P.M. This they did, but by this time the enemy had established a strong line of posts with Machine Guns about 500 yards in front and the patrols were unable to get out more than 300 yards.

Meanwhile at about 9 A.M. the enemy had started to shell LES BOEUFS very heavily. This shelling continued throughout the whole day but as the shelling was confined to LES BOEUFS and the Sunken Roads on the West of the Village and did not touch our new trenches East of the Village, casualties were not so heavy as might have been expected.

Casualties during this Action were as follows :-

U n i t.	Killed. O.	O.R.	Wounded. O.	O.R.	Missing. O.	O.R.	Total.	
2nd Bn. Gren. Gds.,	4	108	5	222	-	12	-	351.
2nd Bn. Cold. Gds.,	3	15	3	64	-	5	-	90.
3rd Bn. Cold. Gds.,	-	20	3	113	-	11	-	147.
1st Bn. Irish Gds.,	1	32	7	191	-	7	-	238.
Bde. M.G.Company.	-	4	-	9	-	-	-	13.
1st Gds. T.M.Btty.,	1	1	-	5	-	-	-	7.
Total :-	9	180	18	604	-	35	-	846.

Orders had been received earlier on the 26th that the 1st and 3rd Guards Brigades would be relieved during the night by the 2nd Guards Brigade. All Infantry of the 1st Guards Brigade were relieved by the 2nd Bn. Irish Guards. The relief of the Brigade was complete by 11-30 P.M. and the 2nd and 3rd Coldstream Guards moved to bivouac ar CARNOY: the 2nd Grenadier Guards and 1st Irish Guards to the CITADEL. The Machine Gun Company was not relieved until the next night.

There is little that calls for criticism in the action of Sept. 25th. The fact that patrols were unable owing to our barrage to push forward and seize good ground for observation after/

after reaching the final objective has already been mentioned. With reference to this point, it must also be borne in mind that the ridge was entirely unexpected and that the situation on the left flank of the Brigade being very obscure up to an early hour on the 26th, prevented the pushing forward of our line 800 yards apparently into the air.

Artillery Liaison with the front line was not good and several chances were missed. It is true that Liaison Officers were sent up early on the morning of the 26th to H.Q., of the 2nd Grenadier Guards and 1st Irish Guards but only one of these had a wire up to him which he was unable to maintain owing to repeated casualties. What was wanted was an O.P. with a wire to it in the front line the position of which all Liaison Officers were aware.

The lesson to be learnt both from the attack of Sept. 25th and that of Sept. 15th appears to be that there must always be the closest touch between Infantry and Artillery. Prior to an attack Infantry Officers with Artillery representatives must inspect the wire and if necessary the Infantry must send out patrols at night to make further reconnoissances. In an attack where Battn. H.Q., move forward into the blue and not by bounds from one definite line of trenches to another it is of little use sending Artillery Liaison Officers with Battn. H.Q., but they should be sent up when Battn. H.Q., have been finally established. Liaison Officers are most useful when Battn. H.Q., move forward from line to line. Some arrangements must be made before an attack for the establishment of an O.P. with a wire to it in a certain forward area as soon as possible after an attack so that Liaison Officers can know where to look for it and to communicate the requirements of the Infantry quickly through the most direct channel. The question of some kind of light signal etween Infantry and Artillery has been raised as a result of se attacks and it would seem possible to evolve a simple code i the coloured lights already in existance. It is possible to ve a code of 7 signals if 1½" Very Pistols are used i.e. 3 co red lights used singly or in combination.

om/

From the attacks on Sept. 15th and Sept. 25th, many of the lessons from the previous fighting on the SOMME have been emphasised while new points have been brought to light. The latter are :-

(1) The advantage of a good jumping off line parallel to the objectives to be attacked.

(2) Every man to carry a tool; if possible, some lighter tool with some definite arrangement for carrying it is required. The 1st Irish Guards arrived at the final objective short of shovels owing to the fact that men had begun to dig after the capture of the first and second objectives and when they advanced to the final objective they left their tools behind.

(3) Every man to be a bomber and to be trained if possible in use of German bombs. Bombing Sections are of little value in big attacks as they are too slow and get easily broken up. Badge men always come to the fore and set an example to the remainder.

(4) Machine Guns.

(a) Must not be expected to keep pace with the Infantry. They must be given definite objectives and advance in their own time and by the best route.

(b) Some Guns to be detailed for defensive flanks.

(c) Some kind of cover for Guns to prevent them being clogged by mud are required.

(5) Lewis Guns.

(a) Like Machine Guns cannot be expected to keep pace with Infantry and should be handled as in para's. 4. (a) and (b) above.

(b) A larger supply of hoppers is necessary.

(c) Most valuable with a bombing party. A Lewis Gun was found to keep the German bombers heads down while our own bombers could stand up and show their heads over the parapet without any enemy interference.

(6) Communications.

(a) Visual of no use owing to smoke, haze, and to their liability to be picked up and shelled.

(b) Pigeons of great value but baskets for single birds required.

(c) Runner Relay Posts essential but runners must carry no equipment except smoke helmets. They should dump their kit at their Post. They are invaluable for guiding individuals or parties.

(7)/

(7) Arrangements to be made for our barrage to get well beyond the final objective so that patrols may get out.

(8) Objectives to be very carefully marked on all Maps. They must not be marked by thick lines drawn at random across the Map.

(9) Units must be prepared to do their own carrying on and after the day of attack, but Brigade assists by formation of Dump as far forward as possible and by maintaining it by convoys of pack animals.

(10) The use of pack animals for bringing up rations, etc.,

(11) If held up by uncut wire a few men to go forward and cut the wire while the remainder lie down and shoot as hard as possible to keep enemy heads down.

(12) <u>Contact Aeroplane</u>.

(a) The Battalion Code Numbers to be carried on one sheet.

(b) A larger supply of flares necessary.

The following lessons learnt in previous fighting are the most important of those emphasized by the fighting on Sept. 15th and 25th.

(1) Necessity for keeping close to the creeping barrage.

(2) Necessity for getting as many men as possible across 'No Man's Land' as soon as possible after Zero. On Sept. 25th within 1 minute of Zero the German barrage came down on our front line.

(3) Necessity for consolidating any position gained without delay, since this is always the quietest time and preventing all unnecessary movement of men on account of the momentary lack of hostile shelling.

(4) Necessity for pushing out patrols and establishing them on good positions in front of the final objective.

(5) Necessity for thinning out from front to rear as soon as possible after final objective has been taken. Troops required for purposes of consolidation must not be forgotten.

(6) Forward Dumps of all Stores (rations, bombs, water, S.A.A., R.E. Material) to be organised by Brigade H.Q., as far forward as possible for Units to draw from on and after the day of attack.

(7)/

(7) Reconnaissance of captured positions by Staff and R.E. Officers.

(8) The absolute reliance that may be placed on the reports of Contact Aeroplanes as to the positions reached by our troops.

Captain,

Brigade Major, 1st Guards Brigade.

APPENDIX "A".

September 15th.

	Advanced Dump. (WATERLOT FM. GUILLEMONT RD.)	Brigade H.Q., Dump.
Wire cutters	200	-
Mills Grenades	4,800	3;600
Mills Rifle Grenades	2,400	2,000
Blank S.A.A., (rounds)	7,000	5,000
"P" Grenades	500	500
S.A.A., (rounds)	100,000	-
Water (2 gallon tins)	200	100
Flares	400	-
Rockets, sticks, & port-fires	100	-

September 25th.

	Advanced Dump. T.8.central.	Brigade H.Q., Dump.
Shovels	200	-
Mills Grenades	4,800	4,800
Mills Rifle Grenades	2,400	1,000
Blank S.A.A., (rounds)	7,000	5,000
"P" Grenades	500	500
Flares	400	400
Rockets, sticks, & port-fires	50	-
Rations	1,800 (90 Boxes)	-
S.A.A., (rounds)	100,000	100,000
Water (2 gallon tins)	170	100
Wire cutters	-	200

NARRATIVES OF EVENTS 13th to 17th
September 1916

2nd Grenadier Gds.
2nd Coldstream Gds.
3rd Coldstream Gds.
1st Irish Gds.
CONGRATULATORY MESSAGES

Narrative of Events from Sept., 13th - 17th, 1916.

On Sept. 13th the battalion was holding the Northern Sector of the GINCHY line. Orders were received that we were to straighten the line by an attack that night in order to form a good jumping off place for the big attack on the 15th. No.4 Company was detailed for this and No.2 Company were ordered to protect their left flank and join up with them. The operation was a difficult one as the left of the attack had to advance further than the right in order to form a line facing N.E.; there was also a bright moon which showed up our attacking party very plainly. 30 or 40 shrapnel were fired at the German trench just North of the Orchard but did very little good and the Germans were on the alert and met No.4 Company, under 2/Lieut., Minchin, with heavy rifle and machine gun fire causing some casualties. The ~~Orchar~~ party cleared the Orchard, killing some Germans who were in shell holes, and dug in, a line to the edge of the Orchard, after a fruitless attempt to push on. They were shot at heavily the whole time but completed their trench before morning.

On the 14th the whole of the battalion front was bombarded all day by 4'5 and 5'9 shells and the line was much knocked about and the Coys. all rather shaken. We were relieved that night by the 2nd and 3rd Bn's. Coldstream Guards and went into bivouac in shell holes a few hundred yards behind GINCHY, where rations were given out and rum issued. A bitterly cold night and no great-coats.

At 6-20 A.M. on 15th our bombardment began and we moved off in two lines of platoon blobs. The German barrage dropped before we reached GINCHY and we went through the middle of it, on the whole losing extraordinarily few men considering the intensity of the fire. At about 6-40 A.M. we halted in GINCHY, luckily the bulk of the barrage was on the South edge but we lost a good many men and Captain Lloyd.

About 20 minutes later we decided to push on out and clear of GINCHY and remained for a short time in shell holes. We saw nothing of the Coldstream Battalions. At 7-20 A.M. we moved on towards our objective with our right on the SUNKEN ROAD. We came at once under machine gun fire from our left front and after a while rifle fire from our right and a good many men went down, including several Officers.

The left Companies were held up by rifle fire from the Green Line, which appeared to be held strongly from about T 8 d 3.8 to T 8 a 8.4.

The right Companies pushed on into the Green Line and our right was in touch with some of the 3rd Bn. Grenadier Guards, 2nd Guards Brigade; who were attempting to stop the Germans from turning their right flank. One platoon of No.1 Company and a Machine Gun was rushed over and succeeded in forming a defensive flank and preventing the Germans, of whom there were a considerable number, from working up behind us. The Division on our right had apparently failed and the Germans were very thick in their trenches and were shooting hard at us. We lost the bulk of our casualties during this period.

The centre of the battalion then rushed a part of the Green Line and bayoneted all Germans they found. The left were unable to get on. Almost as soon as the centre got in the Germans began bombing down the trench very strongly having 3 or 4 men throwing. Our bombers could not stop them and C.S.M. Norton, who was lying out by the wire with some men rushed them and stopped the attack for the time.

All availavle bombs were then collected and a party began to work up the trench but was met by a furious bomb attack and driven back some way most of the bombers being knocked out. We were forced back some way and to relieve the pressure, as the men were rather overwhelmed by the shower of bombs, and all British bombs had been finished, Captain Hancourt Vernon organized and led a bayonet charge over the top, killing the bombing party and driving the remainder back 40 or 50 of whom surrendered.

Our bombing party worked North along the trench until the Germans broke and ran across the open towards the Blue Line. Having cleared the trench for some way we began to consolidate. Two small parties of Germans tried to enter the trench on the left but were dealt with by our Lewis Guns.

During the evening our troops retired from the Blue Line across our front followed at not more than 100 yards by a large body of Germans. They were shot at and lay down in the grass. As it was getting dark it was difficult to see them and fire was ordered to be withheld in the hopes that they would attack, and they were being continually reinforced.
Nothing happened, however, during the night.
On the 16th we were very heavily shelled for most of the day from the front and direct enfilade from the left. We were shot at continuously from our right rear, but this eased after our snipers had killed a good many.

We were relieved on 17th about 2 A.M. by the 13th K/R.R.

19/9/16.

(Sd.) C. de CRESPIGNY, Lt-Col.;
Commdg., 2nd Bn. Grenadier Guards.

1st Guards Brigade.

Narative of operations 14th to 16th Sept., 1916.
2nd Bn. Coldstream Guards.

Ref Map 57C S.W. 1/10,000.

On the evening of the 14th Sept. 2nd Bn. Coldstream Guards (1st Guards Bde.,) marched from CARNOY and reached GINCHY Village about midnight. Taking over trenches held by part o the 2nd Bn. Grenadier Guards to 2nd Coldstream Guards moved into its attack formation thus :-

No.3 Coy. { ——— ——— } No.4 Coy.

No.1 Coy. { ——— ——— } No.2 Coy.

Battn., H.Q.,

On a front of 250 yards with a distance between lines of 50 yards the objective being the enemy trench running from about T.8.d.2.9. to T.8.a.4. the assault having to be made over a distance of about 1000 yards.

At ZERO 6-20 A.M. on the 15th the Battn., with 3rd Bn. Coldstream Guards on the left and the 1st Bn. Coldstream Guards (2nd Guards Bde.,) on the right advanced to the assault. The 2nd Bn. Grenadier Guards being in Support, the 1st Bn. Irish Guards in Reserve.
On emerging from the GINCHY Wood the Battn., became under very heavy machine gun fire from the front and the left flank and the 3rd Bn. Coldstream Guards were momentary checked; this caused the 1st Bn. Coldstream Guards and the 2nd Bn. Coldstream Guards to swing slightly round and when the line again advanced the direction of the attack had changed a point to the North. The 3rd Bn. Coldstream Guards having satisfactorily dealt with the machine gun fire on the left the line advanced behind our artillery barrage and captured an unexpected enemy trench, killing and taking prisoner many of the enemy.

The enemy artillery now opened and the advance continued under a galling fire.

Another unexpected line of trenches was encountered about 600 yards from the start but by this time the enemy were in full retreat and our own artillery barrage having lifted the first objective (Green Line) was rushed and captured with little opposition at 7-15 A.M.

Casualties up to this point had been very heavy and I was only able to find 2 Officers to assist in the reorganization of the Battalion.

After a consultation between the O.C., 3rd C.Gds., O.C., 1st C.Gds., and myself it was decided that it was impossible to advance further until a strong point, still held by the enemy (about T.8.d.4.5.) commanding the whole ground in front of the 2nd objective had been captured.
About 11 A.M. this was accomplished by the troops on the right and a further advance was made by 2nd and 3rd C. Gds., thro' an appalling enemy barrage to the 2nd objective (Brown Line) and the continuation of it running East to LES BOEUFS.
The line held by the 1st Guards Brigade then being roughly from T.2.c.4.7 to T.2.d. central.

This line was occupied about 1 P.M. and posts were sent forward to the FLERS - LES BOEUFS road where they weremained till dark when they were ordered to fall back on the trench which was being consolidated.

About 7 P.M. a counter-attack was made on our right exposed flank; this was easily repulsed. At the same time the 2nd Bn. Scots Guards attempted to reinforce but were prevented by the enemy barrage, a few men only succeeded in reaching our position. Except for a continuous enemy barrage behind our line the night of the 15th/16th was comparatively quiet; the line was strengthened and the troops reorganized.

From daylight on the 16th the enemy shelled our position and the lines in rear continuously all day but our casualties were not heavy.

The night 16th/17th was quiet and at dawn on the 17th the line was relieved by a Battalion of the Lincolnshire Regiment.

The casualties of the Battalion during the above mentioned dates were :- Officers killed 4: Died of wounds:2; Wounded 10; Other Ranks approximately :- Killed wounded and missing 400.

I submit herewith a list of Officers, N.C.O's and Men who I consider worthy of some special award for personal bravery, devotion to duty and steady behaviour.

18/9/16.

(Sd.) R.B.J.CRAWFURD, Lt-Col.,
Commdg., 2nd Bn. Coldstream Gds.,

3rd Bn. Coldstream Guards.

Operations from the 14th to 16th Sept., 1916.

At 8.0 P.M. on the 14th the Battalion marched from CARNOY by Coys. and relieved 2nd Bn. Grenadier Guards in the line at North end of GINCHY (T.13.a.). The Battalion formed up for the attack in rear of the line.
Order of attack.:- Battalion in 4 waves of half coy. columns at 50 yards distance.
No.1 Coy. on Right Front. No;2 Coy. Left Front.
No.4 " " " Support. No.3 " " Support.

2nd Bn. Coldstream Guards on Right, K.O.Y.L.I. on left.

A fine clear night and a beautiful morning.

At about 5-30 A.M. we could see the Tanks operating on our left, and the line on that flank advanced without meeting any opposition.

At 6-20 A.M. the attack was launched. The leading waves were immediately caught and literally mowed down by M.G. and rifle fire; apparently from 'Sunken Road' about 400 yards ahead. The advance was momentarily checked and then swept on and on, over the 'Sunken Road', through another position 600 yards further on, and without a check to the "Green Line", where the line was established at 7-15 A.M. I established my H.Q., on this line and put out my H.Q., Signal for the aeroplanes.

The line was halted with difficulty. It was a collection of Grenadiers, Coldstream and Irish of both 1st and 2nd Brigades. The casualties had been very heavy and there was very few Officers left. I consulted with Lt-Col., R.B.J.Crawfurd, D.S.O. 2nd C.Gds. Lt-Col., the Hon. G.U.Baring, 1st C.Gds., and Lt-Col. R.C.A.McCalmont, 1st I.Gds., and decided that we had got to our 3rd objective. This information I sent back by pigeon.

Consolidation was started under great difficulties owing to constant barrage, lack of Officers, and enfilade fire from a hostile strong point on our right. Later, I discovered that the line we were holding was only the 1st objective. I therefore ordered all officers to reorganize and to pass the men of 2nd Guards Brigade to the Right to turn the enemy strong point, and prepared for a further advance.

At about 10.0 A.M. I ordered the Coldstream to advance, and took the Brown Line. The barrage was intense and M.G. enfilade fire from the right made the advance very difficult. At about 11.0 A.M. the strong point was taken and our line advanced and reached the 2nd objective (Brown Line) which the enemy had evacuated. Posts were put out 600 yards to the front and consolidation was begun, and a message sent back to the Irish Guards to come on.

At 1.45 P.M. I reported that a further advance could not be made without reinforcements as I had only a few men left. The enemy barrage continued throughout the day and we could see the enemy gradually coming back towards us.
One Coy. of Scots Guards reached us about 5 P.M. and shortly afterwards the enemy counter-attacked our right flank. There was not much sting in his attack and by dark we had cleared the situation in our immediate front, and established communication with 2nd Guards Brigade or our right.
After dark a line of outposts was put out and we continued to dig. We had a fairly quiet night and no enemy attack. During the night our Rations, wtar and ammunition came up.
We maintained our position throughout the night and the next day without much incident until relieved at 6.0 A.M. on the 17th by the Bde.,

19/9/1916. (Sd.) J.V.CAMPBELL, Lt-Col., Commdg. 3/C.Gds.

To:
The Brigade Major
1st Guards Brigade.

Herewith narrative of the operations of the 13th–16th September as far as my unit was concerned:

Four STOKES MORTARS under the command of Lt R. J. PINTO, COLDSTREAM GDS, and Lt. T. A. COMBE, GRENADIER GDS, were attached to the 2nd Batt. GRENADIER GDS during the recent operations. The guns moved up with the infantry to the 1st objective where they came into action. A good deal of firing was done during the day and night of the 15th September in one case a direct hit being secured on some Germans who were believed to be attempting a counter attack. The casualties were 4 killed and 6 wounded of the 26 men in action. No guns were damaged.
I should like to recommend the following N.C.O's for general good work during the operation:

9342 Sgt. W. JACKSON 3rd Coldstream Gds
6634 L/cpl W. SPARKES " " "
19473 L/cpl J. RYDER GRENADIER GDS

17.9.16.

H Rheatkin, Capt
1st Guards T.M.B.

ATTACK OF THE 1st GUARDS BRIGADE, SEPTEMBER 15th & 16th. 1916.

1st BATTALION IRISH GUARDS.

The Battalion formed up its right on S.24.b.9.5. facing NORTH EAST, in two lines. Nos. 3 & 4 Coys. were in the front line, Nos. 1 & 2 Coys. in the 2nd Line. We formed up at 9:30p.m. on September 14th. and at 6:20 the following morning, the Battalion moved off as ordered. The two leading Platoons of No. 3 Coy. and probably some of No. 4 Coy. rushed the German First Line (called Vat Alley on some maps)running almost due East and West from the point where the SUNKEN ROAD leaves the NORTH End of GINCHY. These Platoons seem to have closed in on the two Battalions of the Coldstream Guards attacking. Our men got their blood up and it was here that our first wave went forwardin an irresistable rush with the Coldstreamers. They contrived to keep their direction but on the way the 2nd Gds Brigade closed in on the right of the 1st heading too much towards the NORTH. The Right half of the Brigade Area was the more heavily shelled, the German Barrage extending particularly to the hollow about 300 yards Southof the GREEN LINE. This helped to sheer portions of the 2nd Guards Brigade still further Northwards. ~~xxxx~~

Battalion HdQrs. reached the ~~1st German Line~~ wire in front of the 1st German Line (about T.8.4.5.) towards 7:50a.m. By this time the whole Battalion was either in front of the wire or in the GREEN Line, the RIGHT FRONT COMPANY being about T.8.d.2.8. to 1.9.and part of the RIGHT 2nd LINE COMPANY being about the same spot. The remainder were at the WESTERN END of the objective.

By this time three of the original Company Commanders had become Casualties and all the Officers of the LEFT REAR COMPANY (No. 2) were out of action. Before entering the GREEN LINE Battalion HdQrs. despatched a pigeon message to the Brigade, and as there appeared to be no movement in the position, Battalion HdQrs. entered the GREEN LINE which was found to be densely crowded, every unit of the 1st and 2nd Guards Brigades being represented. The Commanding Officer of the 2nd Bn. Irish Guards with several of his Officers was found here as well as fresh troops of the 14th Division waiting to attacktheir 2nd objective.

It appears that the Officers Commanding the two Battalions of the Coldstream Guards were under the impression that they had gained at least two objectives and this was responsible for the delaythat ensued. The further reorganisation of the position was considerably hampered by a party of Germans who were clearly visible in the Communication Trench about T.8.b.2.8. with a Machine Gun and snipersunder the direction of an Officer. The remaining Coy. Comdrs. (Lieut.J.K. GREER) fell a victim to one of these Snipers. Three Lewis Guns were turned on to the enemys position by the Commanding Officer's Orderbut each jammed in succession. Presently a large party of Germans who had surrendered were seen returning on our left front, probably owing to the advance of the 14th Division.

Every effort was now made to get the men of the 2nd Guards Bde. to move along the GREEN LINE TRENCH towards their own area and the Coldstream Gds., the two Battalion mixed together, with a few men of the 1st Battalion Irish Guards,gradually pushed forward. In the meanwhile, despite rather heavy shelling a certain amount of consolidation was done on the trench while the work of reorganisation was continued. Abo t 11:15a.m. word was received that both ~~Company~~ Commanders of the Battalions of Coldstream Guards had advanced on the next objective. At 11:25a.m. the remainder of the Battalion consisting of the Comdg. Officer, The Adjutant and 2/Lieut. G.V.Williams, together with Lieut. L.C.Whitefoord, of the Machine Gun Coy. 1st Guards Bde. followed the Coldstream Guards with every available man that could be collected, Coldstreamers included.

On clearing the top of the ridge the whole panorama of the landscape between ~~XXX~~ FLERS and LES BOEUFS was disclosed, in full view on the further slopes a German Battery of Field Guns shelling our advance. There was a good deal of shelling during our advance down the slope to the BROWN LINE which consisted of shallow trenches with a badfield of fire and no traverses. By 11:45a.m. we had assembled in this line about 60 of the 1st Battalion Irish Guards, on the left, about 30 of the 2nd Bn. Grenadier Guards under Capt. A.F.S.Cunningham and some hundred Coldstream Gds. on the right under the command of Colonel Campbell as Senior Officer present. There was again considerable uncertainty prevailing as to our correct position on the map but it was discovered by compass bearing that our correct position ranfrom T.2.B.2.3. to T.2.c.6.8., a distance of about 400 yards. We discovere to our left front, about 300 yards away, a small party (15) of the 1st Irish Guards, in touch with the 9th Battalion Rifle Brigade. The right of the Coldstream Guards was in the air and the 150contour line was just in front of us. Under more or less heavy shelling which caused a good many casualties everybody began digging themselves in. In accordance with an order sent to him by the Commanding Officer through a wounded man Captain L.R.Hargreaves, who had been left behind in TRONES WOOD by previous arrangement, when the Battalion went into action, now rejoined.

A line was now pushed out about 300 yards in front of the BROWN LINE, over the crest of the ridge by Capt. L.R.Hargreaves together with Lieut. L.C.Whitefoord and 2/Lieut. J.N.Ward and G.V.Williams. This line consisting of a number of disconnected shell holes was held for the remainder of the afternoon under grave difficulty, being shelled by a field battery clearly visible on the further ridge, about 600 yds. away, and continually swept by machine gun fire from the right and by snipers. With the aid of their entrenching tools the men dug themsleves into their shell holes, as best they could, and some of them picked off such enemy targets as presented themselves from time to time. The line formed by this party (about 50 strong, including a Brigade Machine Gun Detachment) was not carried on to the right but it constituted a very effective covering party for the BROWN LINE which was reinforced by the arrival of Lieut. W.C.Mumford and 2/Lieut. F.S. L.Smith with some parties of Irish and Coldstream Guards.

The Germans were reported as massing about the ~~[illegible]~~ Blue LINE for a counter attack and parties of troops were in effect descriedadvancing in artillery formation along the further slope, whilst considerable transport activity was observed on the roads. At nightfallour forward line was regarded as ~~unfavourable~~ untenable and by Col. Campbell's order was withdrawn so that all energies might be concentrated on the consolidation of the BROWN LINE. During the afternoon the 2nd Scots Guards attacked on the right of the Coldstream Guardsbut were beaten back with the exception of a few men who remained in the BROWN LINE. By nightfall nearly 100 of the 1st Bn. Irish Guards had joined the party holding the BROWN LINE besides more Grenadiers, Coldstream. ~~Before dawn~~ Pigeon messages were sent by Colonel Campbell to the Brigade explaining our position and we also indicated it to the contact aeroplane by flares. Lieut. L.C.Whitefoord, 2/Lieut.J.N.Ward, the whole Machine Gun Team and a considerable number of the party holding the forward line had become casualties in the course of the afternoon.

The night was fairly quiet. In the absence of anymaterials and of Verey Lights a screen of men was put out on the high ground about 100 yards in front of the position and kept there throughout the night in touch, on the left with the D. of Cornwalls L.Infy. who had relieved the Rifle Brigade, and on the right with the Grenadier Guards. During the night water was sent up by the Brigadeand rations were obtained from a Dump on the GINCHY — LES BOEUFS Road where the 2nd Bn. Grenadier Gds. were holding the GREEN LINE.

At 9:10a.m. the Battalion on our left (? Somerset L. Infy.) attacked the German system of trenches South of GUEDECOURT but failed and the Germans maintained a barrage over the BROWN and GREEN LINES. ~~so that~~ Communication with the GREEN LINE was practically impossible owing to the sloping ground being in full view of the enemy. The number of stragglers had increased so much that the BROWN LINE was now dangerously crowded.

The line was intermittently shelled throughout the day but the casualties were fortunately not heavy. On several occasions swarms of German Aeroplanes came out to reconnoitre and cruised about until driven off by our machines. During the afternoon the troops on our left made a second attack in the direction of GUEDECOURT. The only instructions received from the Brigade were one message to say that troops in the BROWN LINE would maintain their position but might be called upon to support an attack on the BLUE LINE by the 3rd Brigade. The troops in the GREEN LINE were ordered to be in Divisional Reserve under O.C. 2nd Battalion Grenadier Guards, these troops including about 40 men under 2/Lieut. T.F.McMahon. After dark further consolidation was done and some wire was moved [redacted] and put out in front of the portion of the BROWN LINE held, while the same covering party was sent out as on the previous night. We were warned of a probable counter-attack by the enemy to take place at 2a.m. but it did not materialise. During the night orders were received that the Division would be relieved so Guides were sent back and No. 2 Company, Lincoln Regiment, 62nd Bde. arrived in 2 parties about 5:15 and 5:30a.m. respectively. Their arrival was evidently observed in the early morning light and drew shell fire, in the midst of which a very rapid relief was effected with some difficulty. The various parties concentrated as ordered on the SOUTHERN EDGE of BERNAFAY WOOD where the total strength of the Battalion including 2/Lieut. T.F.McMahon's party, was found to be approximately 7 Officers and 209 Other Ranks.× The Battalion marched to Camp at the CITADEL (F.21.) arriving there about 9a.m.

× excluding the working platoon which rejoined the Battalion here.

Congratulatory messages
for
Sept 15th

2nd Bn. Grenadier Guards.

As your Brigadier I wish to say in a few words how deeply I appreciate the gallant work done by you in the recent operations at GINCHY.

On the 12th September you took over GINCHY trenches and the following night you drove the Germans out of GINCHY Orchard. This work caused you 100 casualties, but by your fine work you cleared the ground for the advance on the 15th September and ensured that it would not be held up at the very beginning.

On the 15th September your first advance was through a heavy Artillery barrage but owing to the splendid discipline in your Regiment you went through it as if on parade.

Your opportunity came later on when you cleared trenches at the point of the bayonet having run out of bombs, and when you charged a trench strongly held and in the face of Machine Gun fire.

You have shown the Germans what they have to expect when they meet the pick of the British Army.

In the near future you may be called on to do as much again and I know that you will not fail.

In the Field. Brigadier General,
18th September 1916. Commdg., 1st Guards Brigade.

2nd Bn. Coldstream Guards.
3rd Bn. Coldstream Guards.

As Coldstreamers you have just taken part in what is certainly the biggest event in the military history of the Regiment. The 1st, 2nd, and 3rd Battalions of the Regiment attacked in line, this alone may be a matter of interest but if you consider the results of the attack you may pride yourselves that you have upheld the traditions of the Regiment. Your losses have been very severe but you have left a mark on the German that he will not forget.

Your undaunted advance under heavy Machine Gun fire in spite of severe losses was what the Regiment expected you to do and you have set a high standard of valour and steadiness under the most trying circumstances that will be maintained by you and by those who succeed you in the Regiment.

You have done your duty as Coldstreamers and let that be enough praise and remember that as Coldstreamers you may have to do as much again in the very near future and I know you will not fail.

In the Field.
18th September 1916.

Brigadier General,
Commdg., 1st Guards Brigade.

1st Bn. Irish Guards.

As your Brigadier I wish to express my feelings as to your most gallant work on the 15th September 1916, in the operations at GINCHY. The advance from the Orchard in the face of Machine Gun fire is equal to anything you have yet accomplished in this Campaign and once more the 1st Bn. Irish Guards has carried out a magnificient advance and held ground gained in spite of the most severe losses.

In this your first Campaign you are setting the highest possible standard of bravery and efficiency for your successors and more praise than that I cannot give you.

You may be called upon in the very near future to carry out similar work and I know that you will not fail.

In the Field.
18th September 1916.

Brigadier General,
Commdg., 1st Guards Brigade.

D I A R Y.

Sept.,12th. Brigade relieved left portion of 3rd Guards Brigade on N.E. edge of GINCHY. 2nd Grenadier Guards in front line - 1st Irish Guards in support. Relief complete 12

Sept.,13th. Fairly quiet day.

Sept.,14th.

12-30 A.M. 2nd Grenadier Guards delivered an attack with one Company and 1 Platoon up sunken road N. of GINCHY and advanced about 150 yards - 60 casualties. Clearing the orchard.
8 P.M. 2nd and 3rd Coldstream Guards started moving from their bivouacs at CARNOY to assembly positions at GINCHY.

Sept.,15th.

1 A.M. All Units in their assembly positions. Quiet night.
5-30 A.M. Tanks heard moving to their positions. They did not seen to attract any fire.
6-25 A.M. Attack and barrage started.
6-30 A.M. A light barrage put down round S. and S.W. of GINCHY. Rifle and Machine gun fire heard S. and S.E. of GINCHY - possibly Tanks.
7-20 A.M. Message from Liaison Artillery Officer with 1st Irish Guards timed 6-30 A.M. Barrage only 77's and Battn., had advanced about 500 yards.
7-30 A.M. 2nd Guards Brigade reported their attack gone half left - Started well.
8-5 A.M. 1st Coldstream Guards reported 1st objective taken - about to attack 2nd objective.
8-20 A.M. Message received that 3rd Guards Brigade moved forward to S.W. of GINCHY at 7-50 A.M.
8-25 A.M. Pigeon message from 3rd Coldstream Guards saying they reached 3rd objective blue line at 7-15 A.M. This message queried.
8-40 A.M. 1st Irish Guards reported their H.Q., in Green Line.
8-55 A.M. Captain Alexander, 2nd Irish Guards reported he was in Flers line from W. side of Les Boeufs - Ginchy road at 6-55 A.M.
9 A.M. Aeroplane dropped map showing our dispositions.
10 A.M. Request for bombs from 2nd Grenadier Guards. Division asked for carrying party.
10-10 A.M. Officer of 2nd Irish Guards reports his position as T.3.b.7.4.
10-12 A.M. Barrage on Ginchy reported to have ceased.
10-15 A.M. 74th Bde.,R.F.A. ordered to move up.
11 A.M. Carrying party of 100 Pioneers for 2nd Grenadier Guards with bombs left.
11-55 A.M. 2nd Grenadier Guards reported on line T.8.d.4.6. to T.8.a.6.4.
12 noon. Line through to 2nd Grenadier Guards.
12-20 P.M. 3rd Coldstream Guards reported advance on Green line held up by strong point T.8.d.9.7. - Not understood.
12-35 P.M. Fox said R.E. could not get up on account of barrage.
12-40 P.M. Brigade Bombers returned from 2nd Grenadier Guards.
12-50 P.M. Lieut., Kelsey with Pioneer carrying party reported back.
1-10 P.M. Carrying party of 100 1st Grenadier Guards sent up with bombs etc., to 2nd Grenadier Guards.
1-15 P.M. Conference with G.O.C., 2nd Guards Brigade.
2 P.M. Another detachment of Stokes sent up to 2nd Grenadier Gds.,
2-10 P.M. Cavalry Officer reported situation verbally.

2-30 P.M.	3rd Coldstream Guards reported they are in Blue Line.
2-32 P.M.	3rd Coldstream Guards asked for support.
2-50 P.M.	Enemy reported massing between Les Boeufs and Morval.
3 P.M.	Division asked to send up a Battalion to support Blue line.
3-30 P.M.	Carrying party of 100 1st Grenadier Guards with 20 bandoliers S.A.A. sent up to 2nd Grenadier Guards.
3-30 P.M.	2nd Grenadier Guards reported Green Line clear of enemy and asked for S.A.A.
3-35 P.M.	R.E. sent up to reconnoitre position.
3-45 P.M.	Orders issued to 2nd Scots Guards to support 3rd Coldstream Guards.
4 P.M.	Lending Brigade of 20th Division ordered to Waterlot Farm.
4-35 P.M.	Orders to consolidate ground gained ~~gained~~ received.
6-15 P.M.	2/Lieut., Marris, 76th Coy., R.E. reported Irish Guards at T.3.a.9.8. at 2-45 P.M.
6-20 P.M.	Message from Irish Guards reporting remnant of Brigade holding ground in T.3.a.
6-25 P.M.	3rd Coldstream Guards asked for reinforcements.
7-0 P.M.	1st Welsh Guards warned to be ready to move up and support Blue or Hreen Line.
7-0 P.M.	Major General visited Brigade H.Q.,
7-50 P.M.	Relay posts - water and ration convoy - work platoons and R.E. with S.A.A. and material sent up. Water and rations to 2nd Grenadier Guards. R.E. to Blue Line (3/C.G.)
8-45 P.M.	2nd Grenadier Guards reported enemy crawling through grass.
9-45 P.M.	Lieut., O'Brien returned with report on Green Line.
9-50 P.M.	Orders sent to all Battalions not to take part in next days operations.

[signature]

Captain,
Brigade Major, 1st Guards Brigade.

1ST GUARDS BRIGADE.

Diary of Operations 12th - 17th September 1916.

<u>12th Sept.,</u> The Brigade relieved the 3rd Guards Brigade taking over the N.E. half of GINCHY, the 2nd Grenadier Guards in the front line, 1st Irish Guards in support in TRONES WOOD, 2nd and 3rd Coldstream Guards remained in reserve in CARNOY. Brigade H.Q., were in DUMMY TRENCH West of BERNAFAY WOOD.

<u>13th Sept.,</u> There was considerable shelling of GINCHY by hostile artillery at times.

<u>14th Sept.,</u> The Germans were firmly established along a line running through the N. point of the Orchard at GINCHY, it was essential to have this part cleared of the enemy in order to get troops assembled for the attack in GINCHY and to prevent the assault being held up at the very start and at 12-30 A.M. the 2nd Grenadier Guards delivered an attack with one Company and one Platoon up the Sunken Road on the N. of the Village and through the Orchard; this attack was stubbornly opposed and no great advance was made up the Sunken Road which was swept by Machine Guns, but the Orchard was cleared of the enemy and our line advanced 150 yards at a cost of 60 casualties. This fine ~~work~~ bit of work on the part of the 2nd Grenadier Guards was most valuable.
At 8 P.M. the 2nd and 3rd Coldstream Guards relieved the 2nd Grenadier Guards and all four Battalions took up their assembly formations during the night, the two Coldstream Battalions in the Village in the most suitable positions they could find, in any case their assembly and jumping off off presented a very difficult problem owing to the ruined Village being cut up by huge shell craters and the irregular front held did not face in the direction of the advance; the other Battalions and 75th Field Coy., R.E. to which were attached the 4 battalion work platoons of 30 men each who have been trained with the R.E., assembled in five lines which had previously been pegged out on ground 500 yards E. of WATERLOT FARM.

<u>OBJECTIVES.</u> The Brigade assaulting area ran in a N.E. direction 500 yards in breadth at the start gradually widening to 800 yards. There were four objectives -
1st objective - A trench 1,200 yards distant;
2nd objective - A switch trench running N N W out of it;
3rd objective - Another trench 1,200 yards beyond the 1st objective;
4th objective - A road beyond LES BOEUFS Village.

<u>PLAN OF ATTACK.</u> The 2nd and 3rd Coldstream Guards were to assault the 1st, 2nd and 3rd objectives, the 2nd Grenadier Guards were to follow them and form a defensive flank to either side if required; on reaching the 1st objective the 2nd Grenadier Guards were to remain there until the 1st Irish Guards had passed through them and if the flanks were all secure were to follow on after them and support them.
The 1st Irish Guards were to pass through the 2nd and 3rd Coldstream Guards at the 3rd objective and take and consolidate the 4th objective, their support was the Grenadiers or failing them was to be furnished by the Coldstream.

M.G's.
T.M.Bty.. Each Battalion had a section of Machine Guns attached to them, the 2nd Grenadier Guards had 4 Stokes T.M.B. Guns, the remaining 4 being kept in reserve.

COMMUNICATIONS. Arrangements were made for Visual and relay posts which was gradually to be supplemented by cable.

TANKS. Three armoured tanks were to start on the left outside the Brigade Area, they should have passed into it at the N. of the cutting which we knew would be a troublesome place on the left flank and then have gone more or less up the centre of our area, but they failed in their programme.

15th Sept., By 1.0 A.M. all Units were in their assembly positions, the night was quiet.

5-30 A.M. The tanks were heard moving to their positions, they did not attract any fire.

6-20 A.M. The attack left the trenches two front battalions in 4 lines 50 yards apart an interval of 150 yards and the 2nd Grenadier Guards in 2 lines 100 yards apart followed by the 1st Irish Guards 150 yards behind in two lines 100 yards apart.
The Field Coy., R.E. and 4 battalion work platoons remained in reserve in the assembly place.
Brigade Headquarters were in dugout near GUILLEMONT Railway Station.

Battalion narratives give the detailed account of their action during the assault and the following is a general review of events -
Soon after leaving the parapet Battalions came under heavy flanking machine gun fire from both flanks, particularly heavy from the left, the leading waves only faltered for a few moments and Lt-Col.,J.V.Campbell, D.S.O., immediately led them forward again.
It is calculated that 75% of the casualties occurred in the early part of the advance to the 1st objective;
Lt-Col., de Crespigny, D.S.O. states that the 2nd Grenadier Guards passed through a considerable artillery barrage but that as the shells approached the men laid down and owing to soft ground they caused very few casualties.
On leaving the front line the ground over which the attack was to be made was seen for the first time and so no line of advance could be previously selected. Compasses were to be used and were used by some Officers but the control of men in such an advance and under heavy fire of all descriptions makes reliance on a compass rather problematical.
The leading Battalions of the 2nd Guards Brigade on our right started off in the wrong direction and edged the 1st Guards Brigade half left. The 2nd Grenadier Guards guided by a road kept their direction and after considerable fighting established themselves on the Right of the 1st objective and carried out their orders to the letter as they secured this flank, which was quite in the air, after heavy fighting.
The 2nd and 3rd Coldstream Guards and 1st Irish Guards were very greatly reduced in numbers and battalions were considerably mixed. An unexpected and unmarked trench was mistaken for the 1st objective. A fresh advance was made and the real 1st objective was next carried, finally a third line was captured and there all three battalions started to consolidate and reorganize; But instead of being in the third objective they were in the second objective facing North and just out of the Brigade Area.

It is difficult knowing all the circumstances to see how this loss of direction could have been avoided but it did lead to great difficulties in communications with Brigade H.Q., and in bringing up supplies. Had the Contact Aeroplane taken the message sent to them showing the positions of the various Battalion Headquarters, great confusion and anxiety would have been saved.
Brigade Staff Officers failed to find these Battalions.
The 2nd objective or FLERS line was incorrectly shown on the Map as joining in a switch with the 1st objective, in reality it ran on in the direction of LES BOEUFS and Commdg., Officers were absolutely mislead by this.

<u>COMMUNICATIONS.</u> It was hoped to establish a Visual Station on the E. side of GINCHY Village after the advance was begun but all Stations were immediately shelled away.
Wire were laid out but constantly cut, finally relay Posts were established and would no doubt have become a going concern but until the position of the left battalion was definately established this was not possible and previous efforts at communication had been made with the idea that they were in the blue line and failed in consequence.
Rapid and reliable news came by pigeon post and contact aeroplane.

<u>SUPPLIES.</u> All ranks had two days rations i.e. 15th and 16th, therefore on the night of the 15th the question was to get water, rum, and a few minor comforts selected by Quarter Masters. A pack convoy was conducted by Captain Shaw Stewart, B.T.O. and with considerable difficulty. At 11 A.M. one Company of the Pioneer Battalion passed through a heavy barrage and took Bombs, S.A.A. and Stokes Mortar Ammunition to the 2nd Grenadier Guards; later on one Company of the 1st Grenadier Guards supplied 100 men for a second journey.

<u>REINFORCEMENTS.</u> At 2-50 P.M. the left battalion reported that the Germans were massing for a counter-attack and asked for reinforcements, the 2nd Bn. Scots Guards was lent by the 3rd Guards Brigade and sent to reinforce the Battalion holding the 2nd objective.

<u>16th Sept.,</u> There was no change in the situation; the 2nd Bn. Grenadier Guards was heavily shelled at times.
At 4-30 P.M. orders for relief were received. The 59th Infantry Brigade relieved the troops in the 1st objective 2nd Grenadier Guards and detachments of the other Battns., whilst the 62nd Infantry Brigade relieved the remainder of the 1st Guards Brigade on the left; these troops only just completed their relief as daylight broke.

The Brigade marched out 970 strong and went into bivouac at the CITADEL, 1 1/2 miles South of FRICOURT.

Brigadier General,

19th September 1916.

Commdg., 1st Guards Brigade.

Narratives of events

21st to 26th

SEPTEMBER 1916

Diary of Operations
Brigade Headquarters
2nd Grenadier Guards
2nd Coldstream Guards
3rd Coldstream Guards
1st Irish Guards
CONGRATULATORY MESSAGES

Diary of Operations on September 25th 1916.

12 noon.	Battalions in front reported situation normal and the enemy not apparently expecting any attack.
1 P.M.	Advanced Visual Station reported heavy German barrage about the front line and SUNKEN Road and also on the reserve trenches in T.8.
1-5 P.M.	5th Division on right reported to have reached their 1st objective in 10 minutes and sending back large numbers of prisoners.
1-20 P.M.	Artillery reported barrage heavy in T.8.d - T.8.a - T.7.b but not heavy about our front line.
1-30 P.M.	Aeroplane report received saying that our 1st objective had been gained except at T 3 d 3.4.
1-35 P.M.	3rd Guards Brigade reported 1st objective taken and being consolidated in touch with 64th Brigade on their left.
2-0 P.M.	F.O.O. reported Infantry going forward to 2nd objective.
2-10 P.M.	5th and 6th Division reported gained 2nd objective and 3rd Guards Brigade reported they had taken the WINDMILL and had 1/2 a company in the SUNKEN Road M 33 d 6.4.
2-15 P.M.	Our Advanced Signalling Station reported our men in the Brown Line.
2-25 P.M.	Aeroplane reported that we had gained 2nd objective.
2-45 P.M.	Large number of prisoners passed back.
3-0 P.M.	Message received from 1st Bn. Irish Guards timed 2-15 P.M. and reporting H.Q., in 1st objective with one company 3rd Bn. Coldstream Guards. Battn., gone forward and reported through LES BOEUFS. Consolidating Brown Line.
	Captain Beaumont Nesbitt who had been wounded at 1st objective reported wire in front of 1st objective uncut in many places and troops held up in consequence there. Troops got in on flanks and working outwards the position was soon won. He had seen our men go into the Brown Line without difficulty and with practically no casualties.
3-10 P.M.	H.Q., 3rd Bn. Coldstream Guards reported at T 3 d 1.6 at 2-35 P.M.
3-15 P.M.	1st Bn. Irish Guards message stated Blue Line captured - shovels required - resistance feeble.
3-20 P.M.	3rd Bn. Coldstream Guards ordered to send up 80 shovels to 1st Bn. Irish Guards.
3-25 P.M.	2nd Bn. Grenadier Guards reported that at 2-45 P.M. they were advancing through LES BOEUFS - supported by 2nd Bn. Coldstream Guards. Only one officer left with 2nd Bn. Grenadier Guards.
3-25 P.M.	Irish Guards work platoon ordered up
3-30 P.M.	Staff Captain sent up to visit Battn., H.Q., with orders to O.C., 3rd Bn. Coldstream Guards to be prepared to relieve 2nd Bn. Gre,adier Guards and 1st Bn. Irish Guards with 2nd and 3rd Bn's. Coldstream Guards.
	Orders for a convoy of Mules with shovels for advanced Brigade Dump issued.

3-45 P.M.	3rd Bn. Coldstream Guards message timed 3-20 P.M. stated LES BOEUFS in our hands - in touch with Left Brigade - 4 of Support Companies sent up - remainder consolidating 1st objective.
3-50 P.M.	75th Field Coy., R.E. instructed to take up shovels when moving up.
3-55 P.M.	2nd Bn. Grenadier Guards message timed 3-7 P.M. stated LES BOEUFS taken and Battn., H.Q., at T 4 c 4.8.
4-20 P.M.	1st Bn. Irish Guards reported they were digging in on line 100 yards East of SUNKEN Road, with patrols pushed out in front - Gap between them and 1st Bn. Grenadier Guards on Left rear filled by one Company 3rd Bn. Coldstream Guards.
4-40 P.M.	3rd Bn. Coldstream Guards reported all objectives taken - no enemy in sight - 2nd Bn. Coldstream Guards in touch with Brigade on Right in 2nd objective.
4-45 P.M.	Situation (as per B.M.689.)
4-50 P.M.	1st Bn. Irish Guards and 2nd Bn. Grenadier Guards instructed to push out posts on suitable ground in front of their position Brigade on Right doing same.
5-40 P.M.	Our Artillery shooting short and told to lengthen.
5-45 P.M.	Mule convoy with shovels left Brigade H.Q., for Advanced Dump.
5-45 P.M.	R.E. and Work Platoons ordered to move up and consolidate Blue Line at dusk.
6-0 P.M.	R.E. ordered up at once with all available tools.
6-45 P.M.	Staff Captain returned - reporting situation in LES BOEUFS very quiet and the shelling in rear slackening considerably - Battalions in front in good spirits with nothing in front of them except a few snipers - 3rd objective being consolidated - 6 Machine Guns in position - Battns., disposed as follows :-

2nd Gren.Gds., and 1st Irish Gds.,	-	All in 3rd objective half each.
2nd Cold.Gds.,	-	2 Coy's. up with 2nd Gren.Gds., 2 Coy's. in 2nd objective (Brown Line.)
3rd Cold.Gds.,	-	2 Coy's. in LES BOEUFS in close Support of 1st Irish Gds., 2 Coy's. in 2nd objective (Brown Line.)

7-0 P.M.	Battalions ordered to hold the ground they occupy no relief of leading Battamions to take place.
	1 Company 4th Cold.Gds., and 2 Sections 76th Coy.,R.E. sent up to consolidate 2nd objective (Brown Line.)
7-40 P.M.	2nd Bn. Grenadier Guards report that they had an excellent line of trenches 100 yards East of LES BOEUFS with posts in front - no Germans in front and good opportunity for Cavalry.
7-45 P.M.	Battns., told to hold the line in depth - withdrawing as many troops as possible from front line.

<u>September 26th.</u>

7-30 A.M.	Quiet night - four strong points made during night about the Blue Line - unarmed enemy seen running about during early morning on ridge 800 yards in front of Blue Line.
10-30 A.M.	2nd Gren.Gds. and 1st Irish Gds., instructed to try and push patrols forward onto ridge 800 yards in front. This was eventually found to be impossible owing to snipers the patrols were able to get out three or four hundred yards. These were withdrawn after dark. During the day LES BOEUFS was very

heavily shelled but the front line was not touched.
Casualties during the day were not heavy and after dark the Brigade less Machine Gun Company was relieved by 2nd Bn. Irish Guards and withdrawn to CARNOY and the CITADEL.

Captain,

29th September 1916. Brigade Major, 1st Guards Brigade.

1st Guards Brigade - Narrative of Operations 21st to 26th Sept. 1916.

The 1st Guards Brigade relieved the 61st Infantry Brigade on the night of the 20th/21st September having been out of trenches to rest since the morning of the 17th inst., every spare moment having been taken up by reorganizing Units, absorbing drafts, preparing narratives of the previous operations and submitting recommendations for awards. The weather had broken and three very wet days had made the rest camp very comfortless. On the night of relief all roads and tracks were seas of mud and progress across acres of shell holes made the relief a very slow one. It took 10 hours and the 2nd and 3rd Bn's. Coldstream Guards arrived in the new line in a very tired condition. A very large draft had detrained at MERICOURT, marched to the Citadel and thence into the trenches in the pouring rain - a bad beginning for a long tenure of trenches previous to the assault.

On the night of the 21st/22nd Sept., the Brigade moved to its left so as to be on its Battle Front - T 3 d 4.2 SUNKEN ROAD inclusive to T 3 a 7.3. the 3rd Guards Brigade being on the left and the 18th Brigade of the 6th Division on the right. Their front line was parallel to what was our first objective 300 yds ahead and South of our front line. The 2nd Bn. Coldstream Guards were on the right; 3rd Bn. Coldstream Guards on the left; 1st Bn. Irish Guards in TRONES WOOD; 2nd Bn. Grenadier Guards in BERNAFAY WOOD; ~~Battn.~~, Bde., H.Q., near GUILLEMONT Railway Station (T 19 a 0.1 1/2.)

A communication trench was dug West out of SERPENTINE TRENCH, so that access could be gained to it without being seen over the crest. A second line was dug behind the firing line as a Support and Assembly Trench, finally on the night of the 24th/25th 500 yards of communication trench was dug in the centre of our area to join up with an old unconnected German communication trench up to the firing and support line.

It was a great advantage that this trench was dug at the last possible moment as it was not barraged throughout its length by the Germans since it was not known to them.

An existing German communication trench along our N. boundary was worked at but was too deep with mud for it to be possible to get into really serviceable condition and so 150 yards of trench boarding were put in the worst places.

For communications relay posts and wire were organised up to the firing line, the wire being laid along the N. boundary communication trench.

A Wireless Apparatus was installed in SERPENTINE TRENCH to be erected after the 1st objective was carried, but it proved to be of no value.

A large dump was formed near the entrance of the communication trench into the SERPENTINE TRENCH with Water, Rations, Ammunition, R.E. Stores etc., for use when operations began. Brigade H.Q., maintained this dump, Units were to provide carrying parties to draw their requirements. A convoy of pack mules was used by day to fill this dump and in addition this convoy carried up water and rations to Battalions in front at night. The SERPENTINE TRENCH was bridged to allow the mule convoy to get up to the front lines.

<u>24th September.</u>

The 2nd 3rd Bn's. Coldstream Guards had been heavily shelled off and on whilst they held the front line and support trenches. After dark on the evening 24th/25th Sept., the Brigade assembled for the attack, on the Right 2nd Bn. Grenadier Guards; on the left 1st Bn. Irish Guards in the front line and support trench; 2nd and 3rd Bn's. Coldstream Guards in communication trenches and SERPENTINE TRENCH to feed into the two front lines as vacated by the assaulting Battalions.

One Section of Machine Guns was to follow up as each objective was captured paying particular attention to the Right flank; as this Machine Gun Section moved forward another from the line in rear was to take its place, the third Section was kept in Reserve with O.C., 3rd Bn. Coldstream Guards so that on reaching the last objective 4 guns would be in position on the East side of LES BOEUFS and 8 guns on the West side of LES BOEUFS.
Owing to casualties during the operations of the 15th and 16th Sept., it was not possible to man more than 12 guns.
The Stokes T.M.Battery was posted on the right of the front line covering the SUNKEN ROAD. It was thought that in the event of our being successful in capturing LES BOEUFS and troops being held up in the attack on MORVAL it might be necessary to form a defensive flank to the South taking advantage of the SUNKEN ROAD, fortunately this precaution was not necessary as the SUNKEN ROAD leading into the West side of LES BOEUFS was liable to direct enfilade fire, but for a start it would have provided immediate cover and a strong position.

25th September.
ZERO was 12-35 P.M. and our available trenches were packed with troops fortunately the morning was exceptionally quiet as regards shelling, but no sooner had the 1st assaulting line left the trenches than a very heavy enemy barrage was put on our trenches.
The 2nd Bn. Grenadier Guards and 1st Bn. Irish Guards sent two lines at 75 yards interval to capture the first objective keeping some troops in hand so as not to crowd the first captured trench as the assault was not to be launched from there until 1-35 P.M.
The assault moved steadily to the attack. Where wire was damaged the trench was captured. It was not well cut anywhere ~~with~~ but on the right of the 2nd Bn. Grenadier Guards by the SUNKEN ROAD there was a stretch of unbroken wire three lines deep which the artillery had not been able to observe.
As soon as our barrage lifted the Germans lined the parapet and opened with rifle and machine gun fire. Captain Cuninghame, Commdg., No.1 Company, 2nd Bn. Grenadier Guards ordered his men to open fire on the Germans and under this murderous fire began cutting the wire, other Officers followed his example and the Grenadiers losses on this spot were very heavy but they achieved the almost impossible and they filled the trench with German dead.
The next two assaults at 1-35 P.M. on the West side of LES BOEUFS and 2-35 P.M. on the Eastern limits of the Village were only lightly opposed.
As soon as the 2nd Bn. Grenadier Guards and 1st Bn. Irish Guards moved forward to the assault the 2nd and 3rd Bn's. Coldstream Guards began moving forward to the vacated front and support lines.
The Battalions moved by the new communication trench dug the night before and in consequence their casualties their casualties were slight. Throughout these Battalions were in close support and in touch with the leading Battalions, 2nd Bn. Coldstream Guards on the right and 3rd Bn. Coldstream Guards on the left. Two Companies of 2nd C.G's were eventually sent up to support the 2nd G.G's. in the Blue Line and one Company of the 3rd C.G's. was sent up to protect the left flank of the 1st I.G's.
The orders for the Brigade were to consolidate all captured lines and push out posts to seize any favourable ground to the front with a view to eventually forming a front line further to the front.
Two things prevented this, in the first place our atillery barrage was close to LES BOEUFS on the first favourable position for digging in, this barrage caused us some casualties including two Officers killed in the 1st Bn. Irish Guards. The second difficulty was that the left of the 3rd Guards Brigade was in the air and the most suitable ground to push forward to was 800 yards to the front, under the circumstances the hopes of gaining this ground were nil.

On the 26th inst., Commanding Officers were ordered to push out patrols to ascertain if this ground was strongly held or not, but it was unfortunately too late. The patrols pushed out gallantly and suffered considerably as the enemy were by now established and nothing short of an organized attack by a couple of Companies with Artillery preparation would have given us the ground.
The Brigade was heavily shelled on and off during the remainder of the 25th September and the 26th September and the garrison of the front trenches was gradually lightened Companies being sent back to SERPENTINE TRENCH, our original firing line and the first objective. Fortunately however the bulk of the enemy shelling was directed against the Village of LES BOEUFS and the SUNKEN Roads West of the Village. Our trenches East of the Village were not shelled and in consequence our casualties were comparatively slight.
During the evening of September 26th the Brigade was relieved by the 2nd Guards Brigade, the relief being an exceptionally quiet one.
Communications worked extremely well except the Wireless Apparatus which for some reason was useless. In spite of heavy shelling it was possible to telephone to the 1st Bn. Irish Guards during the 26th almost without interruption, and messages went to other Battalions by means of the sounder. Our new communication trench helped the wire as far as our original ~~from~~ firing line but after that it had to take its chance across the open.
The 1st Bn. Irish Guards had at times telephone communication to their Companies. A system of relay posts is essential to supplement wires, these posts are also invaluable in providing guides to anyone going to any part of the line. Relay men left their rifles and equipment in the posts and travelled unimpeded.
The system of dumps for water and supplies worked well and all the requirements were met.

Artillery liaison work in the front was not good. One Artillery O.P. was established East of LES BOEUFS but not until about midday on Sept., 26th. At my request another was sent up. These were essential to take advantage of fleeting targets which could not be dealt with by O.P. pushed forward to the first objective.
Artillery liaison Officers had no means of communication with their Batteries or Group except by Runner which proved too slow in many cases.
Liaison Officers with Battalions should know where these O.P's. are situated and do liaison between them an Commanding Officers.
All information gained by O.P's. should be transmitted to Brigade H.Q., by the Group Commander as theyvare in the most favourable position to report on the general situation. During heavy shelling a Commdg., Officer fully realizes what is happening in his immediate vicinity but it is no time for him to be ~~messing~~ moving about, a back O.P. can possibly give all the information required.

Brigadier General,

29th September 1916. Commdg., 1st Guards Brigade.

Narrative of Events from Sept. 24th - Sept. 26th 1916.

On the night of Sept., 24th the Battalion moved from BERNAFAY WOOD, where we had been in bivouac, and relieved the 2nd Bn. Coldstream Guards in the front line, our right being on the GINCHY - LES BOEUFS road, and the Battalion after relief being formed up in our Assembly Area - Two Companies and H.Q., in the front line and two Companies in the support line 150 yards behind. A good deal of shelling was going on during the relief but we only had a few casualties.

The morning of Sept., 25th was a very bad one for us as the trenches were very narrow and the men shoulder to shoulder and almost unable even to sit down. It was quite impossible to lie down.

At 12-35 P.M. our barrage opened and we advanced in two waves of two Companies each. The Germans evidently knew that an attack was imminent as within one minute they began putting heavy shell into the waves and at the same time a terrific barrage was opened on our front line.
About 12-35½ our leading Companies caught up our barrage and lay down. About 12-39 or 12-40 P.M. the 1st Objective was gained with a certain amount of difficulty as our Artillery had entirely failed to cut a single strand of the wire: While the Companies were cutting it and making their way through the Germans picked off almost all our Officers with the rifle and caused us some casualties by throwing bombs. Many Germans were killed in this line and a nice bag of prisoners made, also a Machine Gun was captured. Some Germans who were lying in holes in 'No Man's Land' were also killed.
At 1-35 P.M. we moved forward to the edge of the Village of LES BOEUFS, killing more Germans who emerged from dug-outs in the Sunken Roads and taking some prisoners. All dug-outs were bombed and no doubt many Germans were killed that way, as one or two were seen to be full of dead.
Two Companies pushed rather too far into LES BOEUFS and were forced back by our own Artillery fire.
At 2-35 P.M. we advanced through the Village meeting with little opposition and taking a few more prisoners. We gained the Eastern edge of the Village and consolidated. The Germans were seen retiring over the next hill in small parties and ones and two's; some loss was inflicted on them.
While we were consolidating we were sniped at heavily bya few Germans in a trench in the hollow to our immediate front, causing us some casualties.

During the evening the Village was severely shelled by heavy guns but except for a few stray shells, the front line was left alone. Sniping and shelling continued all night and the next morning.

During the afternoon of 26th we were heavily shelled. The Germans could be seen counter-attacking about half a mile to our left and also digging in all along the ridge to our front.

During the whole of the Operations we were ably and closely supported by Captain Verelst and the 2nd Bn. Coldstream Guards.

The observation from the front of the Village was perfect but no Artillery lines or Observation Posts were formed up to the time we were relieved on the night of the 26th by the 2nd Bn. Irish Gds.

The dash and   of the Infantry was magnificent in spite of large numbers of recent drafts and totally untrained men being in the ranks, but the co-operation of the Artillery was remarkable for its absence and a great deal of ammunition was uselessly expended on ground where no Germans were, and places where Germans could be seen were left untouched.

I should like to record my thanks to the 2nd Bn. Coldstream Guards for the admirable way in which they supported me.

(Sd.) C. de CRESPIGNY, Lieut-Colonel,
Commdg., 2nd Bn. Grenadier Guards.

28/9/1916.

Report on Operations carried out by the
2nd Bn. Coldstream Guards from Sept., 21st - 26th inclusive.

20th Sept., Evening :-
The Battalion relieved the Shropshire Regiment and Oxford & Bucks. No's 1 and 2 Companies being in the front line.

21st — Considerable enemy shelling.
No. 1 Company was relieved by the 11th Essex on right of GINCHY - LES BOEUFS Road and joined No. 4 in Reserve in BERNAFAY WOOD; No. 3 took over from the Grenadiers.

22nd — Our Artillery bombarded LES BOEUFS, enemy retaliating on our support trench held by No. 3 Company.
No. 2 Company after being relieved by No.4 went back to BERNAFAY WOOD.

23rd — Slight Artillery activity only.

24th — Fog in morning - Our front line heavily shelled - Lt. Barny wounded.
At night No's 1; 2 and 3 Companies dug a communication trench from Support line to Assembling trench.

25th — 5 A.M. The Battalion occupied newly dug trench until ZERO.
Order - No's 1; 2, 3, 4.
ZERO (12-35 P.M.) Intense enemy barrage and Machine Gun fire opened on assaulting trenches and communication trenches.
1 P.M. Battalion moved up toward their assaulting stations as previously ordered, meeting with considerable delay.
ZERO+ 1 1/2 (2-5 P.M.) No. 2 Company went over to Green Line, but only remained there 10 minutes before pushing on to rear of Brown Line, thus making up for previous delay - Dug-outs in Sunken Road across their line of advance were dealt with - Very little barrage. No. 2 with Bn. H.Q., closely supported by No. 1 occupied Green Line.
At ZERO +1 3/4 No. 2 reached rear of Brown Line.
At ZERO +2-10 min. the Grenadiers owing to casualties among their Officers had not moved forward - No. 2 Company Officer, leaving Mr ST. Leger to carry out his orders went forward and took charge of all visible. No. 2 Company found little to do beyond searching the Village, and about 3 P.M. were sent for to help dig in along Blue Line and furnish parties for bringing up tools.
No. 1 Company occupied Brown Line and commenced consolidation. with No. 3 lying up in shell holes to their rear.
No. 3 Company then filled gap on left of No. 1 created by Grenadiers moving up, and carried on consolidation.
Later, having completed Green Line, No. 4 and H.Q., joined them.
About ZERO+ 3 1/2 owing to large carrying parties being told off, half No. 1 Company to support of Blue Line.

26th — 2 A.M. No. 2 Company and half No. 1 were relieved by No. 3 Coy. who held front line on right of LES BOEUFS - TRANSLOY Road.
10 A.M. No's 2 and 4 went into Bn. Reserve in Green Line, H.Q., and No. 1 remaining in Brown Line.
In early afternoon Captain Verelst, Lieut., Clerke, and Lieut. MacGregor were killed by explosion of Bomb Store in Brown Line, which had been heavily shelled all day.
Front line quiet.
About 9-30 P.M. the Battalion was relieved by 2nd Bn. Irish Guards and returned to bivouacs at CARNOY.

Sept., 28th 1916. (Sd.) G.P.FILDES, Lieut.,

3/Cold Gds

Narrative of Operations 20th - 26th Sept., 1916.

20th Sept., The Battalion moved from the CITADEL at 7-15 P.M. and relieved the 12th K.R.R. and 12th R.B. in the trenches at T.9. The relief was not fully complete until 6 A.M. owing to the mud and bad state of the ground.

21st Sept., The following night the Battalion was relieved by the Durham Light Inf., and 1st Bn. of Buffs, and in return it relieved the 1st Bn. Grenadier Guards taking over the left sector of the Brigade frontage.
During the next three days the enemy kept up intermittent heavy shelling - especially on the front line. During the night the Battalion supplied 100 men to dig the assembly trenches, and also tried to clean out the old C.T. T.8.b.-T.2.d. but this was not successful owing to the state of the ground and the fact that the enemy continually shelled this trench.

24th Sept., On the night of the 24/25th the two front companies were relieved by the 1st Irish Guards and the Battalion took up its position for the attack, in the main support trench. During the night the Battalion supplied a fatigue party to assist digging a new C.T. at T.8.b.3.3. joining up with an old trench in T.9.a.

25th Sept., There was a good deal of shelling in the morning up till ZERO - 12-35 P.M. The Battalion then moved up the new C.T. under a heavy German barrage in which there was a good number of casualties. There was much delay here, as the trench was blocked by the Support Companies of the Irish Guards. On nearing the end of the trench companies advanced across the open to the Green Line.
At ZERO + 2 hours No. 3 Company moved forward and cleared the Northern portion of LES BOEUFS. Soon afterwards the three other Companies advanced to the 2nd objective and dug in.
About 3-15 P.M. the Irish Guards were not in touch with the 3rd Brigade on their left. Half a Company was sent up, but on arrival found they were not wanted in the front line, so dug in, in close Support.
As the Irish Guards were some way in advance of the Blue Line the rest of the Battalion less 1/2 Company left in Reserve, moved up in close Support to the Irish Guards and dug in along the LES BOEUFS - GAUDECOURT Road.

26th Sept., From about 9 A.M. onwards the enemy kept up very heavy shelling throughout the whole day. About 50% of the casualties of the Battalion occurred during this bombardment.
The Battalion was relieved by 1 Company of the 2nd Irish Guards about 9-30 P.M.

29/9/1916.

(Sd.) F. LONGUEVILLE, Captain,
3rd Bn. Coldstream Guards.

1st BATTALION IRISH GUARDS.

NARRATIVE OF THE ACTION 25th/26th SEPTEMBER, 1916.

Battalion left its bivouac in TRONES WOOD at 9p.m. 24th; and after a somewhat difficult march across the ground broken up by the action of the 15th/16th reached its Assembly Trenches about midnight, with a very few casualties. No. 1 Coy. (Capt. L. R. Hargreaves) and No. 2 Coy. (Capt. Hon. P. J. Ogilvy) were in the front line, the latter on the RIGHT, No. 3 Coy. (Lieut. Blom) and No. 4 Coy. (Capt. R. J. P. Rodakowski) in a Second line about 150 yards in rear, with Battn. Headquarters in a diagonal communication trench.

There was some shelling during the night and following morning, but the trenches being narrow casualties were not numerous, but unfortunately included 2nd Lieut. GIBSON who was hit during the march up, and was replaced in No. 3 Coy. by 2nd Lieut. McMahon, who had been left in Reserve.

The task allotted to the Battalion was to take 3 objectives, supported by the 3rd Battn. Coldstream Guards, who were to consolidate the first objective and to send one Company in close support for the purpose of clearing the Northern part of LES BOEUFS Village. The 2nd Battn. Grenadier Guards, supported by 2nd Bn. Coldstream Guards, had similar objectives including the main portion of the village on our right, and on the Left the 2nd Bn. Scots Guards were to take the 1st objective, after which the 1st Battn. Grenadier Guards were to go through them to the same line. Battalion Orders were to secure the flanks of each objective above everything else, and these points were fortunately visible and clearly defined, excellent aeroplane photographs also being available.

The hostile positions were steadily bombarded all the morning and during the previous day, and at 12:35p.m. on 25th instant, a creeping barrage was put down, behind which Nos. 1 and 2 Coys. together, with the whole line, advanced in 2 waves on the first objective. This was known as the GREEN LINE, and consisted of a complete single trench, with wire and half completed dug-outs about 300 yards away: it was reached by the two Companies without much opposition and with very few casualties, but the Grenadiers on the right suffered severely owing to uncut wire.

Immediately after the two Companies had advanced, a hostile barrage was put on our assembly trenches, which very much hampered Nos. 3 and 4 Coys. whose orders were to move into the front assembly trench under cover: there were a good many casualties including Capt. R. J. P. Rodakowski (Lieut. Mumford taking over No. 4 Coy.), and the Medical Officer. Eventually these Companies got so held up by the shelling that they advanced "over the top" to the first objective, soon after 1p.m.

In accordance with programme, the advance was continued at 1:35p.m. by all 4 Companies, to the BROWN LINE, a sunken road on the West or near side of LES BOEUFS, with the Left Flank thrown forward -- this advance of about 500 yards, like the first was on a downward slope and again resistance was weak and casualties were not numerous - Lieut. BLOM had become a casualty at the first objective and 2nd Lt. McMahon took command of No. 3 Company.

Battalion HdQrs. which had been rather broken up by the hostile barrage reached the GREEN LINE about 1:45p.m. immediately in front of No. 4 Company, 3rd Battn. Coldstream Guards.

On reaching the BROWN LINE the Companies came under shell fire from a Southerly direction, probably from some of our own guns, and there were a number of casualties.

This was reported by a pigeon message from Battn. HdQrs. at 2:15p.m., the capture of the BROWN LINE having been similarly notified at 1:50p.m.

At 2:35p.m., as per programme, the advance was continued, the 3rd and final objective (BLUE LINE) was on the far or EAST side of the village, and had been shewn on map as just EAST of another sunken road, this was also reached without great opposition, such clearing up of houses and dug-outs as was necessary being done by theBattn. as the 3rd Battn. Coldstream Guards Company had not quite closed up.

The whole Battalion advanced about 100 yards beyond the Sunken Road in accordance with the map and orders, and in order to get a field of fire -- here they proceeded to dig in, and patrols were sent forward to keep in touch with the enemy who were visible in small parties, some of which surrendered. Unfortunately our creeping barrage appears to have stopped almost on the line on which the Companies were digging, and it failed to lift forward for at least 15 minutes (this is the subject of a separate report) -- during this time Capt. HARGREAVES was so severely wounded that he died while being carried back, and there were other casualties including Capt. DRURY-LOWE, Commanding the King's Company, 1st Bn. Grenadier Guards, which was digging-in on our ~~left~~ ~~RIGHT~~ LEFT. The 2nd Bn. Grenadier Guards were in line on the Right, though practically without any Company Officers left, but our left was still doubtful, except for the one weak Company of the 1st Bn. Grenadier Guards -- subsequently however a defensive flank was formed by the 3rd Guards Bde. facing GUEDECOURT, where the attack had been held up. Battalion HdQrs. moved forward ~~about~~ before 3p.m. to the BROWN LINE, and subsequently into a German dug-out on the road which formed that line.

A Company of 3rd Bn. Coldstream Guards was moved up to help to secure the Left, and another Company in support of our line.

Digging was continued throughout the afternoon and night, most of the hostile shelling being directed on the village and BROWN LINE. After dark our line was thinned by the withdrawal of No. 1 Coy. (under 2nd Lieut. F.S.L.Smith) into the German dug-outs in the sunken road. A counter attack was launched during the afternoonagainst troops on our left, but was a complete failure, and the enemy Infantry made no other attempt to molest us.

The situation remained unchanged throughout the 16th, shelling of the village and of the sunken road on the west side being almost continuous and being responsible for casualties amongst all 4 Battns. of the Brigade.

In accordance with Corps Orders 3 patrols were pushed forward during the afternoon towards the ridge about 500 yards distant to endeavour to establish posts there, but although they went out with much gallantry they were held up by machine guns and snipers, and had to return after having casualties but having located at least one machine gun.

At 9p.m. the 2nd Battalion of the Regiment arrived and took over the whole village of LES BOEUFS from the Brigade, the Battalion returning via BERNAFAY WOOD to Camp at "THE CITADEL" arriving there about ~~2~~ 2:30a.m. on the 17th instant.

Approximate Casualties :---

1 Officer Died of Wounds.
5 Officers (includi g Medical Off.) Wounded
and some 230 casualties amongst "other ranks".

The Battalion went into action under 600 strong (10 Officers), including over 300 who had joined, in drafts, since the action of 15th/16th.

Congratulatory messages
for operations on Sept 25th
1944

(In pads of 50 dupls.)

"C" Form (Duplicate).

Army Form C. 2123.

MESSAGES AND SIGNALS.

No. of Message ....

Bm. Jas 49 M3 Spondmanes

Charges to Pay. £ s. d.

Office Stamp.

Service Instructions. G.O.R.

Handed in at .... Office 7-7p m. Received 7-21p m.

TO Gam.

Sender's Number	Day of Month	In reply to Number	AAA
GD 907	26		

Following from army Commander aaa Begins aaa Please convey to Guards Division my thanks and admiration for the excellent manner in which they carried out their attacks today aaa added all units

to be sent to others

FROM Guards Div.

PLACE & TIME 9 pm 9m

W 15660 M/151. 75,000 Pads. McC. & Co., Ltd., London. 1/16. Forms/C.2123.

"C" Form (Duplicate).

MESSAGES AND SIGNALS.

Army Form C. 2123.
(In books of 50's in duplicate.)

No. of Message ....

Charges to Pay. £ s. d.

Office Stamp.

Service Instructions.

Handed in at .... Office 7-45 p.m. Received 8-4 p.m.

TO Open.

Sender's Number	Day of Month	In reply to Number	AAA
BM67.	25.		

406 and all Ranks of 2nd Guard Bde wish to congratulate 1st and 3rd Guards Bdes on their splendid success today.

FROM Gauntlet.
PLACE & TIME 7-45 pm.

Wt. 432—M437 500,000 Pads. H W V 5/16 Forms C. 2123.

"C" Form (Duplicate). Army Form C. 2123.
(In books of 50's in duplicate.)

MESSAGES AND SIGNALS. No. of Message..........

Sm AC 43. M 9 [illegible]

	Charges to Pay.	Office Stamp.
Service Instructions. G.D.R.	£ s. d.	

Handed in at.......... Office 8-15 p.m. Received 8-10 p.m.

TO Gain.

Sender's Number	Day of Month	In reply to Number	AAA
GB 885	25th		

following from 14 Corps begins aaa Army Commander sends his best congratulations to all ranks on their great success aaa ends aaa addressed 1st 2nd 3rd Guards Bdes reptd. G.D.A. C.R.E. Pioneer Bn. Adms Q Signals

FROM Guards Divn.

PLACE & TIME 8 pm.

Wt. 432—M437 500,000 Pads. H W V 5/16 Forms C.2123.

"C" Form (Duplicate).
MESSAGES AND SIGNALS.

Army Form C. 2123.
(In books of 50's in duplicate.)

No. of Message..................

1813 Spudmane GDR 2adds	Charges to Pay. £ s. d.	Office Stamp.
Service Instructions.		

Handed in at.................. Office 6-5? m. Received 6-7? m.

TO Gain.

Sender's Number	Day of Month	In reply to Number	AAA
G.B. 897	25		

Following received from Corps Commander aaa Hearty thanks and sincere congratulations to you all aaa a very fine achievement splendidly executed aaa Ends aaa addressed 1st 2nd 3rd Guards Bdes repted. pioneer Bn. GDA CRE "Q" adms. Signals.

FROM
PLACE & TIME

Guards Divn.
5-50 pm

Wt. 432—M437 500,000 Pads. H W V 5/16 Forms C.2123.

"A" Form.

MESSAGES AND SIGNALS. No.

Prefix .... Code .... m.	Words	Charge	*This message is on a/c of:*	Recd. at .... m.
Office of Origin and Service Instructions.	Sent		.... *Service.*	Date ....
	At .... m.			From ....
	To			
	By		(Signature of "Franking Officer.")	By ....

TO SCANT

Sender's Number.	Day of Month.	In reply to Number.	AAA
* B.2. 706	25th		

Very many thanks for most valuable assistance ~~given by~~ of your machine gun which ~~off~~ gave material help to Gallant in capturing Green line on your left today

From Sam

Place

Time 3.40 pm

The above may be forwarded as now corrected. (Z) W.B. Smith Capt.

.... *Censor.* Signature of Addressor or person authorised to telegraph in his name.

* This line should be erased if not required.

225,000 W 14042—M 44. H. W. & V., Ld. 12/15

"A" Form. Army Form C. 2121.

MESSAGES AND SIGNALS.

No. of Message

Prefix .... Code .... m. | Words | Charge

Office of Origin and Service Instructions.

Sent — At .... m. To .... By ....

This message is on a/c of: .... *Service.*

(Signature of "Franking Officer.")

Recd. at .... m. Date .... From .... By ....

TO: Corps Commander XIV Corps.

Sender's Number	Day of Month	In reply to Number	
* SC 908	26		AAA

Your old Brigade very proud to be able to present you with Les Boeufs AAA All ranks most gratified by your kind congratulations

From: 1st Guards Brigade
Place:
Time: 11. am

The above may be forwarded as now corrected. (Z) [illegible]

.... *Censor.* Signature of Addressor or person authorised to telegraph in his name.

* This line should be erased if not required.

T. & W. & J. M. Ltd., London. W 14042/M44. 75,000 12/15. Forms C 2121/10.

All units

You have again maintained the high traditions of the 1st Guards' Brigade when called upon a second time in the battle of the Somme. For five days previous to the assault the 2nd and 3rd Bn's. Coldstream Guards held the trenches under constant heavy shell fire and dug many hundred yards of assembly and communication trenches, this work being constantly interrupted by the enemy's artillery. The 2nd Bn. Grenadier Guards and 1st Bn. Irish Guards though under shell fire in their bivouacs were kept clear of the trenches until the evening of the 24th September and were given the task of carrying by assault all the objectives to be carried by this Brigade, nothing deterred them in this attack not even the fact that in places the enemy wire was still intact and the enemy strongly posted there; this wire was cut in the face of rifle and machine gun fire and in spite of all resistance and heavy losses the entire main enemy defensive line was captured.

Every Battalion in the Brigade carried out its task to the full.

The German 52nd Reserve Division which includes the 238th, 239th and 240th Regiments and which opposed you for many weeks at Ypres, left the Salient on the 18th September. You have now met them in the open, a worthy foe, but you have filled their trenches with their dead and have driven them before you in headlong flight.

I cannot say how proud I am to have had the honour of Commanding the 1st Guards Brigade in this battle, a Brigade which has proved itself to be the finest in the British Army.

The Brigade is now under orders for rest and Training and it must now be our object to keep up to the highest standard of efficiency and those who have come to fill our depleted ranks will strive their utmost to fill worthily the places of those gallant officers and men who have laid down their lives for a great cause.

C. Pereira

Brigadier General,

28th September 1916. Commdg., 1st Guards Brigade.

GENERAL SIR H. RAWLINSON,

COMMANDING FOURTH ARMY.

O.A.D. 151. *17th September.*

The great successes won by the Fourth Army on the 15th are most satisfactory and have brought us another long step forward towards the final victory. The further advance yesterday after such severe fighting was also a fine performance highly creditable to the troops and to Corps, Divisional and Brigade Staffs. Our new engine of war, the heavy Section Machine Gun Corps acquitted itself splendidly on its first trial and has proved itself a very valuable addition to the Army. My warmest congratulations to you and the Fourth Army on a very fine achievement.

D. Haig. Genl.

Commanding-in-Chief,
British Armies in France.

ARMY PRINTING AND STATIONERY SERVICES A—9/16.

LESSONS LEARNT FROM THE OPERATIONS

OF 15th & 25th September

Lessons from the recent Attacks on Sept., 15th and Sept., 25th

by 1st Guards Brigade.

LOSS OF DIRECTION on Sept., 15th.

The primary reason for this was probably the fact of the attack being momentorily checked from the direction of T.13.b. 4.8. and the attack in order to overcome this resistence closing in on the place in question.
On the other hand the attack of the 2nd Guards Brigade on our right was driven from the line of it's attack by the failure of the attack of the Division on their right and the consequent very heavy barrage and Machine Gun fire from that direction which the enemy brought to bear on their right flank; This also tended to drive our attack further to the left in too Northerly a direction.
Another reason for the loss of direction was the uneveness of the jumping off line along the whole front. These combined with the facts that the whole country was an unrecognisable desert of shell holes and that ~~the~~ it was impossible to obtain a view of the country in front of our jumping off line owing to the position of that line just on and not over the crest contributed to the loss of direction in the attack. Precautions had been taken beforehand to lay out direction stakes for the Grenadier and Irish Guards but this was not done for the leading Battalions.
The question of the feasibility of withdrawing the line in order to improve the jumping off line is doubted seeing that it had been extended to the point of the Orchard and was a place of considerable recrimination. The front line was only partially dug and free movement was difficult. An enterprising enemy might have noticed the withdrawal and the fruits of seizing the point of the Orchard would have been lost.
An important fact which considerably increased our casualties is that a Tank should have passed over the N. end of the Sunken Road just previous to our attack, this spot we know held a Machine and we afterwards took 4 Machine Guns from this spot. Not only did the Tank never get to this place, but there was the 100 yards gap in the barrage along the intended tract of the Tank, so that the barrage never touched the point where Machine Guns were known to be, with the result that they opened fire the moment our troops left their trenches.
These two factors combined to make the most formidable task of the assault. It was overcome bybthe spirited determination of the attack but at a very severe cost.
Immediately North of our Area on our left flank was a German Salient that was to be dealt with by a Tank just previous to Zero. The conditions for launching our attack could not have been more difficult and I am certain that it is worth a small minor operations to ensure a straight run for the begibbing of the assault and to make it possible to have a straight barrage in front, instead of the semicircular barrage which had to be put down at the beginning of the attack on Sept., 15th.

ARTILLERY BARRAGE.

When the final objective is indefinite i.e. a line drawn across the Map as on Sept., 25th the Artillery barrage must not be put down too close as thus suitable ground for the digging of trenches is denied to our troops - Also the question of the lifting of the barrage in order to allow patrols to go even further forward must be considered.

ARTILLERY F.O.O's. F.O.O's must be pushed forward to our new front line trenches as for example at LES BOEUFS on Sept., 25th. They must have a telephone wire forward to them so that they can deal instantly and effectively with local situations.

ARTILLERY LIAISON OFFICERS. When Battn., H.Q., are going forward as on Sept., 15th they are of little value. On the other hand when Battn., H.Q., move forward as on Sept., 25th they could be of great value but they must know the position of the nearest F.O.O's and O.P's and get such Artillery Support as Commanding Officers require.

COMMUNICATIONS. On both Sept., 15th and 25th it was found possible to lay and keep a wire going to Battn., H.Q., as soon as they were definitely established in a position.
Pigeons and runners were also invaluable but Visual owing to shell fire, smoke and haze was of little use.
The relay posts of runners are most useful for providing guides to the front.

MACHINE GUNS. These should only be sent forward from objective to objective and not expected to go forward and keep up with an attack. They must choose their own time and set their own pace.

REORGANIZATION. As soon as the final objective has been reached all lines of trenches should be thinned out and the garrison organised in depth in order to lessen the number of casualties. Commanding Officers must not be afraid of sending parties back to rear lines of defence; this does not refer to necessary Working Parties.

FORWARD DUMPS. A Dump of all Stores - (rations, bombs, water, S.A.A. R.E? Material) must be organised by Brigade H.Q., as far forward as possible for all Units to draw on in an emergency.

BRIDGING of TRENCHES. Trenches should be bridged by R.E. to allow pack animal convoys to take up supplies to the attacking troops. Paths can also be marked out if required.

CHANGE OF S.O.S. ROCKETS. If a change of S.O.S. rockets and flares is to be made it should be done a reasonable time before the attack. It is not fully realised the time necessary to draw stores and get them distributed to the front line.

GUIDES. If the party requiring a guide is an important one at least two guides should be provided, but relay posts remedy this.

Captain,

3rd October 1916. Brigade Major, 1st Guards Brigade.

2nd Bn. Grenadier Guards.

During recent operations several points cropped up as being most important.

1. If possible every N.C.O. and man should be a Trained Bomber. It was found that men would not throw bombs although they all knew how to. Only men with badges came to the fore and took charge of the situation.

2. All N.C.O's and men must understand German Bombs.

3. A Lewis Gun should invariably work with a bombing party. On Sept., 15th it was found that a Lewis Gun kept down enemy rifle fire of covering party and also kept down the heads of the observers, while our observers were able to stand well up on the parapet and observe fire.

4. All ranks should be impressed with the very local effect of the German bombs. They make a lot of noise but do very little damage.

5. Close Artillery co-operation most necessary to Infantry in the attack. Many good chances were lost on 15th, 16th and 25th by the Artillery Observing Officer having no communication to their Batteries and apparently making no effort to do so.

6. Importance of keeping close to our own creeping barrage was again shown on 25th, also all waves should be got clear of our jumping off place as soon as possible. The Germans can and do drop their barrage within one minute of assaulting troops appearing. It is well worth risking packing troops into our front line very tightly.

7. In the event of wire not being cut, all ranks should understand that certain men must cut the wire while everyone else shoots at the enemy parapet and bombs it. This is bound to save many lives if everyone is prepared for it.

8. A light shovel for carrying in the attack should be invented and issued to troops. The present shovel is too heavy and cumbersome.

9. It makes all the difference if the objectives are made known two or three days beforehand, so that every man in the Battalion has a chance of knowing exactly what to do and where to make for.

4/10/1916.

(Sd.) W.R.BAILEY, Captain,
Commdg., 2nd Bn. Grenadier Guards.

2nd Bn. Coldstream Guards.

Lessons from the Attack - September 15th 1916.

ARTILLERY BARRAGE.
The attack was held up by Machine gun and Rifle fire about 150 yards from the start. The creeping barrage consequently advanced without the Infantry and when the Infantry did advance, some 15 to 20 minutes later, they did so without a creeping barrage. It is difficult to see how this could have been avoided, direct communication with the Artillery being out of the question.

TANKS.
The Sunken Road on the left which was the enemy's strong point and from which the Machine Gun and Rifle fire which held up the advance, mostly came, was practically untouched by the barrage. This may be accounted for by the fact that this road was one of the routes of advance of the much vaunted "Tanks".
Owing to the failure of the Tanks to advance in this particular locality, enormous casualties occurred.
Had the creeping barrage been used on the Sunken Road instead of relying on the success of these Tanks, it is possible, or even probable, that the advance would not have been held up at this point at all.

DIRECTION.
The Brigade lost it's direction during the attack on the 1st objective and I attribute this to two causes -
(a) The fact that is was necessary to change our direction during the advance.
(b) That the 2nd Brigade on our right, bearing too much to the left forced us out of our course.

I think that (a) might have been avoided had the jumping off trench been dug even at the expense of bringing it slightly back, so that it lay more or less parallel to the objective.
(b) was probably due to the same cause - i.e. that the 2nd Brigade had also to change direction and failed to do so.

COMMUNICATIONS.
After leaving the 1st objective, communication with Brigade H.Q., became very difficult. What few pigeons survived the 1st advance were used from the 1st objective and it was subsequently necessary to use runners over a long distance and frequently through heavy barrages.
Messengers from Brigade H.Q., were unable to find their way to Battalion H.Q., and it was not until a late hour on 15th or early on 16th that any messages from Brigade recahed Battalion in Brown Line.
A Brigade relay post established in 1st objective would have been invaluable.
Runners from Brigade had little difficulty in their way there and runners sent back from Battalions to such a relay post could have brought messages back to Battalions.

ROBBING THE DEAD.
I would suggest that more attention be given to the conduct and discipline of parties sent out to clear the Battle-field and bury the dead. I have made enquiry and without doubt an impression exists among the troops that all valuables viz. watches - rings - cash - etc., become the property and are the perquisites of these parties.

TOOLS.

Although more than 50% of men carried tools on 15th and nearly every man carried a tool on 25th it wad difficult to find either pick or shovel to work with towards the end of day. Once the soldier has unslung his tool he either forgets, or do not wish, to carry it further especially if he is going to attack a new line.
The number of tools lost on these two days must have been colossal.

SENTRIES ON EXPLORED DUGOUTS & CELLARS.

This was forgotten in many cases. In one case in LES BOEUFS an Officer coming upon a cellar which might contain enemy preceded his descent by a Mills Bomb. Three frightened private soldiers of another British Regiment were shortly afterwards seen leaving hurriedly by the alternative exit.

HEAVY ARTILLERY.

About 2-45 P.M. on Sept., 25th the Heavy Artillery were firing very short over LES BOEUFS and causing many casualties among our own men. This was reported and two hours later rectified.

WORK PLATOONS.

The possibility of being able to bring up the 'Work Platoon' (fresh men and tools) to consolidate a position might be considered.

COVERS FOR STEEL HATS.

Men of the new drafts arrived in steel hats which were of a very obvious colour and which on a bright day made a good target for the enemy.

BOMBS.

The system of carrying two bombs per man was very satisfactory and useful in emergencies.

USE OF COVER.

There was a great tendency in both attacks for men to hang about in batches after the capture of a position instead of taking cover and getting to work with the consolidation.
It almost invariably happened that for the first half-hour or so after the capture of a position there was little or no enemy fire and it is during this lull that much valuable work could be done.

LEWIS GUNS.

It was found that the best method of getting Lewis Guns forward during the attack was to leave it to the Lewis Gun Team to work their way up in their own time with the maximum of speed and the minimum of danger, but the trouble of this was that they frequently lost their Companies.
Liaison is therefore necessary between Coy's. and their Lewis Gun Teams.

4/10/1916.

(Sd.) R.B.J.CRAWFURD, Lt-Col.,
Commdg., 2nd Bn. Coldstream Guards.

3rd Bn. Coldstream Guards.

Notes and suggestions on the recent operations.

EQUIPMENT.
That there should be some better method of supplying the front line with bombs, S.A.A., and rations. At present Battalions have to carry these up on their way to the trenches, which means a man has to carry either S.A.A.- a box of bombs - a tin of water - rum - charcoal - rations or flares etc., up to the trenches which is a heavy nights work over such rough ground, especially if it is at all wet, before an attack.

TOOLS.
Every man including the leading waves should carry either a pick or shovel, as it is impossible to say who will reach the objective, and tools are then essential. A lighter tool with some definite arrangement for carrying it is required.

BOMBS.
The pocket seemed an unsuitable place for the men to carry their two bombs, as it is impossible for them to get them out quickly owing to their equipment. The best method seemed to be to carry 20 rounds of S.A.A. from the extra bandolier in the pouches, and then carry the bombs in the bandolier.

ARTILLERY.
There should be some form of signal with Very Light or some such method, between the leading waves, of the Infantry and the Artillery, so that the Infantry can control our barrage. It is impossible to work to a definite time table as if things are very successful it is far better to push on immediately from one objective to another, which under the present system where halts are arranged necessitates our men running into their own barrage. If a system of Signals was arranged a halt could be had if necessary, or the Infantry could advance if an opportunity occurred.

AEROPLANES.
The ground sheet with the Signal call at Battn., H.Q., gives away the position of Battn., H.Q., to hostile aeroplanes. It is necessary that it should be left out the whole time - when once the Contact Aeroplane signals that it has seen the signal the ground sheet might be taken in, and put out again the next time Battn., H.Q., moved.

CONCEALMENT.
When a position has been gained it should be impressed on all ranks not to walk about even if the enemy do not shoot at them, as men are very much inclined to walk about and give the position away.

4/10/1916.

(Sd.) F.LONGUEVILLE, Captain,
Commdg., 3rd Bn. Coldstream Guards.

1st Bn. Irish Guards.

In accordance with your No.287, I wish to bring forward the question of Artillery co-operation, as having been hardly satisfactory either on 25th, 26thn 15th or 16th, more especially on the last two dates.

1. As regards the 1st action, I was accompanied on 25th by a Liaison Officer who was, through no fault of his own, quite useless. He was never in touch by wire, and I doubt whether any of his messages by runner were of any use. He was wounded during the afternoon and although a N.Z.R.F.A. Officer was with me for a short time, he was equally dependent upon runners, who would have been useless had a barrage been urgently required.
I had no further communication with Artillery before being relieved early on 27th.

2. On the morning of the 15th a Heavy Artillery Officer was in my assembly trenches, endeavouring to find a spot to observe a portion of the Green Line which he indicated to me on the map, and which he said he had to deal with. I mention this because I know that the 2nd Bn. Grenadier Guards suffered heavily from a portion of trench which had been inadequately dealt with, and it appeared to me that this particular Officer's task had been left till very late.

3. As regards the 15th, I was again accompanied by a Liaison Officer, who was again dependent upon orderlies, and who was only able to send the same reports on the situation as I was sending to my Brigade - Subsequently, at my suggestion, he went forward after the taking of the final objective to report upon a proper barrage line. He was relieved early on the 16th, and partly as a result of my urgent representations a wire was eventually laid to connect the new Liaison Officer with his Battery - this wire was only maintained with difficulty, and was finally cut after several men had been hit while repairing it. It was only at a late hour that night that I discovered, by accident, that the Liaison Officer with 2nd Bn. Coldstream Guards had been occupying an O.P. in LES BOEUFS all day, with a wire to his Battery, which, had I or my Liaison Officer known, would have been of the greatest assistance, and I submit that it was some Artillery Officer's business to have notified all Units in the vicinity, of this means of Artillery Co-operation ?

4. The most serious matter that I have to report is that on two occasions on 15th, my Battalion suffered quite a number of casualties from our own guns - Firstly on reaching the 2nd Line (BROWN) about 1-45 P.M. they were under intermittent shell fire from what appeared to be their Right Rear (from a Southerly direction), and this continued until 2-35 P.M. Secondly on reaching the BLUE LINE at scheduled time, it appeared as if the creeping barrage failed to lift forward for at least 15 minutes, with the result that the Companies found themselves digging-in on the BLUE LINE in the midst of their own barrage, with disastrous results.
In this connection I would point out, that the BLUE LINE as shewn on the Map issued to me was distinctly to the East of the Sunken Road, and my orders were quite clear viz. that the line to be occupied would be well beyond the Sunken Road, where in fact it was essential, in order to obtain a field of fire - on the other hand I found the BLUE LINE <u>on my Liaisons Officer's map</u> was <u>along</u> the Sunken Road. This may or may not have been an error in copying Maps, but it would have been quite sufficient to account for what was evidently a very serious discrepancy. I consider this a most important point for future guidance. (Sd.) R.McCALMONT, Lt-Col.,

4/10/1916. <u>Commdg., 1st Bn. Irish Guards.</u>

Report on the actions of Sept., 15th and 25th, regarding the Machine Guns of the 1st Guards Brigade Machine Gun Company.

Two attacks were made by this Company. One on Sept., 15th and one on Sept., 25th. In the first attack one section (4 guns) went with each of the assaulting Battalions.
This was ordered because it was thought that by so doing they would escape the heavy barrage which was anticipated.
Two guns went with Battn., H.Q., and one gun with each of the two flank Companies.
There was strong opposition to the attack and the distance to the first objective was so great that few of the guns of the attacking Battalions reached it.
The pace was also too hot for Machine Gunners to be able to keep up.
The casualties on the 15th in the Company were 4 Officers and 90 O.R.
No control was possible by the O.C., Machine Gun Company.

On the 25th the Machine Gun Sections were not attached to Battalions, but arranged as follows :-
There were two objectives which immediately concerned the Machine Coy., i.e. the BROWN LINE and the BLUE LINE.
The Company was organized into three sections of four guns each and known as the BLUE SECTION, the BROWN SECTION, and the RESERVE SECTION.
Operation Orders for the attack on LES BOEUFS showed that one section was ordered to occupy the BLUE LINE after the Village had been taken and two Sections to occupy the BROWN LINE. The BLUE SECTION dug themselves in just behind the jumping off line during the night of the 24th.
The BROWN SECTION did the same except that two guns were at either end of the Brigade Frontage. Their role was to help from a defensive flank if necessary.
The RESERVE SECTION was held in reserve and was not sent for until the BLUE LINE was occupied.
The machine Gun teams were kept in hand by their commanders and did not advance until the line in front of them was captured. They chose their own time and route to do this. All twelve guns reached their objectives and were withdrawn again on relief with the loss of only 4 killed and 7 wounded. No Officer Casualty occurred in this attack.
Control was exercised throughout by the O.C., M.G.Company who was with the H.Q., of the supporting Battalions.

It is of vital importance that correct and up to date Maps of the trenches to be attacked should be issued a day or two before the operations are to take place. In these operations Maps were issued two or three days previous in which at least two lines of German trenches which had to be crossed, were unmarked. These unmarked trenches were all manned by Germans. Through having incorrect Maps much confusion was caused in the minds of the Officers conducting the Operations and others who naturally could not properly distinguish when they had reached their various objectives.
Covers for the guns were found to be absolutely essential.
At one period in the assault all four guns of one section were unfit for action through being clogged with mud, earth, etc., and if it had been a wet muddy day this would have been even worse.
Light tripods were found to be of the greatest use.
Range-finders were found to be an encumberance during the assault and were in some cases thrown away. They should be left behind until the final objective is gained and consolidated; Then they should be brought up and ranges taken.
Every endeavour should be made to develop shutter signalling and if possible there should be a shutter to every gun and as many men as possible should be trained in the use of it.

4/10/1916. (Sd.) R.BINGHAM, Capt. Commdg., M.G.Coy.,

Report on the actions on Sept., 25th and 26th of the
1st Guards Brigade Trench Mortar Battery.

This Battery took part in the attack by the 1st Guards Bde., in LES LES BOEUFS on the 25th and 26th Sept., 1916.
Two guns under 2/Lieut. Earle were posted in the assembly trench on the right of the Brigade front previous to the attack, with orders to proceed at the first convenient opportunity after the attack into the first objective with the object of covering the sunken portion of the GINCHY - LES BOEUFS Road in case of a counter-attack.
These orders were carried out. The advance being made about 1-35 P.M. (nearly an hour after ZERO) when the enemy barrage had considerably slackened.
Two temporary emplacements xere dug in the old German front line trench or Green Line at a point about 150 to 200 yards from a Sunken Road enabling considerable stretches of the two roads to be covered. A bomb store was constructed and a stretch of 30 or 40 yards of trench was consolidated.
Each of the ammunition men carried 7 bombs during the advance and a further supply was brought up later in case of the attack was held up at any point.
These guns did not come into action and took no further part in the offensive as the attack by the Brigade was a complete success.
The other two guns under Captain Meakin were under the orders of Colonel Campbell to come into action if any part of the line was held up. Unfortunately Captain Meakin was killed and one gun was put out of action by shell fire.
Lieut., Combe came up about 3 P.M. and took Command of the remaining 3 guns on the right of the Green Line.

It would appear from experience gained in this and the previous attack that the real use of the Stokes Gun in the attack is either to help in beating off counter-attacks or assisting the Infantry with overhead fire when attacking a definite or limited objective with bombs. The guns teams cannot be of any assistance to assaulting Infantry owing to the weight they are obliged to carry.
Owing to the difficulty of getting ammunition up to the front line it is most important to have several large dumps near the front line where they can easily be got at in case of need.
It is most important to have guns on the flanks and it is desirable for the gun teams under the Officer to advance in their own time.

4/10/1916.

(Sd.) T.A.COMBE, Lieyt.,
1st Gds. T.M.Btty.,

1st Guards Bde., No.329.

Headquarters,

Guards Division.

The following points arose during the recent operations. I think that 'A' has been dealt with in the Divisional Summary of Notes on the operations.

"A". The necessity of a daily joint inspection of the results of wirecutting by C.O's or Coyw Commdrs. and Artillery Officers, so that all concerned are satisfied as to the results and can decide if patrols are necessary to gain further information.

"B" The problem of arriving at the last objective with sufficient tools is unsolved. All men carried one tool apiece in the Attack on 15th Sept., many less tools were available on the 25th Sept.,
Men cannot fight and carry a tool. Even if they are in the later waves and have started consolidating some captured position they are probably under heavy shell fire and when they next advance many tools are probably left behind.
The entrenching tool is quite futile and useless when one considers the amount of protection required against heavy Artillery.
The only solution that I can see is to have some smaller tool than the full sized one, it should have a carrier which is easily attached and detached from a man's equipment and which will not unduly hamper his movements. These tools to be issued only when an attack was intended.

"C" Points affecting Contact Aeroplane -

(1) The two numerals of Battn., H.Q., Code Numbers should be on the same sheet, it happened that D 29 arrived at one objective with the 2 but without the nine. This will make a heavier load, but the half only of the lighter load is of no use.

(2) When the final objective E of LES BOEUFS was captured flares were duly burnt, but there was no Aeroplane to see them and as this line lay in a hollow the Signal was not visible from the back, also flares by this time were very scarce owing to casualties among men carrying them.

(3) Battn., H.Q., complain that Aeroplanes do not acknowledge their Signals and that they have to constantly send men out to repeat them and that they suffer casualties in consequence.
I understand that the probable reason of this is that several Battn., H.Q., may be sending messages and if close together they might confuse the acknowledgement if the Aeroplane did not have time to reply with the Battn., Code Call.

(4) Contact Aeroplanes appeared to drop their message at Corps H.Q., it is suggested that in cases where Battn's ask for assistance in the form of Artillery support, they would get it earlier if the reports were dropped at Divnl. H.Q.,

11th Oct., 1916.

Brigadier General,
Comdg., 1st Guards Brigade.

6 copies

SECRET

HEADQUARTERS,
GUARDS' DIVISION.
No. 2339 /G
Date 8.10.16

1st Guards Brigade.
2nd Guards Brigade.
3rd Guards Brigade.
****

The attached copy of the Major-General's Report, rendered to Head Quarters XIV Corps, on the operations carried out by the Guards Division on 15th and 25th September, is forwarded for your information.

[signature]

Captain,

8th October,1916. General Staff, Guards Division.

Secret

XIV Corps 'G'.

With reference to your G.142/2/7, I herewith forward to you a report on the actions of the 15th and 25th September, and a copy of the War Diary, which shows the various objectives and the formations employed.

The attack made on the 15th was one full of difficulties: which were somewhat as follows :-

GINCHY stood out as a salient in our lines as on the right the enemy were in possession of the QUADRILATERAL in N.14.d.8.2, and the trench running North of it which joined the FLERS line at T.8.d.4.3. This trench was admirably placed as it gave flanking defence to the German line should any attack be attempted from GINCHY.

On the left, the Germans were in possession of certain trenches between GINCHY and DELVILLE WOOD which would also flank any advance that we might attempt to make. Besides which, the enemy were holding the various Sunken Roads with machine guns about N.14.a.1.5. The result of this salient was to make the forming up of two brigades for the attack a very difficult matter. Two brigades had to attack out of a very limited area and out of trenches which were by no means parallel to the first position which was to be assaulted.

This first objective was 1250 yards distant and between this first objective and GINCHY there would necessarily be a lot of fighting.

From GINCHY, the top of the tower of the Church of LES BOEUFS was just visible; but from GINCHY the ground fell for about 400 yards in a gentle slope so that once the troops had left GINCHY they had no more any landmarks which were really prominent to guide them. The ground then runs in a gentle glacies to the FLERS line which was heavily wired and a magnificently placed line of defence.

In this attack great reliance had been placed on the tanks. The barrage was arranged for them. They were /expected

expected to clear the enemy out of the trenches between DELVILLE WOOD and GINCHY, out of the Sunken Roads in front, and out of the QUADRILATERAL on our right. As a matter of fact none of these things happened. The tanks had been given a great start on account of the slowness of their movements and the barrage started with the tanks with the result that our infantry as soon as they advanced came under a heavy flank fire from both right and left and also from in front. However, the troops pushed on and by the time that they had reached the FLERS line they had suffered not only heavy casualties but they had gone 1250 yards and had taken trenches not marked on any map and fought with enemy in all sorts of places with the result that they thought that they were very much further than they really were.

The lesson that we learn from this operation is that the tanks should be used so as to clear the enemy out of such positions as may hamper the immediate formation of trenches for the attack, that they should have been used a few days before to assist in taking the QUADRILATERAL and the trenches on our left which would have allowed the 6th Division to come up into line with us for the attack on the 15th.

An attack such as we had to make with the Division on our right starting 500 yards behind us with an enemy's strong point in line with us and with enemy on our left having a gap between us and the Division on our left is a hazardous operation.

That for a main attack tanks are of no use.

However, the Division took the first objective and even pushed as far as 500 yards beyond establishing posts which were most valuable as it was on the line of these posts that trenches were dug from which the attack on the 25th started.

I herewith forward a map showing how the enemy had positions in front of our first objective, positions which were unexpected to our troops and therefore led them to believe that they had taken three lines of trenches when they had really only reached their first objective. The accompanying German map

/shows

shows how in the ground in front of the FLERS line there was one whole battalion whereas in the FLERS line itself there were only two companies. Four machine guns were captured in the Sunken roads alone. This shows how very determined the enemy were that we should only reach the FLERS line after heavy fighting.

On September 25th, the main and final objective was a line East of LES BOEUFS. The different objectives are given in the order and notes herewith. The main features were that the Division on our right were holding OX Trench south of the GINCHY - LES BOEUFS road from T.9.b.4.9 to T.9.d.7.7, whereas the enemy held the line of trenches north of the Sunken Road and also held a loop line in front of that T.2.b.6.8 to T.3.a.2.5.

The result was that the Division had to take two lines of trenches to get into line with the Division on our right preparatory to the attack on LES BOEUFS.

A few days before the attack we were ordered to extend our front by 400 yards to our right and extra artillery was given to us for this purpose.

Now the main difficulties that occurred in this attack was first that the loop line mentioned above was not sufficiently prepared with artillery, only ten minutes before the attack commenced the Captain commanding in this part of the line telephoned and said that the artillery fire was not effective and was very wild. This was too late to allow for remedy; the result was that when the attack was launched there were very heavy casualties and the line of trenches were not captured until the following day.

It was eventually captured by the use of a tank.

Now the second place where difficulty was met was at T.3.d.2.6 where for about 100 yards the wire was not cut; which caused very heavy casualties. Now I have been to the place from which the attacking troops for this part of the line started. The wire is quite visible, and it is quite easy to see that it is uncut. Now the lesson that we learn from both these misfortunes is that the

/Company

Company Officer must be in closer touch with the Artillery Observation Officer and should let them know early whether or not they are satisfied with the shooting of the artillery. Wherever possible, the C.O. or senior infantry officer should go round with a senior Artillery Officer and settle with him what parts of the enemy's line have not been sufficiently treated.

From the whole of these operations, the following points have been brought to notice.

(1) The very closest liaison between the Infantry actually in the trenches and the Artillery is absolutely necessary.

(2) That for an attack, Bombing Sections are of no use. These get quickly broken up and even when they can be kept together they are not quick enough. All men must be trained as bombers, and all men should be trained in the use of German bombs of which they will probably find an ample supply.

(3) Pigeons were very useful; but baskets for single birds would be most useful so as to minimise the chance of losing all birds.

(4) Lewis Guns which got through were very short of hoppers. It is suggested that an extra issue be made.

(5) A larger number of flares is urgently recommended to make sure that isolated advanced parties may be able to show the contact aeroplanes where they are. On the 15th 520 were issued to the Brigade but many of the advanced troops found themselves without any.

(6) The discharge of S.O.S. rockets often involves much delay. It is recommended that an S.O.S. Signal which can be fired out of a Very pistol be instituted.

(7) After the final objective has been gained, the barrage should creep on so as to cross any high ground that there may be in front. On the 25th our troops were stopped from pushing on by our own barrage.

(8).

(8) Machine guns should be given their tasks but told to push forward in their own time, a number always being kept in hand to form a defensive flank. The light auxiliary tripod was invaluable.

(9) Eavery man should carry a pick or a shovel. A lighter tool with some definite arrangement for carrying it is required.

(10) Cover for machine guns is absolutely essential. At one period in the assault all four guns of one section were unfit for action through being clogged with mud.

(Signed) G. Feilding

Major General,
Commanding Guards Division.

5th October 1916.

GUARDS DIVISION.
****

"OPERATIONS OF THE 25TH/26TH SEPTEMBER 1916.

TRENCH MAP, FRANCE. SHEET 57 C S.W.

HEADQUARTERS.
BERNAFAY WOOD. SEPTEMBER 25TH.

DISPOSITIONS BEFORE ATTACK.

The detailed dispositions of the attacking Brigades previous to the attack were :-

1st Guards Brigade. Right Sector.
1st Bn. Irish Guards on the left, 2nd Bn. Grenadier Guards on the right.
3rd Bn. Coldstream Guards left support, 2nd Bn. Coldstream Guards right support.

3rd Guards Brigade. Left Sector.
4th Bn. Grenadier Guards on left, 2nd Bn. Scots Guards on right.
1st Bn. Grenadier Guards in support, 1st Bn. Welsh Guards in reserve.

OBJECTIVES.

The objectives and dividing lines between Brigades and Divisions are marked on the attached map.

First objective GREEN.
Second objective. BROWN.
Third objective. BLUE.

10.30 a.m. The General Staff of the Division moved up to BERNAFAY WOOD as in the previous operations.

BRIGADES IN POSITION.

11 a.m. All three brigades were in their assembly positions.

GERMAN MESSAGES TO BE DROPPED.

12.15 p.m. The Corps sent a message to say that our aeroplanes were going to drop false message in German over the enemy lines to confuse them.

ZERO HOUR.

12.35 p.m. The infantry attacked.
12.50 p.m. F.O.O. reported the infantry had gained most of the first objective.

FIRST OBJECTIVE CAPTURED.

1.5 p.m. Contact patrol report received showing that Guards Division held their first objective with the exception of points at T.3.d.3.4 - 4.2 and T.3.a.8.1 - 1.0. Here the enemy was still holding out.

Note. The latter co-ordinate was a trench which should have been dealt with by a 60 pounder battery specially detailed for this purpose but which failed to knock out the machine guns and 4th Bn. Grenadier Guards, the left battalion 3rd Guards Brigade, suffered heavily from here.

The 21st Division reported that the 64th Bde. had taken GIRD TRENCH and SUPPORT. This information subsequently proved to be incorrect as the 64th Bde. had not moved.

ENEMY BARRAGE. The enemy barrage was on T.8.b and d.

XIV CORPS GAIN 1ST OBJECTIVE. XIV Corps reported having captured all its 1st objective except the two points already mentioned.
Note. By this time these points had been captured. They also reported that the French had taken RANCOURT.

ENEMY REINFORCEMENTS. G.D.A. reported that the enemy were seen massing in LE TRANSLOY, and the guns had been turned on.

2ND OBJECTIVE CAPTURED. Contact aeroplane message timed 2 p.m. reported we held whole of the BROWN Line from N.33.b.8.0 to T.16.a.7.6 and parties had seized one or two houses in LES BOEUFS. Enemy held N.33.c.1.0 and T.16.b.3.5. Attack was carried out wonderfully without a hitch.

LEFT FLANK EXPOSED. The situation on our left was still obscure and there were still Germans in the 1st objective of the 21st Division which exposed our left flank badly.

RESERVE BNS. MOVE UP. Two Battalions of the 2nd Guards Brigade were ordered to move to the 3rd Guards Bde. H.Q. and were placed under G.O.C. 3rd Guards Bde as a reserve to protect the left flank of the 3rd Guards Bde.

A large number of prisoners were reported to be coming in from LES BOEUFS.

One company of Pioneers and two sections of 76th Field Coy. R.E. were sent to each of the leading Brigades.

O.C. 1st Bn. Irish Guards reported by pigeon his H.Q. in GREEN Line and stated that the infantry were advancing with few casualties.

The left battalion of the 10th Inf. Bde. reported that they were through LES BOEUFS and in touch with our right.

FINAL OBJECTIVE REACHED. Contact patrol reported that we held all our second objective and our final objective from N.34.c.3.10 - T.17.a.8.10 and that MORVAL had also been taken.

21st Division reported that the 110th Brigade were in GUEUDECOURT and their supporting battalions in GIRD TRENCH. There was still no news of the 64th Brigade.

3.45 p.m. Instructions were sent to the 3rd Guards Brigade to Stokes Mortar and bomb the Germans on their left flank in NEEDLE TRENCH but not to make a direct attack.

SITUATION.

3.45 p.m. The situation was as follows. Our line ran from N.34.c.5.7 - T.11.a.1.5. This had practically been consolidated. There appeared to be no enemy immediately in front of our line and no rifle fire. The Left Division held MORVAL along a line T.11.a.1.4, T.11.c.7.3 and down the street to T.16.b.5.9, in the GREEN line the road T.16.a.7.9 - T.16.b.7.9.

4.30 p.m. Message from XIV Corps states that XV Corps airmen report their men lining the road N.26.a.1.9 - 9.8. They appear to be held up in N.26.d. and Germans can be seen in GIRD TRENCH. From N.32.b.3.1 - N.32.d.8.2 LES BOEUFS is completely surrounded by us.

4.30 p.m. The enemy shelled the BLUE line and LES BOEUFS. 9 German aeroplanes were flying high over their own lines.

CONSOLIDATION OF FINAL OBJECTIVE.

5.30 p.m. Message sent to XIV Corps giving the situation as follows. The right brigade were consolidating their final objective in touch with 18th Inf. Bde. on the right. 4 companies of the supporting battalions right brigade had been sent up to LES BEOUFS and the BROWN line and the remaining 4 companies were consolidating the GREEN line. The left brigade was consolidating its final objective and in touch with the right brigade but not in touch with the left division. The left flank was at N.34.c.3.9 with refused flank to N.33.d.8.9 and defensive flank was being made to join up with T.3.a.2.8.

6 p.m. The position of the 21st Division was still obscure and the 3rd Guards Bde was ordered to dig a trench along their left flank and a barrage was arranged along this flank.

7 pm. A message was received from the 3rd Guards Bde. stating that they had received a report from the left battalion in N.34.c. timed 5 p.m. that they were walking about on the top and digging with no difficulty and that there were no Germans anywhere near.

The G.S.O. 1 telephones to the B.G.G.S. reporting this and in consultation with the Corps Commander it was agreed that no big advance should be made but that it was advisable to push out a post to make good the cross roads at N.W. corner of N.34.a.

7 p.m. Orders were received from XIV Corps to keep barrages on all fronts through the night.

7.15 p.m. The 21st Division troops which had penetrated into GUEUDECOURT fell back to GIRD TRENCH and left posts in the village.

8 p.m. The Army Commander sent his congratulations to all rnaks in the Division.

8 p.m. The 1st and 3rd Guards Bdes report that all the C.Os in the front line say that there are no Germans in front of them and ask for the cavalry to be sent through. The G.O.C. consulted the Corps Commander and agreed that in view of the position on either flank this could not be done.

SITUATION DURING NIGHT UNCHANGED. The situation during the night was unchanged. The BLUE line was consolidated all along the Corps frontage and posts were put out in front on the high ground. The situation on our left flank was still obscure and the 21st Division were to use a Tank to clear GIRD TRENCH but no news had been received of it.

CAVALRY SQUADRON. 9.10 am. A message from the XIV Corps stated that a cavalry squadron was on duty at A.15.c and at the disposal of the 5th and Guards Divisions to be used if opportunity occurred to reconnoitre the ground in front and get in touch with the enemy who appeared to be retiring to another line.

One troop was sent to Hd Qrs 3rd Guards Bde and put under their orders.

TANK CLEARS GIRD TRENCH. 9.45 a.m. News was received that the 21st Division had cleared the enemy from GIRD TRENCH by the use of a tank which did good work by driving them up the trench towards us and many were killed and some surrendered including 6 officers and 100 O.R.

The 3rd Guards Bde confirmed this and stated that the 64th Bde were advancing towards the BLUE line with little opposition and the Welsh Guards on our left flank were ordered to conform.

10 a.m. The Corps directs that the BLUE line shall be consolidated and that our main line shall not be advanced without reference to Hd Qrs.

10.5 a.m. The 56th Division and the French occupied COMBLES.

ORDERS FOR RELIEF OF 2 ATTACKING BRIGADES. 11 a.m. Operation Order No. 85 issued concerning the relief of the 1st and 3rd Guards Brigades by the 2nd Guards Brigade on the night of the 26th/27th.

12.30 p.m. Two cavalry patrols were sent out by the 3rd Guards Bde. One went northeast towards GUEUDECOURT and the other through LES BOEUFS and a patrol of the South Irish Horse was reported to have gone through GUEUDECOURT.

ENEMY COUNTER ATTACK. 1.5 p.m. A message was received from the 7th Divisional Artillery, Left Division, reporting that a hostile counter attack with considerable forces was advancing from N.22.central towards N.27.central, that they were caught by six field batteries and retired in the greatest disorder. This report was confirmed by 3rd Guards Bde who reported their left battalion could see hundreds of the enemy retiring in disorder without arms or equipment over the crest toward LE TRANSLOY. The Guards Artillery also got on to this target and a great many of the enemy were seen to fall. About half an hour later these or other of the enemy returned to the line N.21.central and N.28.central and N.35.a. and bagan digging in. During this time various reports of our cavalry being seen going in all directions were received.

GUEUDECOURT TAKEN. THIEPVAL TAKEN. 4.10 p.m. The 21st Division reported that they now held the whole of GUEUDECOURT.

5 p.m. XIV Corps reported that the Reserve Army had taken THIEPVAL village and the ZOLLERN REDOUBT and beaten off counter attack.

The cavalry patrols sent out by the 3rd Guards Bde returned having come up against our own barrage and had nothing to report.

The 3rd Guards Bde reported that the enemy had established a strong point with a machine gun at N.34.a.1.9 and that they had arranged with the 64th Inf. Bde. to attack it at 8 p.m.

The 21st Division reported that they were now on the BLUE Line along the GUEUDECOURT LES BOEUFS road and in touch with us..Again this was incorrect as the enemy still held the cross roads. They were really about 100 yards west of the road and the 3rd Guards Brigade were to make a strong point at N.33.b.9.3 to help them.

SEPTEMBER 26TH.

Orders to 3rd Guards Bde to consolidate a defensive flank along the northern flank where the 21st Division had failed to come up.

Instructions to the 2nd Guards Bde concerning the policy laid down by the Corps for consolidating a strong defensive line on the ground held east of LES BOEUFS.

Operation Order No. 85 concerning the relief of the 1st and 3rd Guards Brigades by the 2nd Guards Brigade.

C A S U A L T I E S

CASUALTIES - September 10th - 17th, 1916.

1st Guards Brigade.

Unit.	Killed.		Wounded.		Missing.		Total.	
	O.	O.R.	O.	O.R.	O.	O.R.	O.	O.R.
2/G.G.	3	105	11	280	-	36	14	421
2/C.G.	6	69	9	254	-	128	15	451
3/C.G.	3	38	8	271	-	90	11	399
1/I.G.	3	35	9	188	1	156	13	379
M.G.Coy.	-	29	4	82	1	10	5	121
T.M.Bty.	-	6	1	7	-	1	1	14
Total.	15	280	42	1082	2	423	59	1785

CASUALTIES - September 18th - 30th, 1916.

1st Guards Brigade.

Unit.	Killed.		Wounded.		Missing.		Total.	
	O.	O.R.	O.	O.R.	O.	O.R.	O.	O.R.
2/G.G.	4	38	5	198	-	98	9	334
2/C.G.	3	16	2	85	-	10	5	111
3/C.G.	-	23	3	118	-	17	3	158
1/I.G.	1	22	4	190	-	43	5	255
M.G.Coy.	-	4	-	7	-	-	-	11
T.M.Bty.	1	7	-	11	-	-	1	18
Total.	9	110	14	609	-	168	23	887

CASUALTIES - September 10th - 30th, 1916.

1st Guards Brigade.

Unit.	Killed.		Wounded.		Missing.		Total.	
	O.	O.R.	O.	O.R.	O.	O.R.	O.	O.R.
2/G.G.	7	141	16	478	-	136	23	755
2/C.G.	9	85	11	339	-	138	20	562
3/C.G.	3	61	11	389	-	107	14	557
1/I.G.	4	57	13	378	1	199	18	634
M.G.Coy.	-	33	4	89	1	10	5	132
T.M.Bty.	1	13	1	18	-	1	2	32
Total.	24	390	56	1691	2	591	82	2672

Subject :- Casualty Return.

Bde Major

Headquarters,

Guards Division.

Casualties to 12 noon 21st Sept. 1916.

	Officers.	Other ranks.								
2nd Bn Grenadier Gds.	-	-	K	1	W	-	M	=	1
2nd Bn Coldstream Gds.	-	1	K	+25	W	-	M	=	26
								Total.	27

+ including 1 at duty

Casualties to 12 noon 22nd Sept. 1916.

3rd Bn Coldstream Guards.	-	-	K	6	W	-	M	=	6
								Total.	6

Casualties to 12 noon 23rd Sept. 1916.

2nd Bn Gren.Gds.	-	1	K	▽2	W	-	M	=	3
2nd Bn Coldstream Gds.	-	2	K	8	W	-	M	=	10
3rd Bn Coldstream Gds.	-	1	K	11	W	1	M	=	13
1st Bn Irish Guards.	*1 W	-	K	⌿3	W	-	M	=	4
Bde.M.Gun Coy.	-	-	K	2	W	-	M	=	2
1st Gds.T.M.Battery.	-	-	K	□4	W	-	M	=	4
								Total.	36

* Capt. The Revd. Father F.M.BROWNE. C.F.
1st Bn Irish Guards.

⌿ includes 1 wounded accidentally.

▽ including 1 at duty.

□ including 1 at duty.

23/9/1916.

Brigadier General.
Commanding 1st Guards Brigade.

CASUALTIES * September 10th - 17th, 1916.

1st Guards Brigade.

Unit.	Killed.		Wounded.		Missing.		Total.	
	O.	O.R.	O.	O.R.	O.	O.R.	O.	O.R.
2/G.G.	3	103	11	280	-	38	14	421
2/C.G.	6	69	9	254	-	128	15	451
3/C.G.	3	38	8	271	-	90	11	399
1/I.G.	3	35	9	188	1	156	13	379
M.G.Coy.	-	29	4	82	1	10	5	121
T.M.By.	-	6	1	7	-	1	1	14
Total.	15	280	42	1082	2	423	59	1785

2nd Guards Brigade.

Unit.	Killed.		Wounded.		Missing.		Total.	
	O.	O.R.	O.	O.R.	O.	O.R.	O.	O.R.
3/G.G.	4	31	9	155	4	209	17	395
1/C.G.	8	26	3	209	3	241	14	476
1/S.G.	4	52	7	184	-	115	11	351
2/I.G.	2	39	5	221	3	177	10	437
M.G.Coy.	7	5	2	27	-	15	9	47
T.M.By.	-	-	-	-	-	-	-	-
Total.	25	153	26	796	10	757	61	1706

3rd Guards Brigade.

Unit.	Killed.		Wounded.		Missing.		Total.	
	O.	O.R.	O.	O.R.	O.	O.R.	O.	O.R.
1/G.G.	3	56	7	256	-	35	10	347
4/G.G.	2	32	3	144	-	12	5	188
2/S.G.	3	26	8	192	-	30	11	248
1/W.G.	5	44	8	230	-	61	13	335
M.G.Coy.	-	5	-	23	-	3	-	31
T.M.By.	-	-	-	4	-	-	-	4
Total.	13	163	26	849	-	141	39	1153

Other Units.

Unit.	Killed.		Wounded.		Missing.		Total.	
	O.	O.R.	O.	O.R.	O.	O.R.	O.	O.R.
4/C.G.	1	2	-	28	-	5	1	35
R.A.	-	4	3	19	-	-	3	23
R.E.	-	4	2	37	-	2	2	43
R.A.M.C.	-	6	6	40	1	1	7	47

SUMMARY.

****

Unit.	Killed.		Wounded.		Missing.		Total.	
	O.	O.R.	O.	O.R.	O.	O.R.	O.	O.R.
1st Gds. Bde.	15	280	42	1082	2	423	59	1785
2nd Gds. Bde.	25	153	26	796	10	757	61	1706
3rd Gds. Bde.	13	163	26	849	-	141	39	1153
4/C.G.	1	2	-	28	-	5	1	35
R. A.	-	4	3	19	-	-	3	23
R.E.	-	4	2	37	-	2	2	43
R.A.M.C.	-	6	6	40	1	1	7	47
T o t a l.	54	612	105	2851	13	1329	172	4792

Officers.

Killed.	54.	
Wounded.	105.	172.
Missing.	13.	

Other Ranks.

Killed.	612.	
Wounded.	2851.	4792.
Missing.	1329.	

Total 4964.

NOTE. One officer, 3rd Guards Brigade, has since died of wounds, making the figures :-

Killed - Officers, 55.
Wounded - Officers, 104.

CASUALTIES * September 18th - 30th, 1916.

The battle of the 25th September accounted for more than 90% of these casualties.

1st Guards Brigade.

Unit.	Killed.		Wounded.		Missing.		Total.	
	O.	O.R.	O.	O.R.	O.	O.R.	O.	O.R.
2/G.G.	4	38	5	198	-	98	9	334
2/C.G.	3	16	2	85	-	10	5	111
3/C.G.	-	23	3	118	-	17	3	158
1/I.G.	1	22	4	190	-	43	5	255
M.G.Coy.	-	4	-	7	-	-	-	11
T.M.By.	1	7	-	11	-	-	1	18
Total.	9	110	14	609	-	168	23	887

2nd Guards Brigade.

Unit.	Killed.		Wounded.		Missing.		Total.	
	O.	O.R.	O.	O.R.	O.	O.R.	O.	O.R.
3/G.G.	-	2	1	21	-	1	1	24
1/C.G.	1	4	3	19	-	1	4	24
1/S.G.	-	4	-	23	-	-	-	27
2/I.G.	-	17	-	50	-	-	-	67
M.G.Coy.	-	-	-	4	-	-	-	4
T.M.By.	-	-	-	-	-	-	-	-
Total.	1	27	4	117	-	2	5	148

3rd Guards Brigade.

Unit.	Killed.		Wounded.		Missing.		Total.	
	O.	O.R.	O.	O.R.	O.	O.R.	O.	O.R.
1/G.G.	1	23	5	172	-	49	6	244
4/G.G.	8	70	3	232	-	143	11	445
2/S.G.	2	40	2	195	-	79	4	314
1/W.G.	-	15	3	62	-	5	3	82
M.G.Coy.	1	10	-	26	-	4	1	40
T.M.By.	-	3	1	7	-	--	1	10
Total.	12	161	14	694	-	280	26	1135

Other Units.

Unit.	Killed.		Wounded.		Missing.		Total.	
	O.	O.R.	O.	O.R.	O.	O.R.	O.	O.R.
4/C.G.	-	4	-	14	-	-	-	18
R. A.	-	8	2	40	-	2	2	50
R. E.	-	-	1	14	-	-	1	14
R.A.M.C.	-	4	2	26	-	-	2	30
Chaplains	-	-	1	-	-	-	1	-

SUMMARY.

Unit.	Killed.		Wounded.		Missing.		Total.	
	O.	O.R.	O.	O.R.	O.	O.R.	O.	O.R.
1st Gds.Bde.	9	110	14	609	-	168	23	887
2nd Gds.Bde.	1	27	4	117	-	2	5	146
3rd Gds.Bde.	12	161	14	694	-	280	26	1135
4/C.G.	-	4	-	14	-	-	-	18
R. A.	-	8	2	40	-	2	2	50
R. E.	-	-	1	14	-	-	1	14
R. A. M. C.	-	4	2	26	-	-	2	30
Chaplains.	-	-	1	-	-	-	1	-
T o t a l.	22	314	38	1514	-	452	60	2280

Officers.

Killed.	22.)	
Wounded.	38.)	60.
Missing.	-.)	

Other Ranks.

Killed.	314.)	
Wounded.	1514.)	2280.
Missing.	452.)	

Total. 2360.

Ref these. Please show officers separately by numbers & type in on narratives done by Wainwright the other day

CASUALTIES.

September 15th/16th, 1916.

Unit.	Killed.	Wounded.	Missing.	Total.
	officers O.R.	officers O.R.	officers O.R.	
2nd Bn. Grenadier Guards.	121	236	12	369
2nd Bn. Coldstream Guards.	135	280	46	461
3rd Bn. Coldstream Guards.	87	301	32	420
1st Bn. Irish Guards.	79	312	31	422
Bde., Machine Gun Company.	24	63	6	93
1st Guards T. M. Battery.	4	7	-	11
Total :-	450.	1,199.	127.	1,776.

CASUALTIES.

September 25th/26th, 1916.

Unit.	Killed.	Wounded.	Missing.	Total.
2nd Bn. Grenadier Guards.	112	227	12	351
2nd Bn. Coldstream Guards.	18	67	5	90
3rd Bn. Coldstream Guards.	20	116	11	147
1st Bn. Irish Guards.	33	198	7	238
Bde., Machine Gun Company.	4	9	-	13
1st Guards T. M. Battery.	2	5	-	7
Total :-	189.	622.	35.	846.

CASUALTIES.

September 15th/16th, 1916.

Unit.	Killed. O.	Killed. O.R.	Wounded. O.	Wounded. O.R.	Missing. O.	Missing. O.R.	Total.	
2nd Bn. Gren. Gds.,	3	118	11	225	-	12	-	369.
2nd Bn. Cold. Gds.,	7	128	9	271	-	46	-	461.
3rd Bn. Cold. Gds.,	3	84	8	293	-	32	-	420.
1st Bn. Irish Gds.,	5	74	10	302	-	31	-	422.
Bde., M.G.Company.	-	24	3	60	1	5	-	93.
1st Gds. T.M.Batty.,	-	4	1	6	-	-	-	11.
Total :-	18	432	42	1157	1	126	-	1776.

CASUALTIES.

September 25th/26th, 1916.

Unit.	Killed. O.	Killed. O.R.	Wounded. O.	Wounded. O.R.	Missing. O.	Missing. O.R.	Total.	
2nd Bn. Gren. Gds.,	4	108	5	222	-	12	-	351.
2nd Bn. Cold. Gds.,	3	15	3	64	-	5	-	90.
3rd Bn. Cold. Gds.,	-	20	3	113	-	11	-	147.
1st Bn. Irish Gds.,	1	32	7	191	-	7	-	238.
Bde., M.G.Company.	-	4	-	9	-	-	-	13.
1st Gds. T.M.Batty.,	1	1	-	5	-	-	-	7.
Total :-	9	180	18	604	-	35	-	846.

The Headquarters,

1st Guards Brigade.

Herewith please find particulars of casualties, in accordance with 1st G.B. No. 596 of 23rd November, 1916.

Lieutenant Colonel,

Commanding 2nd Battalion Grenadier Guards.

24th November, 1916.

ORDERLY ROOM
2ND BN GRENADIER GUARDS

2nd Battalion Grenadier Guards.

Casualties for the period 15th September.

	Killed & Died Wnds.	Wounded.	Missing.	Slightly wounded, remained duty.
Officers.	3	9	-	2
Other Ranks.	110	207	12	8
Other Ranks, attached Trench Mortar Battery.	8	10	-	-

Casualties for the period 25th September.

	Killed & Died Wnds.	Wounded.	Missing.	Slightly wounded, remained duty.
Officers.	4	5	-	-
Other Ranks.	107	210	12	10
Other Ranks, attached Machine Gun Company.	1	2	-	-

ORDERLY ROOM
2nd Bn. GREN. GUARDS

Lieutenant Colonel,

Commanding 2nd Battalion Grenadier Guards.

24th November, 1916.

2nd Battalion Coldstream Guards.

Return of Casualties for 15th and 25th September 1916.

--+++++++++- 15/9/16 -+++++++++--

Officers

Killed	4
Died of Wounds.	3
Wounded.	9

Other Ranks.

Killed.	108
Died of Wounds.	20
Wounded.	271
Missing believed wounded.	10.
Missing.	36.

--+++++++++- 25/9/16 -+++++++++--

Officers.

Killed.	3
Wounded.	3

Other Ranks.

Killed.	13.
Died of Wounds.	2
Wounded.	64
Missing.	5

-++++ Total ++++-

Officers.

Killed.	7
Died of Wounds.	3
Wounded.	12

Other Ranks.

Killed.	121
Died of Wounds.	22
Wounded.	335
Missing believed wounded	10
Missing.	41

J. S. Coats. Lt.
for Captain,
Commanding,
2nd Bn. Coldstream Guards.

27th November 1916.

1st Guards Bde.

Reference 1st Guards Bde. No. 596.

The Casualties sustained by the Battalion under my Command for the periods mentioned are as follows :-

During the fighting about Sept 15th.

OFFICERS.	Killed.	Major G.E. Vaughan.	
		Capt. H.A. Cubitt.	
		" C.E. Tufnell.	3
	Wounded.	Lieut. R. M. Synge.	
		2/ " A. G. Smith.	
		" N. F. Machin.	
		" W. Atkinson.	
		" J. D. Legge.	
		" W. S. Hardwicke.	
		" V. N. Rowsell.	
		" J.D.N. Warren.	8

OTHER RANKS.	Killed	84	
	Wounded	293 (includes 5 Slightly at duty)	
	Missing	23	
	Wounded & Missing	9	409
			420

During the fighting about 25th Sept.

OFFICERS.	Wounded.	2/Lt. J.G. Fortescue.	
		" F. McBride.	
		Capt. J.V. Llewelyn.	3

OTHER RANKS.	Killed	~~22~~	20	
	Wounded	~~1185~~	113 (Includes 3 Slightly at duty)	
	Missing		5	
	Wounded and Missing		6	144
				147

R.B.Y. Crawfurd

Lt. Col.
Comdg.
3rd Bn. Coldstream Guards.

24/11/16

1st G/1077/16.

1st Guards Bde.

In reply to your No 596 of this date, the casualties of the Battalion under my command during the fighting of about Sept. 15th & about Sept. 25th are as under:-

SEPT	KILLED		WOUNDED		DIED of WDS		MISSING	
	Offrs.	OR.	Offrs.	OR.	Offrs	OR	Offrs.	OR.
10th/17th	3	65	10	302	2	9	NIL	31.
22nd/26th	NIL	25	7*	191	1	7	NIL	7

* Includes 2 Offrs attached Bn. (Chaplain + Medical Officer)

Total casualties for each action:-

10/17th. - 13 Officers 398 O.R.
22/26th. - 7 " 223 "

Total:- 20 Offrs. 621 O.Ranks.

23/11/16.

R. McCalmont
Lt. Colonel.
Comdg. 1st Bn Irish Guards.

M. G. A. No 15/25/11/16

Headquarters

1st Guards Brigade.

With reference to your office letter, 1st G.B. No 596 dated 23rd Nov 1916 re casualties during the fighting about Sept 15th & 25th. Herewith amended Nominal Roll please.

SECTION OR BATT.	REGT. No	RANK	NAME		REMARKS	
No 1. Section	–	LIEUT.	Hon. R.V. Agar-Robartes		Wounded	14-9-16
2nd Bn Gren Gds	19136.	Pte.	Clarke	C.H	Wounded	14-9-16
″	20501	″	Jones	G.H	″	″
No 1. Section	16154	L.Cpl	Collier	E.R.	″	″
No 1 Section	23287	Pte.	Anderson		Wounded – Prev reported Missing.	
No 1 Section	14930	Sgt.	Bartlett	J	Killed	15-9-16
No 1 ″	17275	Pte	Clark	J.S.W.	″	″
2nd Bn. Gren Gds	22444	″	Furlonger	V	″	″
″ ″	17207	″	Dawes	H.L	″	16-9-16.
″ ″	16154	L/Cpl	Biddle	J	Wounded	15-9-16
No 1 Section	14071	″	Clark	J	″	″
2nd Bn Gren Gds	15474.	L/Cpl	Brignell	J.	″	since died of wounds
No 1 Section	19517	Pte	Hogan	E.	″	15-9-16
2nd Bn. Gren Gds	11804	″	Fox	E.	″	″
No 1 Sect	23511	″	Sheffield	J	″	″
2nd Gren Gds	15786	″	Richards	R	″	″
No 1 Sect	13058	″	Coleman	J	″	″
″	15566	″	Hodge	F	″	″
2nd Bn Gren Gds	17674	″	Mott	E.	″	16-9-16
″ ″ ″	17274	″	Barker	H.	″	″
No 1 Section	13764	″	Langham		″	″
2nd Gren Gds	17135	″	Tuckey		″	″
No 2. Section	–	LIEUT.	G.M. Perry		Wounded	15-9-16
″	–	2/LIEUT	G.L. Walker		″	″
No 2 Section	11065	L/Cpl	Downing	E	Killed	15-9-16
2 Bn Coldm Gds	12711	Pte.	Biggs	C.S	″	″
No 2 Section	9116	″	Fothergill	G	″	″
″	10990	″	Frogley	A	″	″
″	8791	″	Smith	J	″	″
2 Bn Coldm Gds	10441	L/Cpl	Ayres	G	Wounded	″
No 2 Section	12130	″	Cousens	W	″	″
″ ″	12620	Pte.	Andrews	H	″	″
″ ″	14244	″	Bateman	J	″	″
″ ″	11129	″	Fleet	R	″	″
2nd Bn Coldm Gds	13523	″	Gardener	E	″	″
″ ″	11975	″	Hassell	J	″	″
No 2 Section	10871	″	Hillier	W	″	″
2 Bn Coldm Gds	13462	″	Lanchester	H	″	″
″ ″	11804	″	Lester	W	″	″
″ ″	9267	″	Scarfe	J	″	″
No 2 Section	8555	″	Smith		″	″
″ ″	10524	″	Gates	F	Shell Shock	15-9-16
2 Bn Coldm Gds	12021	″	Le Poucher	J	″	″
″ ″	10838	″	Gibson	B	″	″
″ ″ ″	13443	L/Cpl	Henshaw	S	Missing	″
″ ″ ″	10238	Pte.	Bradley		″	″
No 2 Section	7826	″	Burke		Wounded	15-9-16

Section or Batt	Regt No	Rank	Name		Remarks
No 3 Section	7881	Sgt.	Maddison	R.	Killed - 15-9-16
3rd Bn Coldm Gds	14014	Pte.	Flinkham	J.	″ ″
No 3 Section	8207	″	White	W.	″ ″
3rd Bn Coldm Gds	9304	″	Dewis	J.	″ ″
″ ″	11475	″	Knowles	W	″ ″
″ ″	10626	″	Davis	J	Wounded ″
″ ″	11834	″	Belton	J	″ ″
No 3 Section	11664	″	Cousins	J	″ ″
″ ″	6961	″	Ward	F	″ ″
″ ″	10101	″	Dore	A	″ ″
″ ″	11292	″	Ash	R.	″ ″
3 Bn Coldm Gds	6479	″	Blythe	W	″ ″
″ ″	10745	″	Reeves	W	″ ″
″ ″	11693	″	Whitlam	A	″ ″
″ ″	11920	″	Duckworth	H	″ ″
No 3 Section	13217	″	Steele	W	″ ″
3rd Coldm Gds	4172	″	Brown	A	″ Prev. reported Missing.
No 3 Section	7413	″	Manning	H	″ ″ ″ ″
3 Coldm Gds	9514	″	Colbert	J	Missing. 15-9-16
″ ″	11553	″	Hosker	A	″ ″
No 4 Section	—	Lieut	L.C. Whitefoord		Missing. 15-9-16
No 4 ″	3844	Pte.	Coffey	W	Killed ″
1st Irish Gds	4916	″	Daly	R	″ ″
″	5930	″	Murphy	J	″ ″
No 4 Sect	4821		Lyden	J	″ ″
1st Bn Irish Gds	5901	″	Walsh	W	″ ″
No 4 Section	3494	L/Sgt	Nolan	J	Wounded since died of wounds
″	3973	L/Cpl	Doyle	J	″ ″ ″ ″
″	4323	L/Cpl	Richardson	J	Wounded 15-9-16
1st Bn Irish Gds	4698	—	Roche	M.	″ ″
″ ″	4795	Pte	Gallagher	J	″ ″
No 4 Section	8739	″	McCormack	W	″ ″
	8700	″	Broderick	E	″ ″
1st Irish Gds	7428	″	Kennedy	W	″ ″
″ ″	4708	″	Donnelly	H	″ ″
″ ″	4848	″	Byrne	J	″ ″
No 4 Section	3071	″	Chambers	Jo	″ ″
1 Irish Gds	5437	″	Joyce	H	″ ″
No 4 Sect	9105	″	Deering	J	″ ″
1 Irish Gds	5106	″	Hancox	W	″ ″
″ ″	5905	″	Hearn	J	″ ″
No 4 Section	4836	″	Byrne	[illegible]	″ ″
1st Irish Gds	4198	″	Fisher	P	Killed Prev reported missing
″	3668	″	Rowe	[illegible]	Wounded ″ ″ ″
″	4843	″	O'Keeffe	P	Missing. 15-9-16
No 4 Section	4788	″	Mullenly	[illegible]	Killed Prev reported missing
		25th Sept 1916			
2nd Gren Gds	17350	Pte	Page	W.	Wounded 25-9-16
″ ″	16811	L/Cpl	Wilson	J	″ ″
No 1 Sect	24001	Pte	Woodhams	F	″ ″
No 1 Sect 3.GG	22716	″	Hollis	C.	″ ″
No 1 Sect	14794	″	May	H	Killed 26-9-16
2. Gren Gds	21961	Pte.	Shirley	H	″ ″
No 2 Section	13935	″	Wakefield	J	Shell Shock ″
″ ″	9862	″	Stimpson	D	Wounded 26-9-16
″ ″	16963	″	Garner	H	″ 26-9-16
2/Gren Gds	13787	″	Hall	G	″ 25-9-16
No 3 Sect 1st Welsh Gds	1786	″	Jones	T	Killed 26-9-16
1st Irish Gds	6132	″	Pinder	A	″ ″
No 4 Sect	9225	″	Campbell	J	Wounded ″

BRIGADE MACHINE GUN COMPANY
No. 4/8A
Date 25-11-16
FIRST GUARDS BRIGADE

[illegible signature] CAPTAIN,
COMMANDING MACHINE GUN COMPANY,
1st GUARDS BRIGADE.

Trench Mortar Battery.

2nd Gren. Guards.

No	Rank	Name	Remarks	Date
14423	Pte	Glynn J.	Killed.	13 9/16.
13950	.	Willis E.	" "	" "
15521	L/c	Eustace G.	" "	15 9/16.
16371	Pte	Freeman G.	" "	16 9/16.
9975	"	Pippett J.	Wounded.	15 9/16.
18510	.	Swain C.	" "	14 9/16.
19473	L/c	Ryder J.	" "	15 9/16.

2nd Cold. Guards.

Lieut		R. J. Pinto	Wounded.	15 9/16.

3rd Cold. Guards.

10529	L/c	Morris H	Wounded.	15 9/16
11485	Pte	Gigg H	" "	" "

1st Irish Guards.

2411	L/Sgt	Connors T	Wounded.	15 9/16.

24/11/16.

R J Pinto Capt.
O.C. 1 Gds Bde T. M. Battery.

Trench Mortar Battery.

2nd Gren: Guards.

No	Rank	Name	Remarks	Date
14000	L/C	Bibby J.	Wounded.	25 9/16.

2nd Cold: Guards.

[illegible]370	Pte	Beckett S, J.	Killed	25 9/16.
10866	"	Wright D,	Wounded.	23 9/16.

3rd Cold: Guards.

	Capt	H P Meakin	Killed	25 9/16.
11951	L/C	Wilde H	Wounded	" "
12735	Pte	Savage F,	" "	" "

1st Irish Guards.

8653	Pte	Calnan J.	Wounded.	25 9/16.

24/11/16.

[illegible] Capt.
O.C. 1 Gds Bde T. M. Battery.

Headquarters,

Guards Division.

Herewith List of Officer Casualties :-

KILLED.

2/Lieut., G.A.ARBUTHNOT,	2nd Gren.Gds.,	
Captain A.K.S.CUNINGHAME,	" " "	
Lieut., Hon. W.A.D.PARNELL,	" " "	
Lieut., M.A.KNATCHBULL-HUGESSON,	" " "	
Captain H.W.VERELST,	2nd Cold.Gds.,	26/9/16.
2/Lieut., F.W.T.CLERKE,	" " "	26/9/16.
2/Lieut., J.A.MACGREGOR,	" " "	26/9/16.
Captain H.P.MEAKIN,	3rd Cold.Gds., (1st Gds.T.M.Btty.,)	

WOUNDED, DIED OF WOUNDS.

Captain L.R.HARGREAVES,	1st Irish Gds.,	25/9/16.

WOUNDED.

Lieut., A.F.IRVINE,	2nd Gren.Gds.,	
Captain G.C. FITZ. HARCOURT-VERNON,	" " "	
Lieut., H.G.WIGGINS,	" " "	
Lieut., R.B.B.WRIGHT,	" " "	
Captain W.H. BEAUMONT-NESBITT,	" " "	
Lieut., G.BARRY,	2nd Cold.Gds.,	24/9/16.
Captain B.N.MURPHY, R.A.M.C. attch.	" " "	26/9/16.
2/Lieut., S.O.CROMIE,	" " "	26/9/16.
2/Lieut., J.G.FORTESCUE,	3rd Cold.Gds.,	24/9/16.
~~Lieut., J.V.LLEWELYN,~~	~~" " "~~	~~26/9/16.~~
Lieut., R.J.P.RODAKOWSKI,	1st Irish Gds.,	25/9/16.
2/Lieut., G.V.WILLIAMS,	" " "	25/9/16.
2/Lieut., T.C.GIBSON,	" " "	25/9/16.
Captain P.R.WOODHOUSE, R.A.M.C. attch.	" "	25/9/16.

WOUNDED REMAINING AT DUTY.

2/Lieut., F. McBRIDE,	3rd Cold.Gds.,	24/9/16.
Lieut., J.V.LLEWELYN,	" " "	26/9/16.

TO HOSPITAL (SHOCK.)

Lieut., A.H.BLOM,	1st Irish Gds.,	25/9/16.

Brigadier General,

27/9/1916.

Commdg., 1st Guards Brigade.

Headquarters,

Guards Division.

Casualties of Other Ranks of 1st Guards Brigade during recent Operations September 21st to 27th 1916, are as follows :-

Unit.	Killed.	Wounded.	Missing.	Slightly W. at Duty.	Total.
2/Gren.Gds.,	37	188	98	7	330
2/Cold.Gds.,	11	62	10	-	83
3/Cold.Gds.,	21	100	16	-	137
1/Irish Gds.,	20	171	43	-	234
M.G.Company.	4	5	-	-	9
T.M.Battery.	1	5	-	-	6
Brigade H.Q.,	2	4	-	-	6
TOTAL	96	535	167	7	805

Brigadier General,

28th September 1916. Commdg., 1st Guards Brigade.

CONFERENCES

~~Orders~~ previous to

attack orders for

Sept 15th 1916

(1)

me auf

S E C R E T.

BRIGADE CONFERENCE held at Brigade Hd.Qrs., MEAULTE, 27th Aug.1916.

Tactical Lessons of recent operations.

1. Dress and Equipment.
(a) Great-coats and spare kit packed in valise labelled and stored. Pockets of coats empty in case coats required.
(b) Carried by men (except certain specialists).
(1) Rifle and equipment less pack.
(2) Two bandoliers S.A.A.
(3) Haversack on back containing two tins meat, eight ration biscuits, canteen packed with grocery ration.
(4) Waterproof sheet with jersey rolled inside fixed on the back of the waist with the supporting straps of the pack.
(5) Three sandbags carried under the flap of the haversack.
(6) Two Mills Grenades.
(7) Two Smoke-helmets.

2. Distinguishing Badges.
(a) Carriers - Red band, right arm.
(b) Runners - Blue band, right arm.
(c) ~~Cleaning~~ Clearing up parties - White band, right arm.

3. Work Parties.
Drilled by R.E. by day and night to ensure rapidity of getting on to tasks. Work Platoons will practice with R.E. Section and will after an assault find the working and carrying party for consolidation.

4. Taking over line, from another Unit - great care to ensure no ground lost especially on flanks.

5. Hour of Attack.
Early morn assists assembly and conceals advance, but -
(a) Early mists cause loss of direction and touch.
(b) Aeroplanes cannot see mirrors and flares until some time after the attack.
(c) Artillery observation difficult. Afternoon advantageous, provided it is clear enough for heavy Artillery to do effective counter battery work.
(d) Night affords great concealment and protection from artillery fire when position captured.

6. Assault.
(a) Company frontage about 100 yards.
(b) Four platoon waves.
(c) Intervals 50 to 100 yards.
(d) Steady drill-like advance of each wave to maintain control.

7. Position gained.
(a) Establish posts well to front and send out patrols.
(b) Consolidate strong points on pre-arranged plan, at first only pick and shovel work.
(c) Obtain maximum of protection by digging deep for all lines and Machine Guns and Lewis Guns.
(d) Bold handling of Lewis Guns should there be commanding positions to front.
(e) Early relief of assaulting troops.

/8.

8. Holding of ground ~~see O.B.~~ 1782 para. 4.
 (a) In front chain of posts ~~Machine Guns and Lewis Guns,~~ posts thickened at night.
 (b) These posts protect Machine and Lewis Guns from bombers and snipers.
 (c) Snipers actively employed in killing enemy patrols.
 (d) If inside a Wood consolidate 50 yards inside with posts holding outer edge to deny it to the enemy.

9. Lewis Guns not to go forward earlier than the second wave and Machine Guns until consolidation of new line has begun.

10. Machine Guns.
 (a) Active night work to prevent repairs and hinder reliefs and carrying parties.
 (b) In assault, covering fire on successive targets.
 (c) Forward positions previously selected.

11. Stokes Mortar Guns.
 (a) Work by sections under orders of Battalion Commander.
 (b) Slow bombardment to ensure accuracy for rapid fire later.
 (c) Last two minutes hurricane bombardment until 1 minute after Zero then lift to Support line.
 (d) Consolidation begun move forward to previously selected positions to cover enemy lines of approach.
 (e) Light loads are suggested as more sure of coming up than heavy and Depots should be well forward.

12. Carrying Parties may take up to 25% of Brigade.

13. A case occurred of German prisoners being sent back over 'No Man's Land' unescorted; they picked up rifles and fought again. Company Commanders must be prepared to deal with any prisoners that may surrender. The impetus of the attack must not be checked by any enemy surrendering and a small party will suffice to collect and march off prisoners.

14. Smoke discharges have proved very useful as a screen.

15. German Machine Guns and men have frequently abandoned wrecked trenches and taken up positions in shell-holes and standing crops.

16. Importance of seizing Tactical Positions.
Prompt following up has often found important positions evacuated and enabled them to be denied to the enemy when he has returned to them later. Patrols must not return as a whole but send back a report and hang on to the position seized until support is sent to them.

17. Lessons learnt by 36th Division.
 (a) Hug the barrage.
 (b) Limited objective.
 (c) Stores right up.
 (d) Battalion Commanders upwards always to have a reserve in hand.

18. Communications.
 (a) It takes many hours for orders to reach Company Commanders, each Commander has to digest orders and then issue his own.
 (b) Eight runners per Battalion attached to Brigade H.Q., Relay stations about a quarter mile apart, runners very lightly equipped.
 (c) Assaulting Units carries forward wire which Brigade Signal Section later on supplements with cable.
 (d) Visual signalling.
 (e) Pigeons.

/19.

19. It is essential for all ranks to work with vigour and determination. The position after an assault is generally most obscure and so all ranks must be impressed with the necessity of holding on to what they have gained and of making the utmost use of their weapons, their position and the demoralization of the enemy.

20. <u>Various points to be attended to.</u>

(a) Careful writing of messages; the time of despatch and position when writing must be stated.

(b) Men must be trained to use restraint in drinking, their water bottle will have to last 24 hours. No water in the German lines to be touched until examined by a M.O. and declared free from poison.

(c) The word 'Retire' will not be used or if used will not be obeyed - The Germans have constantly used this word to deceive our troops.

(d) Pay no attention to a White Flag until the enemy come out with their hands up and even then look out for treachery.

(e) Captured guns are rendered useless by punching a hole in the buffer case which is underneath the gun, it can be pierced by a bullet or an entrenching tool or by burring the breech screw with a bullet or heavy stone.

(f) No unwounded man is allowed to bring back wounded men - wounded men able to walk make their own way back to Regtl. Aid Posts, others wait the arrival of stretcher bearers.

(g) Trophy and Souvenir collecting must be sternly repressed, every man must be consolidating or be reorganised for further offensive.

(h) No papers, documents, maps, etc, that may be of value to the enemy must be carried by assaulting troops.

****

Capt.
B.M.
1st Gds Bde

28. 8. 16.

Conference Notes
refer to lessons learnt
at the early July attacks
The conditions which
existed in the middle
of September were very
different & necessitated
changes notably in:—
~~[illegible]~~
~~[illegible] at zero~~
para 9. Lewis gun teams
cannot keep up in these
long advances & must be
allowed to come on in their
own time
Machine guns do, but
must start with assaulting
battalions
para 12. Bns must do their own

carrying it does not
take anything like 25%

18 (a) I cannot find
entirely

1st G.B. No. 226/1.

2nd Bn. Grenadier Guards.
2nd Bn. Coldstream Guards.
3rd Bn. Coldstream Guards.
1st Bn. Irish Guards.
Bde., Machine Gun Company.
1st Guards T.M. Battery.
Bde., Signalling Officer.

COMMUNICATIONS DURING AN ATTACK.

There may be the greatest difficulty in establishing and maintaining communications during an attack. All Officers must be prepared to assist especially in the early stages by knowing where their own Signalling Stations are established, and by directing runners to them. They must also be ready to inform their own Signalling Stations, if some distant Station is calling up and receiving no reply, since it may often happen that whilst part of a line is visible to a forward Station the other part of that line where there is a Signalling Post cannot be seen.

Captain,

8th September 1916. Brigade Major, 1st Guards Brigade.

S E C R E T.

2nd Bn. Grenadier Guards.
2nd Bn. Coldstream Guards.
3rd Bn. Coldstream Guards.
1st Bn. Irish Guards.
Bde., Signalling Officer.

The following instructions with regard to signallers and communication generally in the attack are forwarded for future guidance.

Equipment of Signallers and Runners.

1. (a) The equipment of signallers and runners will be the same as for Infantry vide Conference Notes of August 27th para. 1, with the exception that these will only carry 20 rounds of S.A.A. and no bandoliers of S.A.A. - sandbags or bombs.

Signalling Equipment.

2. (a) Company signallers in the attack will only take forward -
   - (i) Shutters -
   - (ii) Flags -
   - (iii) Possibly pigeons.

   (b) Battn., H.Q., will take forward -
   - (i) Shutters -
   - (ii) Flags -
   - (iii) Pigeons -
   - (iv) A small number of telephones -
   - (v) Lamps -
   - (vi) Panel and numbers -
   - (vii) Wire - Sufficient wire should be taken forward to allow of an extension to Companies when possible.

   (c) All Signalling equipment not required by Battalions will be stored under Battalion arrangements.

   (d) The aim of all communication within Battalions in the attack should be to establish and maintain one main line either by telephone - visual - runner or pigeons with the front line.

   It is almost impossible to maintain more than one line owing to the limited number of personnel to replace casualties and the difficulty of maintaining any line at all.

Codes.

3. (a) XIV Corps Code "A" will be used as much as possible when the situation is normal and communications are working properly.

   (b) A Code known as the Aeroplane Code will be used during active operations between all Units of the Brigade and with the Contact Aeroplane. Copies of this Code are attached and any suggestions for additions to this Code should be sent in as soon as possible.

Contact Aeroplane. 4. (a) Distinguishing marks of XIV Corps Aeroplanes are a black line on each of the lower planes and two streamers from the struts.

(b) To call up Contact Aeroplane, Units will use their Code Call i.e. D.23 - D.27 etc., which the Aeroplane when it has seen will answer by the same Code Call.

(c) Aeroplane calls up Units by sending the Code Call of Unit required and Unit acknowledges this by "T".

(d) Transmission of messages -

- (i) Each word will be acknowledged by "T" -
- (ii) "V.E." will be sent by sender on completion of message.
- (iii) "R.D". will be sent by recipient on completion of message.
- (iv) Code letters of Aeroplane Code will be checked back by recipient.
- (v) White Very Light or hooter means "Where are you?" to the front line troops only and these immediately show their position by every available means.
- (vi) It is hoped to make some arrangement with R.F.C. so that the flares of front line troops may be acknowledged by a coloured 'Very' Light.

Battn.,H.Q., 5. In the event of Battn.,H.Q., moving forward the Brigade, on being informed, will establish a Relay Post at their original H.Q., and will collect messages from them at that Post.

Runners. 6. (a) Runners on arrival at their Relay Posts or Stations will dump all their equipment except their smoke-helmets.

(b) Runners will not be used where Visual is possible and when runners are sent they must be sent in pairs, each runner with a copy of the message and by different routes.

(c) To economise in the exertions of runners, runners will remain at their destinations until a second runner from the same Relay Post or Unit arrives when the first will return with receipts etc.,

(d) All runners will wear blue bands on right arm.

(e) Eight runners per Battalion will be attached to Brigade H.Q.,

Messages. 7. (a) All messages must be carefully written. The time of despatch and the position (map reference or name of trench) of the sender must be included in every message.

(b) Messages sent by Visual must be worded as shortly as possible.

W B[illegible]

Captain,

7th September 1916. Brigade Major, 1st Guards Brigade.

AEROPLANE CODE.

N N	means	"Short of S.A.Amn:".
Y Y	"	"Short of Bombs".
K K	"	"Lengthen range".
O O	"	"Barrage wanted".
X X	"	"Held up by M. G. Fire".
Z Z	"	"Held up by Wire".
F F	"	"The enemy is attacking".
C C	"	"Will attack again at ---".
S S	"	"Have reached objective".
"O K"	"	"Everything all correct".

1st G.B. No. 237.

2nd Bn. Grenadier Guards.
2nd Bn. Coldstream Guards.
3rd Bn. Coldstream Guards.
1st Bn. Irish Guards.

1. Battalions will draw 2 bombs per man from the Divisional Bomb Store F.19.d.2.4. as soon as possible. These bombs must be detonated, when drawn, under Battalion arrangements, so that each man can go into the line with two detonated bombs.

2. Battalions will make arrangements so that 2 bandoliers of S.A.A. can be issued to each man before moving into the line.

3. The three sandbags which are to be carried by each man must be drawn as soon as possible from R.E. Dump about A.13.d.4.2.

4. Petrol tins for all Units are being collected and stored by Brigade H.Q..

5. Material for distinguishing arm badges will be issued tomorrow.

6. S.O.S. Rockets will be issued to Units before moving into the line.

7. Tools will be provided in the line or drawn on arrival nearer to the front.

Captain,

10th September 1916. Brigade Major, 1st Guards Brigade.

S E C R E T.

HEADQUARTERS
No. 237/2
Date 12/9/16
BRIGADE

2nd Bn. Grenadier Guards.
2nd Bn. Coldstream Guards.
3rd Bn. Coldstream Guards.
1st Bn. Irish Guards.

Meal the morning of the Assault.

Arrangements should be made to give the men either a sandwich or fresh bread and cooked meats and if possible hot tea previous to the assault.
There will be an issue of Oxo Cubes and it is hoped that there will be a rum ration.

There will be a bread and fresh meat ration for consumption on the 14th inst., and if extra preserved meat and biscuits and groceries are required to make up for the extra meal before the assault it can be drawn from a Divisional Dump provided authority stating what is required is obtained from this Office.

Captain,

12th September 1916. Brigade Major, 1st Guards Brigade.

Secret — Bns. M. G. Coy

Conference held at [illegible] on Sept 11th 1916

We were informed of

1) The probable date of operation.

(224)

2) The following points govern the formation in which the Brigade will attack

A) Forming up trenches cannot be dug on any considerable scale for want of time

B) The attack will be at or just before dawn

C) As tanks will precede the attack it will not come as a complete surprise to the enemy.

D) The advance to the first objective will be 700 to 800 yds

It will therefore be necessary to have an extension of about 2 paces & interval between waves of 50 yards.

3) ~~As~~ The attack will be on a front of several miles & past experience shows that in this case the hostile barrages are not of the same intensity as when a shorter front is attacked.

4) The leading Brigades will start at Zero the flow of waves in these brigades will be conti

2/

n[illegible] in succeeding waves
small columns according
as Bns are under rifle fire or not.

5) The Brigade frontage is about
500 yards in the first advance;
1000 yards in depth is calculated
as being sufficient for the leading
attacking Brigade.

6) The 1st [illegible] Brigade must be
prepared to form a defensive
flank to the North should attacks on
that flank be held up.

7) Forming up will require very
careful reconnaissance &
marking out of the ground, also
the careful laying out of lines
for ~~the~~ direction on the
initial advance.

8) The C in C has notified the
vital importance of the great
final blow of the Somme battle.
The offensive power of the
Division must be used to the
utmost.

V) C.O.s will submit in roughly the number of Officers & N.C.O.s it is proposed to leave with the first line. These officers & N.C.O.s will join the 1st Line Transport when Battalions leave Camp.

6 Copies

C.P.

GERMAN TROOPS.
****

Within the last 48 hours, the German troops opposite us have changed, 111th Division being relieved by 185th Division and 58th Division by 5th BAVARIAN Division.

The 185th Division has been re-organised and now consists of 28th Reserve Regiment (late 16th Reserve Division) from FRESNES, 65th Regiment, and 161st Regiment (both late 15th Division) from SOISSONS. The two latter regiments are composed of RHINELANDERS.

The 5th BAVARIAN Division has been brought down from LENS.

All the battalions of these two Divisions, which were holding the line during our attack on 9th September, suffered very heavy losses.

The moral of both appears to be considerably inferior to that of the two Divisions they relieved.

The dividing line between the two probably runs N.E.-S.W. through T.14.c.4½.0.

Order of battle from North to South is :-

14th BAVARIAN Regt.
19th BAVARIAN Regt.
161st Regiment.
28th Reserve Regt.
65th Regiment.

Further particulars will be issued later.

H. L. Aubrey-Fletcher

Captain,
General Staff, Guards Division.

11th Sept. 1918.

Secret

C.R.E. Guards Div. No. 1027.

"G".
"Q".
C.R.A.
55th Field Coy. R.E.
75th. Field " " "
76th. Field " " "
Gds. Signal " " "
1st Guards Bde.
2nd Guards Bde.
3rd Guards Bde.

The Advanced Brigade Headquarters for 1st and 2nd Guards Brigades are being constructed at S.24.b.6.1½. and T.19.a.½.3½.

H. [signature] Lt. Col.

H.Q.R.E.G.D.
11th ~~August~~ Sept 1916.

Lieut. Colonel. R.E.
C.R.E. GUARDS DIVISION.

SECRET

S E C R E T. G.D.No. 2149/G

1st Guards Brigade.
~~2nd Guards Brigade.~~
~~3rd Guards Brigade.~~
~~C.R.E.,~~

C O N F E R E N C E
held at Divisional Headquarters, August 28th.

1. The Major General gave outlines of Plans for future operations.

The next objective of XIV Corps, the attack on which will be in conjunction with attacks by the French on the South and by other Corps on the North will be the line

B.2.B.5.5-Cross roads 500 yards E. of GUILLEMONT - GINCHY (to be attacked by XV Corps).

If this attack is successful, the next objective of XIV Corps will probably be the high ground between COMBLES and GINCHY.

The task of capturing this ground is likely to be allotted to Guards and 6th Division in conjunction with other attacks on the South and North.

The enemy, as far as is at present known, in rear of his GUILLEMONT - GINCHY position, has a line running from COMBLES - through T.21.central to T.8.central, i.e. on the rear slope of the high ground, and at an average distance of from 1200 yards to 1700 yards from the objectives now to be attacked by XIV Corps.

There is however the BOIS DE LEUZE which juts out westwards in front of the above line to a distance of 800 yards and is not likely to be given up by the enemy without a prolonged fight, as it lies on a spur commanding the ground to the N.W. and S.E.

We may therefore be required to deal with a situation as follows :-

A. Take over the objectives gained by either the left or right Divisions of the XIV Corps on the line B.2.B.5.5 - T.20.A.0.5, probably some days after the objectives have /been

been gained.

B. Prepare for an attack against the line COMBLES - T.21.central - T.15.C.2.2 which may involve advancing our line anything from 1400 to 800 yards prior to the actual assault.

C. An assault on the line mentioned in para. B above which line is behind the crest.

2. The above is a forecast of events as they may happen but of course much will depend on the success of the next attack, and the situation may develop either more slowly or more rapidly than as outlined above. It is an advantage however, to think over and discuss beforehand situations which may have to be dealt with.

The above plans should only be mentioned to Battalion Commanders and Brigade Majors.

3. As regards taking over the line captured by another Division, the following are points that have mostly been referred to in literature that has been sent round and must receive attention.

(i) Care that the number of men to be relieved in forward trenches is accurately ascertained so as to avoid the crowding involved by the relief of a weak unit by a strong one.

(ii) All troops in support and reserve to at once commence providing themselves with adequate cover against shell fire where such does not exist.

(iii) Where the situation admits a line of posts forming an outpost line to be established. This will allow of our main front line being lightly held.

(iv) Active patrolling to gain command of "No Man's Land" to be at once commenced. Posts to be established in any ground of importance found unheld by the enemy and arrangements made to incorporate such ground in our line as early as possible.

(v) The Major General again wishes to call attention to the great importance of good arrangements for artillery support

/against

against counter attack during the period of preparation for our attack - all "S.O.S" arrangements to be in order and tested - also the importance of machine gun defence, including long range barrage fire into "No Man's Land".

4. As regards making preparations for the attack.

The first essential must be the advancing of our front line to within 200 yards of enemy trenches. This may have been effected in part before we take over the line.

As any advanced line of this description will draw hostile shell fire it is desirable that if possible two or more lines should be dug simultaneously to allow circulation and to reduce losses from shell fire.

5. As regards the actual attack there are certain points on which, as the result of experience of recent fighting, there appears general agreement.

<u>A</u>. The necessity of closely following up our barrage.

<u>B</u>. Brigades and Battalions to adopt dispositions which will allow of some reserves remaining in hand for the purpose of establishing a defensive flank, should troops on their flanks be temporarily held up.

<u>C</u>. The necessity of getting the whole of the troops engaged in the assault across "No Man's Land" as early as possible so as to avoid supporting lines being cut off by hostile barrage. This entails assaulting troops advancing in thick lines with only a few yards between lines.

The advantages of this system in escaping enemy barrage are obvious, but there are also certain disadvantages.

(i) Troops before the assault must be crowded close up to our front line.

(ii) There may be difficulty in finding any form of cover for supporting lines when the objective is reached.

(iii) The thick lines offer an easy target to any hostile machine guns left in action.

/The

The necessity, however, of escaping the enemy's barrage has been found so important as to ~~outway~~ outweigh the disadvantages mentioned above. The risk of a heavy hostile bombardment on our crowded assembly trenches must be run.

It will be reduced by ensuring that our artillery bombardment gives no hint, by an intensive period prior to the assault, of the time of our intended attack.

There appears to be a concensus of opinion in favour of afternoon attacks, owing to the better observation obtainable for counter battery work.

An afternoon attack however obviously has disadvantages when men have to remain crowded in assembly trenches. This question of time of the attack will have to be settled with due regard to the varying considerations affecting the particular situation to be dealt with.

As regards hostile machine guns and the vulnerability of thick lines in the advance. By means of a creeping barrage close in front of our advance, to knock out any hostile machine guns pushed forward, and by means of a stationary barrage on the enemy's front line and any points in rear that can command "No Man's Land", everything possible will be done to ensure that hostile machine gun fire is reduced to a minimum.

6. In the situations that now develop when we successfully capture an objective, there is great scope for local initiative.

The concerted attack ceases when the objective is reached but every endeavour must be made to push forward locally to secure ground in front of the objective.

This should be impressed on Battalion and Company Commanders.

The object to be attained is to advance our line to within 200 yards of the enemy's new line as soon as possible.

The actual establishment of posts (to be developed later into continuous lines) may have to be done by degrees if the intervening distances are great, but patrolling should be pushed right forward up to the enemy's new line on the first night after the assault and continued nightly.

/The

The Division would arrange with Divisions on the flanks that the advancing of the line should be prosecuted along a broad front, and thus ensure that our flanks were not left in the air.

As soon as advanced posts are definitely established on a portion of the front, the Artillery should be informed, and arrangements ~~she~~ made for normal S.O.S. barrages to run in front of these posts - which must be supplied with S.O.S. rockets.

It will be impossible to suspend S.O.S. barrages because our patrols are out. Patrols must, in this respect, take the same risks as in ordinary trench warfare, when S.O.S. barrages are not changed because patrols being out in "No Man's Land".

7. The Major General went through the XIV Corps orders for attack, and discussed the system of Barrages to be employed.

The chief features of the system are

A. Infantry to leave their trenches at ZERO.

B. The following barrages to commence at ZERO,

a fixed barrage on enemy's front line -

a creeping barrage commencing 100 yards in front of our front line -

the creeping barrage to advance at rate of about 50 yards per minute, the pace depending on the extent to which the ground is cut up -

when the creeping barrage reaches the first objective, the fixed barrage lifts back, and the creeping barrage creeps on 200 yards beyond the first objective.

C. When a second objective has to be captured, a time is laid down for the infantry advance to recommence, when barrages as in para. (B) precede it. Similarly with any subsequent objectives allotted.

ACKNOWLEDGE.

C P Heywood

Lieut.Colonel,
General Staff, Guards Division.

29th Aug. 1916.

SECRET

G.D.No. 2284/G.

G.D.A.
C.R.E.
1st Guards Bde.
2nd Guards Bde.
3rd Guards Bde.

CONFERENCE HELD AT 2ND. GUARDS BRIGADE HD.QRS.
19th September 1916.

1. The MajOr General stated that the Division was again called upon to carry out an attack.

It is realised by all the higher authorities that it is a heavy call, but the Commander-in-Chief once more calls upon the Corps to attack the enemy in conjunction with the French on our right. Although we have had a severe time of it, the XV Corps on our left have had a more severe time ~~of it~~ and the 5th Division has had already very heavy fighting in this area since the battle of the SOMME began. This Division is still the strongest in the Corps.

2. Outlines of the next attack were discussed and attention called to the following points:-

A. If the attack is held up on the whole or part of the front of attack, Brigadiers should not order a fresh attack without calling on the Division to provide adequate artillery support.

B. Maintenance of direction by subordinate commanders is a matter of great importance. Also the accurate location of points reached.

If compass bearings are given - two bearings giving an intersection will assist the receiver of a message in locating the sender's position.

C. As far as possible Brigadiers to keep in touch with the fight by means of their Staffs.

D. The capture of LES BOEUFS presents difficulties.

The danger is that if attacking troops rush straight through the village to the final objectives, enemy troops may issue from cellars and dugouts after our troops have passed.

/To

To prevent this situation arising it was agreed by G.O.Cs. 1st and 3rd Guards Brigades that arrangements would be made to have strong parties detailed to follow up the attacking line and clear the village in detail.

E. The necessity of consolidating the Brown Line, and of pushing forward reserves to hold it, when the attack goes forward to the last objective was mentioned.

F. If Brigade Commanders realise beforehand that for any reason an attack cannot start at the hour ordered, they must report the matter at once.

G. One battalion 2nd Guards Brigade will be attached to 1st Guards Brigade, and one battalion 2nd Guards Brigade to 3rd Guards Brigade.

It is proposed that these two battalions should move up to join the Brigades to which they are attached on the night before the attack.

C M Heywood

Lieut.Colonel,

19th September 1916. General Staff, Guards Division.

INTELLIGENCE NOTES

OUR LINE.

Before the capture of GUILLEMONT, the British held a fairly complete trench system between that village and TRONES WOOD. Since the advance on Sept. 3rd the line has fluctuated every day and its actual position is even now uncertain. Probably the only 'prepared' trench now occupied is the section of the German COMBLES - FLERS line, running through LEUZE WOOD. From that point to DELVILLE WOOD, the troops have have dug themselves in along the sunken roads, and have formed isolated trenches by connecting up shell holes. By the time the Guards Division takes over, it is probable that a fairly definite line will have been organised.

Communication trenches from TRONES WOOD to the outskirts of GUILLEMONT are fairly good and deep, the best being GUILLEMONT ALLEY, CORNISH ALLEY, and LONGUEVAL ALLEY.

GUILLEMONT.

There are a fair number of good cellars in GUILLEMONT, but no map of them has yet been made.

The principal German fixed barrages appear to be :-

East side of TRONES WOOD, particularly the Southeast corner.

Road running along the southern edges of TRONES and BERNAFAY WOODS.

Spur south of LONGUEVAL.

In front of, and behind BRIQUETERIE.

ARROW HEAD COPSE and WATERLOT FARM are also favourite targets, and, recently, GUILLEMONT and the WEDGE WOOD - GINCHY ROAD.

SYSTEM OF DEFENCE.

The German system of holding the line is as follows: all three regiments in the line, each having one battalion in the front and support lines, one in reserve and one resting.

The battalion actually holding the line usually has 3 companies in the front trench and one in support.

The rest billets of the 111th Division are reported to be in ST. PIERRE VAAST Wood, and the reserve battalion is probably in the COMBLES - FLERS line.

Headquarters are as follows:-

Divisional Hd. Qrs.		ETRICOURT.
-do-	(advanced)	SAILLY-SAILLISEL.
221st Brigade "		SAILLY-SAILLISEL.
73rd Fus. Regt."		COMBLES (caves).
76th Regt. "		T.16.a.7.6.
164th Regt. "		COMBLES (caves).

Owing to the scarcity of communication trenches and the constant severity of our artillery fire, carrying parties are very seldom sent up to the troops in the front line.

Battalions usually remain only 3 days in the front line and have to take all their supplies with them.

These, for 3 days, consist of:-

3 bottles of soda water, 1 bottle of coffee, 3 tins of meat, 2½ lbs of bread, 2 bags of biscuits and one small spirit stove, per man.

Owing to our complete command of the air, no movement whatever is allowed in daylight for fear of drawing artillery fire. This naturally limits very considerably the amount of work done on the trenches, which, apart from the prepared rear lines are little more than roughly linked shell holes.

Except in villages, the Germans do not appear to use concrete machine gun emplacements, but keep their guns in deep dugouts along the numerous sunken roads and put them up on the parapet to resist an attack.

The position of these sunken roads should be very carefully noted for this reason, as they form the enemy's main centres of resistance between the prepared positions.

The enemy's light signals vary in different Divisions, but the following is the most usual, and is apparently in use in the 111th Division.

Red : S.O.S., calls for barrage.

Green : Lengthen range.

Red and green : Gas alarm.

White : indicate position of infantry.

GERMAN LINES.

GENERAL.

Now that the whole of the German second line of defence has been captured, the enemy has to rely upon trenches which he has dug during the course of the battle. His three prepared lines are described below, but, in addition, there are many isolated trenches, converted communication trenches, sunken roads and connected shell craters from which he has proved himself capable of offering a very stout resistance. Naturally, however, these are not to be compared, for prolonged resistance, with the intricate trench systems prepared during two years of comparative quiet, which have already fallen into our hands. The prepared lines are as follows:-

(1) COMBLES - FLERS Line.

Runs from western edge of COMBLES, through LEUZE WOOD, along the reverse slope of the GINCHY TELEGRAPH Ridge to southern edge of FLERS. Just North of LEUZE WOOD, a newly made branch trench runs through the southern end of BOULEAUX WOOD along the sunken road into COMBLES. The line is connected with the MORVAL - GEUDECOURT line by a trench running through T.8.d., 9.c and d. Just short of FLERS a second line, which at present stops short of T.2.c., will probably also be joined up to the MORVAL - GEUDECOURT line. The line is very well sited, as for nearly all its length it is invisible to any but aerial observation, though we may soon be able to enfilade it from the newly won high ground south of COMBLES.

At present it is only a single trench, but a great deal of work has been put into it, and prisoners report it to be at least 6 feet deep. The line is said to

be/

be well supplied with dugouts 20 feet below the surface, each with two exits. It is very heavily wired, the dimensions being given as 20 feet wide and 5 feet high. There is no information about machine gun emplacements.

(2) MORVAL - GEUDECOURT Line.

Not much is known about this line, but it is probably a complete single trench, with dugouts for ¾ of the garrison, and a large amount of wire in front of it. It has been constantly worked on for the last month.

(3) SAILLISEL - BAPAUME Line.

This line has only recently been commenced and the last air reconnaissance report shows it to be only dug in places - a thousand yards of trench being followed by as much undug.

It must be expected, however, that the line will be more or less complete by the middle of the month. A further report on this line is expected shortly.

MORVAL.

The usual type of village in this area, the houses being brick and wattle, with small cellars.

There are reported to be old quarries near the Church, which is of stone.

There are 3 ponds and 4 public wells, and most houses have private wells.

The brewery at the northern end of the village has cellars large enough to hold 300 - 400 men.

There are a large number of sunken roads round the village.

/LES

LES BOEUFS.

A special map and report on LES BOEUFS is being issued separately.

The principal feature is two underground passages with caverns, running from the Church towards GINCHY and LE TRANSLOY respectively.

The village is surrounded by sunken roads.

LE TRANSLOY.

Also reported to possess an underground passage running from LEMOINES Brewery towards LES BOEUFS.

The two breweries and the sugar factory all possess spacious cellars.

German line of approach.

The following are the principal lines as taken from captured German maps:-

(1) T.16.b.1.5 - North corner of BOULEAUX WOOD - just N. of copse T.21.b.2.8 - T.21.a.6.3.

(2) T.10.c.5.0 - T.15.b.3.4 - just North of sunken road - T.15.c.1.5.

(3) Track from windmill N.33.d.6.3 - T.3.a.8.8 - T.8.b.2.2.

It will here be interesting to give a short description of the German Corps who had been identified as facing the Guards Division on the 25th September 1916

A GERMAN TROOPS.

****

Constitution of enemy's troops

There were two Divisions, the 111th and 56th, and there were

The Guards Division is opposed principally by 111th Division, reinforced by two battalions of 24th Reserve Division. The northern flank, may, however, come in contact with 53th Division.

HISTORY.

The 111th Division was formed in March 1915. It consisted of the 73rd Fusilier Regiment (Hanover), 7th Regt. (Hamburg), and 164th Regt. (Hanover). After one month in the WOEVRE, the Division was moved to the ARRAS front, where it remained until the present battle, when it came into the GUILLEMONT sector on 22nd August. It had previously seen practically no fighting, and when it first came into the line its moral was good. Since its severe handling on 3rd Sept. it has shown signs of deterioration, and it is almost certain to be relieved in a few days.

The 56th Division was also formed in March 1915, but has had a much more active career. It is partly composed of Brandenburgers and partly of Hessians, and consists of 35th Fusilier Regt., 88th Regt., and 118th Regt.

After a short tour of duty in CHAMPAGNE the Division was sent to GALICIA to take part in MACKENSEN'S advance. It suffered heavy losses, and in June was sent back to rest at VALENCIENNES. In September 1915 it was sent to CHAMPAGNE to meet the French offensive, suffered heavy losses, was pulled out and sent in again in November to attack the French. It remained in CHAMPAGNE during the winter of 1915–16, and in May 1916 it was sent to VERDUN where it took part in the heavy fighting on the MORT HOMME, again losing heavily. After a short rest

/in

in the VIMY sector, the Division was brought down to the SOMME and relieved the 26th Division in the DELVILLE WOOD sector on the 24th August.

It arrived with a reputation of only fair moral, but ~~has done~~ did exceedingly well in the ~~present battle~~ fighting at the end of August, resisting repeated attacks and taking part in the very successful counter attack upon DELVILLE WOOD on the 31st. ~~August.~~

~~It has however suffered heavy casualties from our artillery fire, and will probably be relieved very shortly.~~

The 24th Reserve Division, two battalions of which ~~are~~ were sent to ~~reinforcing~~ reinforce the 111th Division, was in ~~this~~ the Somme sector during the latter part of July and, on relief, took over the 56th Division front at VIMY. It ~~is~~ was composed of Saxons.

Preliminary Report on MORVAL.

****

MORVAL is a typical PICARDY village of brick and wattle houses, surrounded by high trees, growing in meadows enclosed by hedges. In the accompanying plan, the houses which are built of wattle are marked with a "T". All the others are of brick. All have cellars, but most of them are quite small and unimportant.

The Church was built of stone dug out of quarries under the Place (No.1) just South of it. These quarries have now of course been covered in, but they cross the main street, and of late years, several accidents have happened owing to carts which were driving along the main street, just S.W. of the Church, falling bodily through the roadway into these old quarries. They said to run from the centre of the Eastern edge of the Place (No.1) to just West of houses No.3.

There are 3 ponds in the village - marked P on map, and 4 public wells - marked W on map. Most of the houses have private wells.

The following are the most important features:-

1. The Place, with trees growing round it.
2. Small stone Church.
3. Two quite new brick houses, with particularly strong and big vaulted cellars, which extend right round the corner of the road.
4. Presbytry, built of brick. Cellars unimportant.
   The water of the well next to the Presbytry, is not good for drinking. The inhabitants of the village never use it except for watering their animals when water is scarce.
5. Brewery belonging to the Maire, M.CARON. It is a strong brick building, with a very deep well. It also has cellars big enough to hold 300 - 400 men.
6. Brick built house with particularly good cellars and a good well.
7. Wattle house with particularly large cellars, which were built to hold beetroots.
8. Old brick house with cellars which run out underneath the field just South of it. (Just under figure 8 on the plan).
9. Two unoccupied brick houses.
10. Brick farm with big cellars.
11. Two strongly built old brick farms.
12. Small brick house with good cellars.
13. Row of brick houses with strong cellars.
14. Absolutely new brick house with specially good cellars.
15. Wattle house with large cellars, capable of holding 100 men.
16. Brick house with small cellars.
17. Brick house with good cellars.
18. Mairie, and school, brick built, but no cellars.

ROADS. Nearly all the roads S. & W. of MORVAL, are sunken though not very deeply (as shown on plan). The road running W. of MORVAL from the W. of LESBOEUFS to the N.W. corner of COMBLES is [illegible] deeply sunken in parts, but it is probably very nearly level for about 100 yards on each side of where it crosses the MORVAL - GINCHY road in T.13.a. Opinions however, differ on this point.

The continuation of the main street of MORVAL towards FREGICOURT is only an earth track and is so bad as to be entirely useless. The villagers do not even take their carts along it.

=

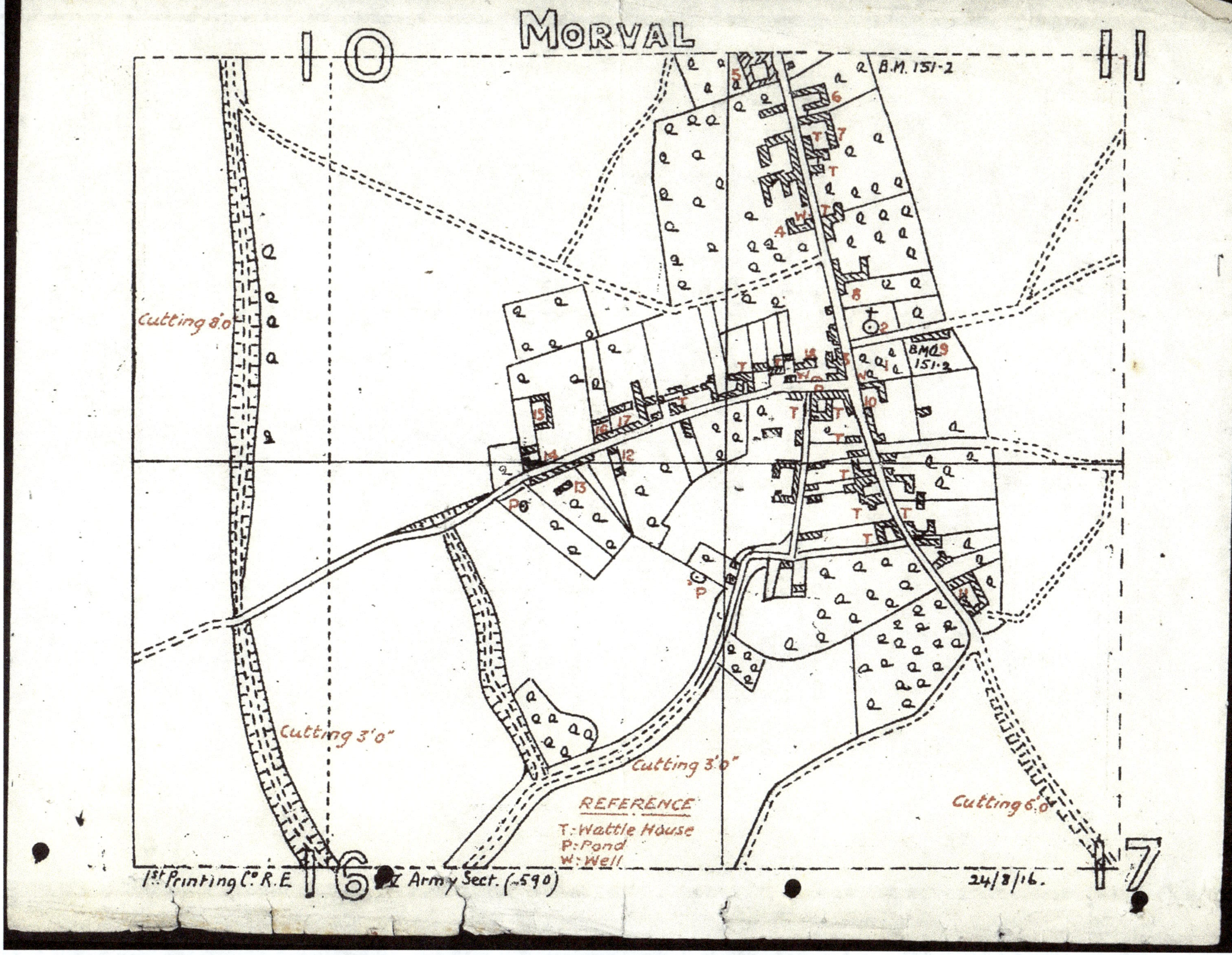
MORVAL
10
11
16
17
B.M. 151·2
B.M. 151·3
Cutting 8'0"
Cutting 3'0"
Cutting 3'0"
Cutting 6'0"
REFERENCE
T: Wattle House
P: Pond
W: Well
1st Printing Co R.E.
I Army Sect. (-590)
24/8/16.

INFORMATION ABOUT LES BOEUFS

****

FROM A REFUGEE.

****

There are two large underground passages, with caverns, dating from the Middle Ages, but fallen in along the greater part of of their length, starting from the Church. The first runs as far as the well W. 1. The second runs in the direction of the well W. 2, and is continued towards the village pond. Eight years ago the pond all ran away into this excavation; the bottom of the pond has apparently been recemented, as it now holds water.

As a general rule all the farms in the village have private wells, and small cellars. Those houses not specially mentioned in the following report are built of wattle, except for one or two feet from the ground, which is of brick.

There is a gap with trees between each of the houses on the Western side of the road leading to MORVAL in T.4.c.

The hollow on the road to GINCHY, the bottom of which is not visible from LES BOEUFS, is called in the neighbourhood LA GATTE. LEUZE and BOULEAUX WOODS have very little undergrowth. They are not so thick as DELVILLE WOOD, nor are the trees so tall.

The Church is surrounded by a cemetery enclosed by a wall. There is no cemetery outside the village.

The following are the most important buildings:-

1. Strongly built farm, belonging to M. BOURDON, slightly raised above the level of the street, with big cellars.

2. Block of well built brick houses, with fairly good cellars.

3. Church, very solidly built. The floor over the crypt is paved with extremely large and solid flag stones.

4. Well built brick house belonging to M. HENRIQUET, slightly raised with cellars big enough to hold 40 men.

5. Brick house belonging to Mm. BOQUET. Cellars big enough for 50 men.

6. A block of brick houses comprising two cafes and a forge at the Southern corner; fairly good cellars.

7. Cafe; cellars particularly strong.

8. Well built brick farm with good cellars.

9. Strongly built brick farm belonging to the Maire, with large cellars.

10. Row of houses with especially big cellars.

11. Presbytery - mostly built of torchies, cellars poor.

12. A house once stood here but was pulled down before the war.

13. Solidly built deserted house with big cellars.

14. Strongly built farm with big cellars.

Guards Div H.Q. 4 Sept 1916 — W.G.

le Transloy
Cemetery
Windmill
Lesboeufs
Morval
Ginchy Telegraph
Ginchy
Bouleaux Wood

Blue represents our present line at 6.10 pm.
I can see no enemy immediately in front of our troops. Looked carefully in all small works & trenches.

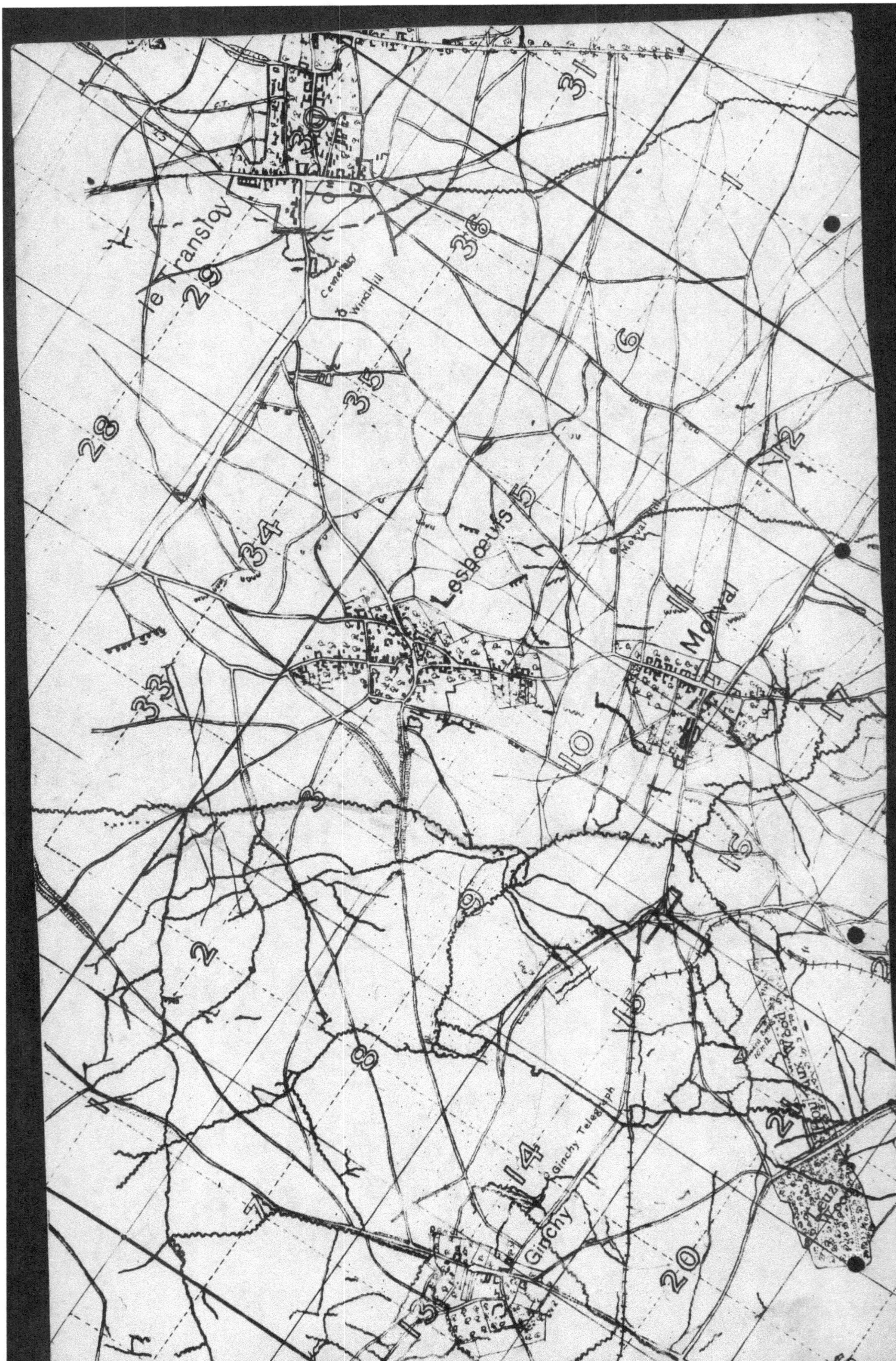

le Transloy
29
30
31
36
Cemetery
Windmill
6
35
28
12
Lesboeufs
5
34
Morval
11
33
10
17
3
16
9
2
15
8
Bouleaux Wood
24
Leuze Wood
14
Ginchy Telegraph
Ginchy
20
7
13

Situation at 1.5 pm.
our troops held up at T3a 17
and T3d 34 – 42.
Corps on left appear to be
doing well.
Red = enemy
Blue = our troops

W G Begg Lt.

Please send on immediately
to 5th & 6th Divs

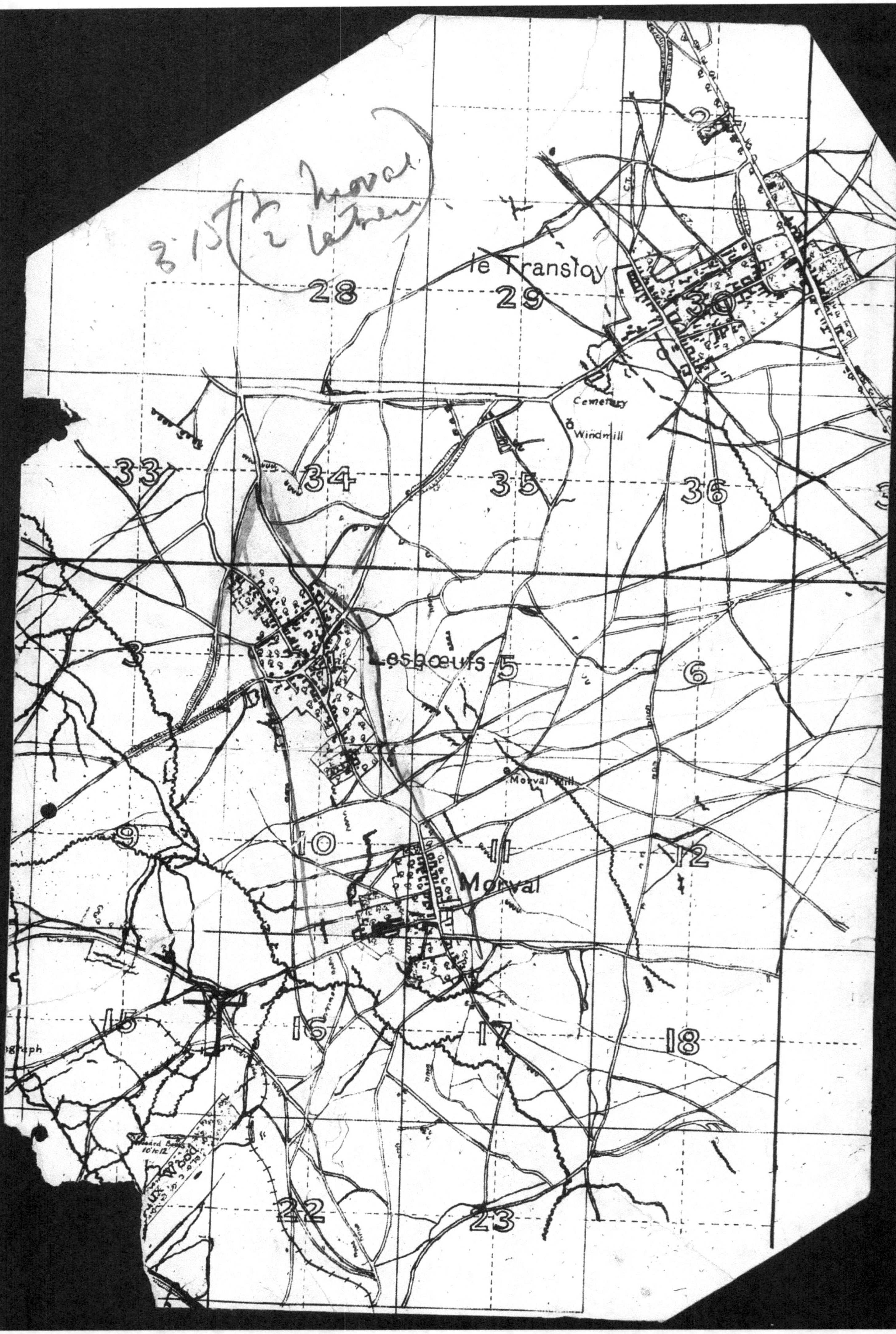
3/15
Morval
2 letters
le Transloy
28
29
30
Cemetery
Windmill
33
34
35
36
Lesbœufs
3
5
6
Morval Mill
9
10
11
12
Morval
15
16
17
18
22
23

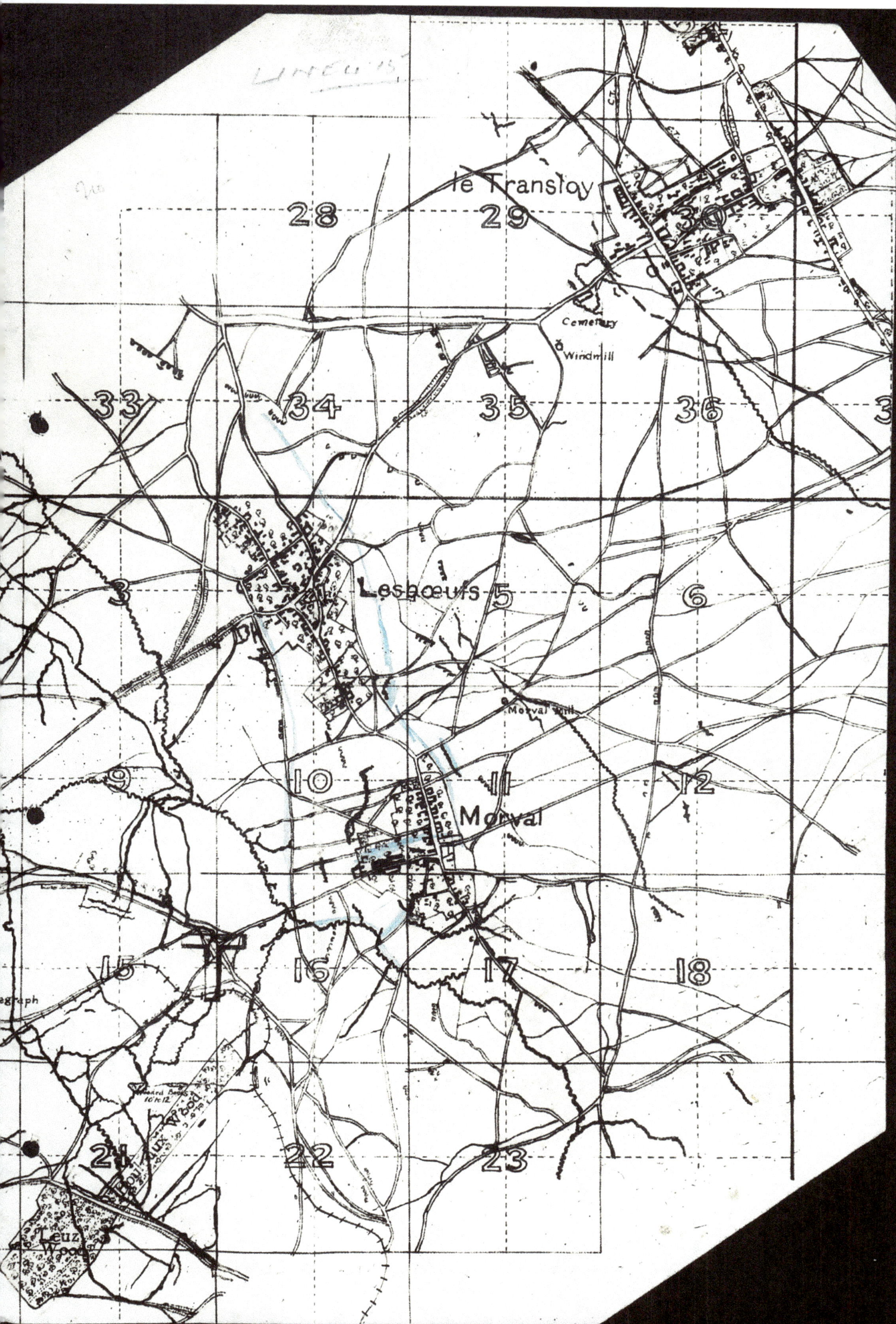
le Transloy
28
29
30
33
34
35
36
Cemetery
Windmill
Lesbœufs
3
5
6
Morval Mill
9
10
11
12
Morval
15
16
17
18
egraph
21
22
23
Bouleaux Wood
Leuze Wood

www.ingramcontent.com/pod-product-compliance
Lightning Source LLC
Chambersburg PA
CBHW080841010526
44114CB00017B/2351
* 9 7 8 1 4 7 4 5 0 1 8 9 7 *